Ghosts, Holes, Rips and Scrapes

Ghosts, Holes, Rips and Scrapes

Shakespeare in 1619, Bibliography in the Longue Durée

Zachary Lesser

PUBLISHED IN COOPERATION WITH
FOLGER SHAKESPEARE LIBRARY

PENN

UNIVERSITY OF PENNSYLVANIA PRESS

PHILADELPHIA

Published by
University of Pennsylvania Press
Philadelphia, Pennsylvania 19104-4112
www.upenn.edu/pennpress

Printed in the United States of America on acid-free paper
10 9 8 7 6 5 4 3 2 1

Library of Congress Cataloging-in-Publication Data
Names: Lesser, Zachary, author.
Title: Ghosts, holes, rips and scrapes : Shakespeare in 1619, bibliography in the longue durée / Zachary Lesser.
Description: 1st edition. | Philadelphia : University of Pennsylvania Press, [2021] | "Published in cooperation with Folger Shakespeare Library." | Includes bibliographical references and index.
Identifiers: LCCN 2020032184 | ISBN 978-0-8122-5294-1 (hardcover)
Subjects: LCSH: Shakespeare, William, 1564–1616—Criticism, Textual. | Shakespeare, William, 1564–1616—Bibliography—Quartos.
Classification: LCC PR3071 .L47 2021 | DDC 822.3/3—dc23
LC record available at https://lccn.loc.gov/2020032184

For Rafa, who tolerated my selfies from all those libraries

CONTENTS

ACKNOWLEDGMENTS

From its beginnings in dialogue between A. W. Pollard and W. W. Greg, bibliography of the Pavier Quartos has been a collective endeavor. This book is the outcome of discussions with numerous colleagues. For those to whom I am most indebted, I fear it may have seemed an endless conversation. In particular, I need to thank Peter Stallybrass. In 2013 we taught a graduate course together, which led to a co-written essay partly on the Pavier Quartos: "Shakespeare between Pamphlet and Book," in *Shakespeare and Textual Studies*, ed. M. J. Kidnie and Sonia Massai (Cambridge University Press, 2015), 105–33. A section of that essay is incorporated in revised form in the pages that follow, and I am grateful not only for Peter's generosity in letting me include it here, but also for his ongoing collaborative curiosity about the Pavier Quartos and many, many other subjects. More than anyone else, Aaron Pratt of the Harry Ransom Center at the University of Texas and Jay Moschella of the Boston Public Library have talked through innumerable mysteries about these quartos with me over the past few years, and I have been as inspired by their shared excitement as I have been enlightened by their expertise. Erin Blake, Claire Bourne, Alan Farmer, Mitch Fraas, Ian Gadd, Adam Hooks, Kathryn James, David Kastan, Ivan Lupić, John Pollack, Tara Lyons, Will Noel, Sarah Reidell, Tony Russ, Adam Smyth, Tiffany Stern, Whitney Trettien, Heather Wolfe, and Henry Woudhuysen also spent time thinking about these playbooks with me over the years and made a number of crucial suggestions that have furthered my research.

It is impossible to undertake a comprehensive study of the extant copies of ten playbooks that survive in hundreds of copies without a great deal of assistance. I have been fortunate that the curators of the special collections that I have not been able to visit personally have been so helpful and learned: John Ball (Akron), Rebecca Baumann and Madeline Keysey (Indiana), Adam Doskey (Illinois), Eric Johnson (Ohio State), Robert MacLean (Glasgow), and Georgia Prince (Auckland). Many other librarians have answered further questions when they arose, as they inevitably do, after I had visited, or have examined other books in their collection for me: Lucy Angus (Birmingham), Karen Attar (Senate House), Erin Blake (Folger), Julie Christenson (Texas Christian), Emily Dourish (Cambridge), Christina Duffy (British Library), Elizabeth Dunn (Duke), Jill Gage (Newberry), Sarah Horowitz (Haverford), Kathryn James (Beinecke), Tanya Kirk (British Library), James Mitchell (National Library of Scotland), John Overholt (Houghton), Phil Palmer (Clark, UCLA), Sandy Paul (Trinity College, Cambridge), Susan Swain (Texas Christian), Stephen Tabor (Huntington), Kyle Triplett (New York Public), Abbie Weinberg (Folger), and Heather Wolfe (Folger). Molly Schwartzburg at Virginia offered very helpful comments on the lost volume once owned by Thomas Randolph, and Kathryn James helped me to understand Henrietta Bartlett's censuses better. Numerous scholars have checked features of books for me, both the 1619 quartos and others, including Adam Barker, Liza Blake, Heidi Brayman, Megan Cook, Sophie Coulombeau, Megan Heffernan, Eve Houghton, Roberta Klimt, Elizabeth Zeman Kolkovich, Thomas Luxon, Erin McCarthy, Ellen McKay, Molly Murray, Duncan Salkeld, Paul Salzman, and Adam Zucker.

My work developed through a series of lectures, where I received many thoughtful critiques and suggestions, including from Erika Boeckeler, Emma Depledge, Lukas Erne, John Jowett, Marina Leslie, Laurie Maguire, Jim Marino, Sonia Massai, Elizabeth Ott, Kristen Poole, Richard Proudfoot, Ben Robinson, Will Sharpe, Emma Smith, Dan Traister, Bart van Es, and Julian Yates.

Alan Farmer, Ben Higgins, Kathleen Lynch, Aaron Pratt, Taije Silverman, Adam Smyth, and Peter Stallybrass each read the entire manuscript in detail and improved it immensely, as did an anonymous reader for the press. The book is much better thanks to the expert editorial guidance of Jerry Singerman, who made smart suggestions all along the way.

Ghost, Holes, Rips and Scrapes was written while I was a visiting professor in the Dipartimento di Lingue, Letterature, e Culture Moderne at the University of Bologna, and I remain grateful to the department, and particularly to Keir Elam, for making my time there so enjoyable and productive.

Introduction

> Nothing, I think, but the hypnotic influence that traditionally accepted facts exercise even over the most critical mind can have prevented Mr. Pollard from suspecting that the ten quartos in question were not merely collected and published in one composite volume in 1619, but that, whatever the dates that appear on the title-pages, the whole set was actually printed by one printer at that one date.
>
> —W. W. Greg, "On Certain False Dates in Shakespearian Quartos"

Our modern understanding of Shakespeare as an author, of what he wrote and how, depends on the development in the early twentieth century of a new way of looking at books. And our modern understanding of printed books as physical objects containing clues to their own process of production—the scholarly discipline of bibliography—would look very different without Shakespeare. At the foundation of this intersection is a narrative of detection and discovery: "traditionally accepted facts" are overturned by a "revolutionary hypothesis," and the "hypnotic influence" of old ways of thinking is pierced by the "critical mind" informed by bibliographic knowledge.[1]

This foundational moment came in 1908, with W. W. Greg's modestly entitled essay "On Certain False Dates in Shakespearian Quartos." Greg's friendly critique of A. W. Pollard's inability to see beyond "traditionally accepted facts," and "the more revolutionary hypothesis" that Greg advanced instead, were central to establishing what came to be called, in a typically modernist formulation, the New Bibliography.[2] This approach to Shakespeare's texts reigned for much of the twentieth century, but over the past several decades scholars have engaged in a sustained critique of its methods, ideology, and unexamined assumptions. Even as we have sought our own "revolutionary hypotheses," however, the "hypnotic influence" of "traditionally accepted facts" has been as hard for us to escape as it was for Pollard. In trying to overturn the arguments of the New Bibliographers, moreover, we have often relied on the very evidence they provided us, imposing our own beliefs—which therefore remain, in important if unseen ways, *their* beliefs—on what we see in Shakespeare's books.

This book is an extended case study, with I hope broad implications, of one of the most important books in the history of Shakespeare studies. Not the First Folio, which has been analyzed more intensely and celebrated more devotionally than any other book printed in early modern England. Rather, the book that started Pollard and Greg on their quests to uncover the truth hiding behind "traditionally accepted facts" was an ordinary-looking quarto volume that Pollard first saw in 1902 (Figure 0.1).[3] It bound together ten plays, or nine playbooks (since one of them is made up of two plays), all in some way connected to Shakespeare. Three of these plays are linked by continuous signatures, the printer's pagination system: *The Whole Contention betweene the two Famous Houses, Lancaster and Yorke* (which comprises versions of the second and third parts of *Henry VI*) and *Pericles*. All the other plays in the group have their own run of signatures: *A Yorkshire Tragedy, The Merry Wives of Windsor, The Merchant of Venice, King Lear, Henry V, Sir John Oldcastle*, and *A Midsummer Night's Dream*.[4] While *Yorkshire Tragedy* and *Oldcastle* are not now considered Shakespearean, they both have Shakespeare's name on the title page, although *Henry V*, like all the other early quartos of that play, does not.[5] *Pericles, Yorkshire Tragedy*, and *Merry Wives* are dated 1619; but *Whole Contention* is undated, and the other five plays are dated either 1600 or 1608. Five of the playbooks list "T. P." as the publisher—the initials belong to Thomas Pavier—but the others have various names in the imprints (Table 0.1). The whole volume is bound in simple brown calfskin, and the name of the early seventeenth-century lawyer and book collector Edward Gwynn is tooled in gold on the front cover. The volume is now in the Folger Shakespeare Library, and the story of its journey there shows the power of the "revolutionary hypothesis" that Greg told about it.

In July 1919, the great Philadelphia book dealer A. S. W. Rosenbach burst into the offices of the Standard Oil Company of New York with a message for its president, Henry Clay Folger. Rosenbach had finally succeeded in acquiring the Gwynn volume from the Rhode Island collector Marsden Perry.

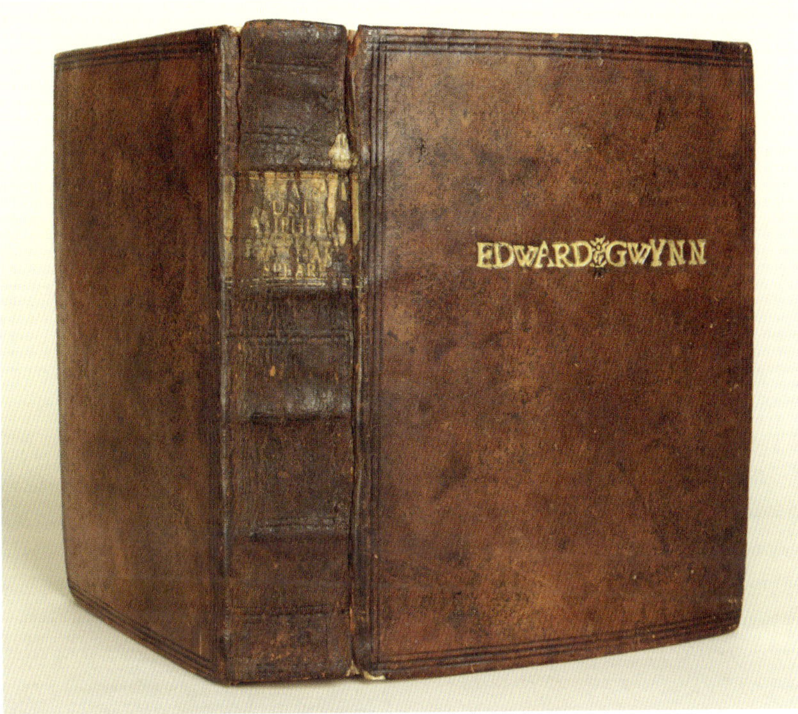

Figure 0.1 Edward Gwynn's set of Pavier Quartos. Used by permission of the Folger Shakespeare Library, STC 26101 copy 3.

Folger immediately bought the book for the staggering price of fifty thousand dollars, more than he ever paid for a book, with the exception of two of his copies of the First Folio.[6] Only eight years earlier, Henry Huntington had paid this same amount for a Gutenberg Bible, said at the time to have set the sales record for a single volume.[7] The price of the Gwynn volume is even more surprising when we realize not only that these are all later editions, not firsts, but also that numerous copies of each of the quartos bound in the volume still survive, far more than is typical for Shakespeare editions. To understand why Folger wanted the book so badly and was willing to pay so much for it, we need to trace its provenance.

The most obvious sign of previous ownership is Edward Gwynn's stamp on the cover.[8] The Gwynn name, with the guarantee it brings that the binding is roughly contemporary with Shakespeare, is crucial to the story. But the twentieth-century provenance is just as important. Pollard recounts that the

Table 0.1. The So-Called Pavier Quartos: Titles, imprints, and signatures

Short title	Imprint	Signatures
The Whole Contention	Printed at LONDON, for T.P.	A–Q⁴
Pericles	Printed for *T.P.* 1619.	χ¹ [=2B2?] R–2A⁴ 2B² (-2B2)
A Yorkshire Tragedy	Printed for *T.P.* 1619.	π¹ [=D4] A–C⁴ D⁴ (-D4)
The Merry Wives of Windsor	Printed for *Arthur Johnson*, 1619.	A–G⁴
The Merchant of Venice	Printed by *J. Roberts*, 1600.	A–K⁴
King Lear	Printed for *Nathaniel Butter.* | 1608.	A–L⁴
Henry V	Printed for *T. P.* 1608.	A–G⁴
Sir John Oldcastle	*London printed for T.P.* | 1600.	A–K⁴
A Midsummer Night's Dream	*Printed by Iames Roberts,* 1600.	A–H⁴

book was brought to him in his capacity as a member of the Department of Printed Books at the British Museum: "Some years ago a letter was received at the British Museum from a German gentleman stating that he was bringing over to England, with some other early books, a volume containing nine Shakespearian (or pseudo-Shakespearian) plays, which he had been advised in Germany were of considerable value. He offered the British Museum the refusal of any that it might want, and stated that he proposed to bring the volume to the Museum immediately on his arrival at Charing Cross, probably about 6 p.m."[9] This "German gentleman" must have been a member of the aristocratic Goertz-Wrisberg family, or one of their agents, since a bookplate on the front pastedown belongs to their library; the effects of the book's sojourn in Germany can also be seen on the spine, where a macaronic label was added that reads: "Plays und pamphlets of W Shak-speare."[10]

Pollard's institution declined to purchase the volume because "all these plays were already in the British Museum," although Pollard himself was already impressed by the book, which "was in such admirable condition and generally such an attractive purchase that some pains were taken, but unavailingly, to find it an English home."[11] The relative lack of interest is telling: at this moment the book must have appeared fairly familiar to collectors, resembling numerous other assemblages of Shakespeare quartos still to be found at reasonable prices, and the plays it contained were among the most common on the market. Purchased by the Quaritch bookselling firm in August 1902, the book was sold two months later to Perry. Pollard seems to have given little further thought to the "charming fat little volume" until 1906, when he saw a book that reminded him of Gwynn's. While "arranging a Shakespeare exhibition in the King's Library" at the British Museum, Pollard had "a chance conversation with a visitor," which led him to another volume of the same plays, although in a different order, in a mid-eighteenth-century binding.[12]

In fact, this encounter was hardly chance: the owner of the book, Edward Hussey, had noted the recent rise in sales prices for Shakespeare quartos and decided the time was right to sell the volume that had been in his family's library since at least the mid-1700s. Hussey's copy may originally have been owned by the minister and bureaucrat William Neile (1560–1624), who signed the title page of *Whole Contention*, the first play in the book.[13] Perhaps it was Neile who, upon acquiring the volume, also added "1622" in manuscript after the dateless imprint of *Whole Contention*; the numerals appear to be in an early hand, and the ink appears similar to that used in Neile's signature, although since both were later bleached, it is hard to be sure. Hussey consulted with the Society of Antiquaries about the book, and on the advice of someone there, "took the book to the British Museum and hunted up Mr Pollard."

Hussey recounts that Pollard was "much impressed by it," declaring it "a very creamy little volume" and estimating that "the price of it would suffice to buy a house with." Following this consultation, Hussey decided to auction the volume at Sotheby's, where each play was pulled out of the binding for individual sale. "A few days afterwards," he continues, he "received a letter from Mr Pollard requesting me if possible to delay breaking up the volume, as he had an interesting and ingenious theory connected with it."[14] Unfortunately, it was too late: the plays had already been prepared for auction. The market for rare books had destroyed this interesting volume, since they were worth more individually than together. Only the binding survives, still at the Hussey estate at Scotney Castle and now containing Hussey's own manuscript account of the story. The whereabouts of four of the nine playbooks once included cannot now be traced.[15] As Pollard wrote, while it may be "to the advantage of every seller to break up the old volume," the "contents, once dispersed, may easily lose all power of telling their collective history."[16]

Not quite all their power: it was this brief encounter with Hussey's book before its dispersal that led Pollard to his hypothesis about the Gwynn volume. Pollard believed that both volumes were made up of remaindered copies, hastily put together in 1622 when "the news of the forthcoming folio of 1623 caused them to be thrown on the market." Four of the five plays with dates earlier than 1619, Pollard noted, had been the second of two editions printed in the same year, and "every publisher knows by sad experience that a first edition of a book may be exhausted so rapidly that to refuse to print a second seems a mere turning away good money, and yet when the second is printed only a few copies are sold," and the remaining copies "become at once dead stock." Bundling them together might create a fresh market for these old wares. "Obviously Thomas Pavier was the prime mover in this device," Pollard wrote, "as most of the editions were his."[17] Seeing an opportunity to unload some copies when news of the First Folio surfaced, Pavier quickly tried to salvage what he could of his investments by packaging them as a nonce volume, a collection of previously printed texts.

Pollard seems initially to have thought that the Gwynn volume was simply a "sammelband," an assemblage of individual pamphlets bound up by a reader at some time after their initial sale. Readers commonly did this, because it was not worth binding a single play, but leaving plays unbound increased wear and tear (Figure 0.2).[18] But once Pollard had seen Hussey's volume, he rejected this hypothesis: "The chances that two collectors, without any determining cause, had bound together precisely the same editions of these plays, without the admixture of any others, seemed very remote."[19] And he knew from Greg's catalogue of the collection of Edward Capell at Trinity College, Cambridge, where Greg was the librarian, that the very same plays were present there in two eighteenth-century bindings (Figure 0.3). Finally, under Pollard's own care at the British Museum was the former collection of David Garrick, which contained the same plays individually bound but of such a uniform size that Pollard could identify them without even looking "for the titles on their backs," easily "pick[ing] out all nine plays from among their fellows simply by their height."[20] Pollard thought it impossible that these same plays had coincidentally been gathered by different readers into the two volumes he had seen, along with the Capell and Garrick volumes he inferred had once existed.

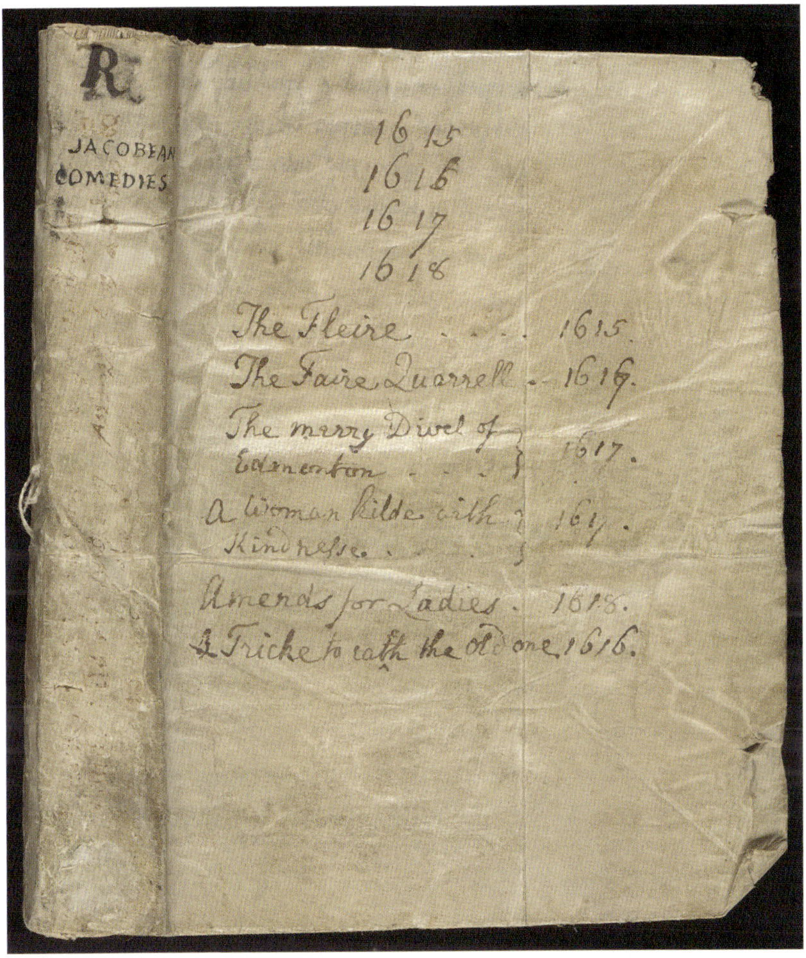

Figure 0.2 A reader's sammelband of drama, probably assembled by the Edward Palmer who signed all but one of the title pages; the table of contents on the front cover is likely later. Beinecke Rare Book and Manuscript Library, Yale University, Ih Sh24 607fc.

Ironically, Pollard thought, Capell himself had likely contributed to the destruction of other bound volumes of these plays by drawing so much attention to the editorial value of Shakespeare quartos in his 1768 edition of *Mr. William Shakespeare, his Comedies, Histories, and Tragedies, set out by himself in quarto, or by the Players his Fellows in folio*: "It cannot be doubted that this (undue) exaltation of the quartos as set out by Shakespeare himself

Figure 0.3 Edward Capell's two volumes of Pavier Quartos. By permission of the Master and Fellows of Trinity College, Cambridge, Capell Q.11 and Q.12.

powerfully directed attention to them, and would cause copies to be searched for." And then the antiquarian market would destroy more evidence: "As soon as a volume containing nine plays was found, the tendency, as we have noted, would be to break it up."[21] Pollard perceived from the outset that to understand this odd bibliographic case we need to consider the full lifetimes of these books across the centuries, as they interact with readers, editors, collectors, librarians, bookbinders, auction houses, and scholars.

For Pollard, "that plays of Shakespeare should have remained unsold for nineteen years or more and then have been worked off in a made-up volume, in the company of others wrongly assigned to him," offered some "consolation for the 'Remaindered'" among contemporary authors. When they saw "their precious works offered in second-hand catalogues for a small fraction of their original price," they could remember the similar fate of the works of their illustrious predecessor.[22] Pollard concluded on this note of historical irony: that the greatest of English writers should have been remaindered like anyone else showed the fickleness of the book-buying public.

Greg soon turned this explanation on its head. With the new tools of analytic bibliography, he transformed Shakespearean consolation into Shakespearean triumphalism, remainders into harbingers. His 1908 essay in the *Library*, which Pollard edited, was a powerful demonstration of the New Bibliography and did much to secure its reputation. Through close analysis of the watermarks in the paper of the playbooks, Greg demonstrated that they all contained the same mix of paper stocks, which is vanishingly unlikely if the plays were indeed printed as much as nineteen years apart.[23] Along with the typographical similarity of the various title pages and the use of the same printer's device on all but one of them, the watermark evidence led to the inescapable conclusion that the plays dated earlier than 1619 were deliberately falsified. In fact they were all printed at the same time in the shop of William and Isaac Jaggard, the same printers who would soon be involved in the First Folio, since in 1619 they owned the printer's device with the arms of the city of Geneva and the motto "POST TENEBRAS LUX" that appears on the title page of *Midsummer Night's Dream* and the one with the Welsh motto "HEB DDIEV HEB DDIM" ("without God, without anything") that appears on all the other plays (Figure 0.4).[24] (Isaac Jaggard took over his father's shop in 1623 when William died, sometime before November of that year, but his name occasionally appeared in imprints even while he was still working in his father's shop, and "it is quite possible that Isaac's position was that of a manager" with control over some publications.[25] Since we do not know which Jaggard

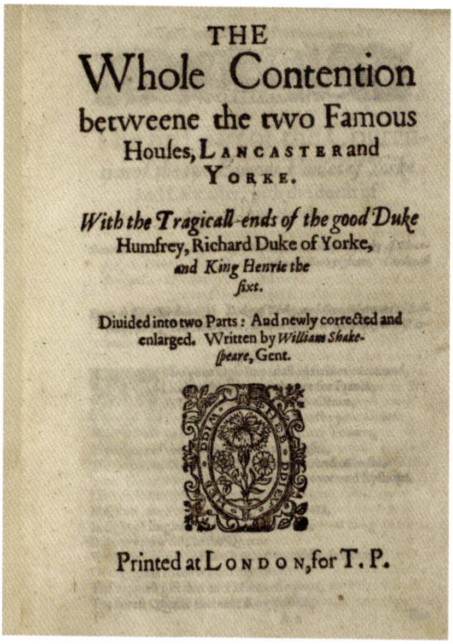

THE
Whole Contention
betvveene the tvvo Famous
Houſes, LANCASTER and
YORKE.

With the Tragicall ends of the good Duke
Humfrey, Richard Duke of Yorke,
and King Henrie the
ſixt.

Diuided into two Parts: And newly corrected and
enlarged. Written by *William Shake-*
ſpeare, Gent.

Printed at LONDON, for T. P.

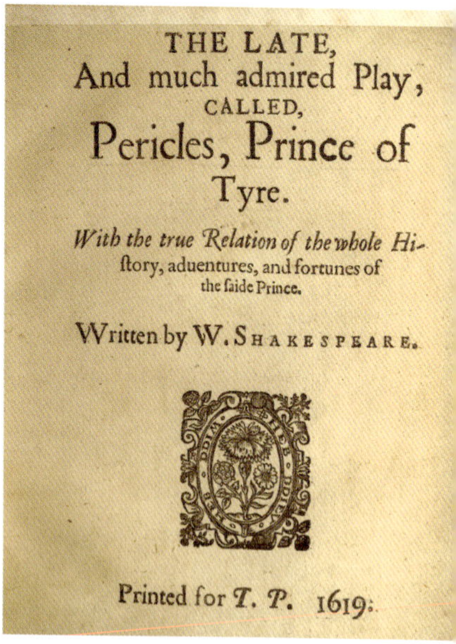

THE LATE,
And much admired Play,
CALLED,
Pericles, Prince of
Tyre.

With the true Relation of the whole Hi-
ſtory, aduentures, and fortunes of
the ſaide Prince.

Written by W. SHAKESPEARE.

Printed for *T. P.* 1619.

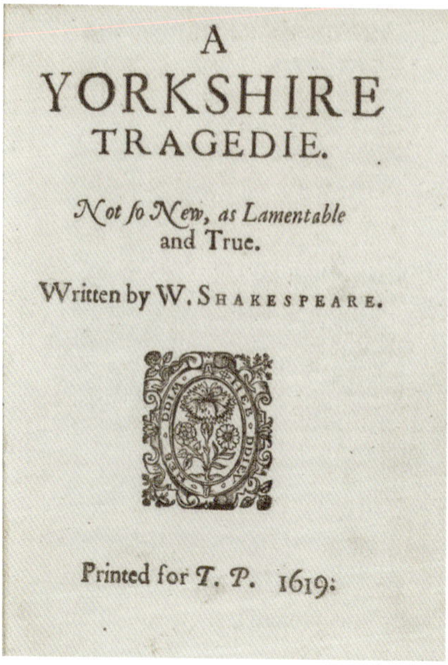

A
YORKSHIRE
TRAGEDIE.

Not ſo New, as Lamentable
and True.

Written by W. SHAKESPEARE.

Printed for *T. P.* 1619.

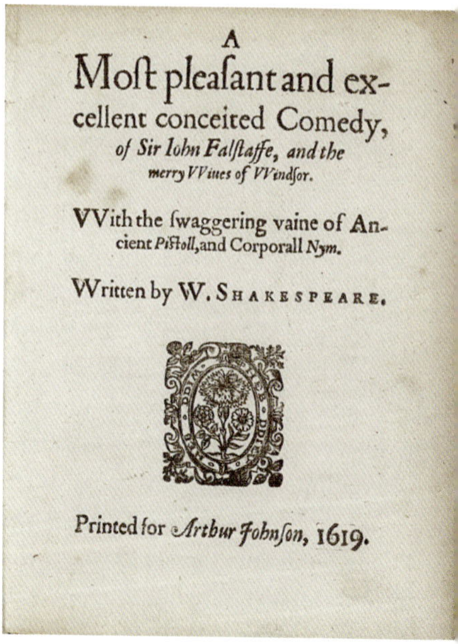

A
Moſt pleaſant and ex-
cellent conceited Comedy,
of Sir Iohn Falſtaffe, and the
merry VVives of VVindſor.

VVith the ſwaggering vaine of An-
cient *Piſtoll*, and Corporall *Nym.*

Written by W. SHAKESPEARE.

Printed for *Arthur Iohnſon*, 1619.

Figure 0.4 Title pages of the Pavier Quartos: *Whole Contention* (Martin Bodmer Foundation), *Pericles* (Ohio State University, PR 2830.A2 1619), *Yorkshire Tragedy* (Folger Shakespeare Library, STC 22341 copy 1), *Merry Wives* (Folger, STC 22300 copy 2), *Merchant* (Folger, STC 22297 copy 2), *Lear* (Folger, STC 22293 copy 2), *Henry V* (Folger, STC 22291 copy 1), *Oldcastle* (Folger, STC 18796 copy 1), *Dream* (Folger, STC 22303 copy 1). Used by permission of the Folger Shakespeare Library, Martin Bodmer Foundation, Geneva, and the Stanley J. Kahrl Renaissance and Restoration Drama Collection, in the Rare Books and Manuscripts Library of the Ohio State University Libraries.

THE
EXCELLENT
Hiſtory of the Mer-
chant of Venice.

With the extreme cruelty of *Shylocke*
the Iew towards the ſaide Merchant, in cut-
ting a iuſt pound of his fleſh. And the obtaining
of *Portia*, by the choyſe of
three Caskets.

Written by W. SHAKESPEARE.

Printed by *J. Roberts*, 1600.

M. VVilliam Shak-ſpeare,
HIS
True Chronicle Hiſtory of the life
and death of King *Lear*, and his
three Daughters.

With the unfortunate life of EDGAR,
ſonne and heire to the Earle of *Glocester*, and
his ſullen and aſſumed humour of TOM
of Bedlam.

*As it was plaid before the Kings Maieſty at White-Hall, vp-
pon S. Stephens night, in Christmas Hollidaies.*

By his Maieſties Seruants, playing vſually at the
Globe on the *Bancke-ſide.*

Printed for *Nathaniel Butter.*
1608.

THE
Chronicle Hiſtory
of Henry the fift, with his
battell fought at *Agin Court* in
France. Together with an-
cient Piſtoll.

*As it hath bene ſundry times playd by the Right Hono-
rable the Lord Chamberlaine his
Seruants.*

Printed for *T. P.* 1608.

The firſt part
Of the true & hono-
rable hiſtory, of the Life of
Sir Iohn Old-caſtle, the good
Lord Cobham.

*As it hath bene lately acted by the Right
honorable the Earle of Notingham
Lord High Admirall of England,
his Seruants.*

Written by William Shakeſpeare.

London printed for T. P.
1600.

A
Midſommer nights
dreame.

As it hath beene ſundry times pub-
likely acted, by the Right Honoura-
ble, the Lord Chamberlaine his
ſeruants.

VVritten by VVilliam Shakeſpeare.

Printed by Iames Roberts, 1600.

was primarily involved in the 1619 quartos, or if both of them were, I use the singular "Jaggard" to encompass the agency of the entire printing house.)

Like Pollard, Greg argued that Pavier was the driving force behind the project. Pavier legitimately held the rights to some of the plays: he had entered *Henry V* and *Oldcastle* in the Stationers' Register in 1600 and published them the same year; he had acquired the rights to *2* and *3 Henry VI* in 1602 from Thomas Millington; and in 1608 he entered and published *Yorkshire Tragedy*. But because he had pirated the other plays, to which he had no rights, he became "nervous about his undertaking" and decided "to issue the rest of the plays he was reprinting," after the ones correctly dated 1619, "under the guise of remainders of earlier editions."[26] In later work on the subject, Greg argued that Pavier's fear of being exposed for pirating other stationers' copies was not the only reason for the fraud. E. K. Chambers had drawn attention to a notice in the records of the Stationers' Company, dated 3 May 1619, from the Lord Chamberlain, William Herbert (one of the dedicatees of the First Folio), forbidding the printing of any plays performed by the King's Men without the "consent of some of them."[27] The King's Men, Greg now believed, had "got wind of Pavier's enterprise," and they "invoked the protection of authority" in the middle of work on the project, presumably in anticipation of their own forthcoming Shakespeare collection.[28] The abandonment of the continuous signatures after *Whole Contention* and *Pericles*, and the fraudulent imprints, revealed the underhanded attempt to evade this order.

The case was clinched when the American scholar William Neidig used the system of composite photography pioneered by Alphonse Bertillon, the inventor of the mug shot, to prove that the title pages of the various plays had all been set from standing type within days of each other. Superimposing photographs of the title pages for *Pericles*, dated 1619, and *Merchant of Venice*, dated 1600, Neidig showed that the author attribution, "Written by W. Shakespeare," matches perfectly (Figure 0.5). Such an exact reproduction was impossible to achieve when composing movable type—unless that line was simply left in place on the printer's forme from one title page to the other. Neidig thereby proved that these title pages were not printed nineteen years apart but rather days or months apart at most, and he was even able to deduce the order in which the plays were printed.[29] Like Bertillon's method, Neidig's scientific analysis identified a criminal, the pirate Thomas Pavier. Greg's and Neidig's views of the Pavier Quartos, as they quickly (though, I will argue, incorrectly) became widely known, held sway for most of the twentieth century.

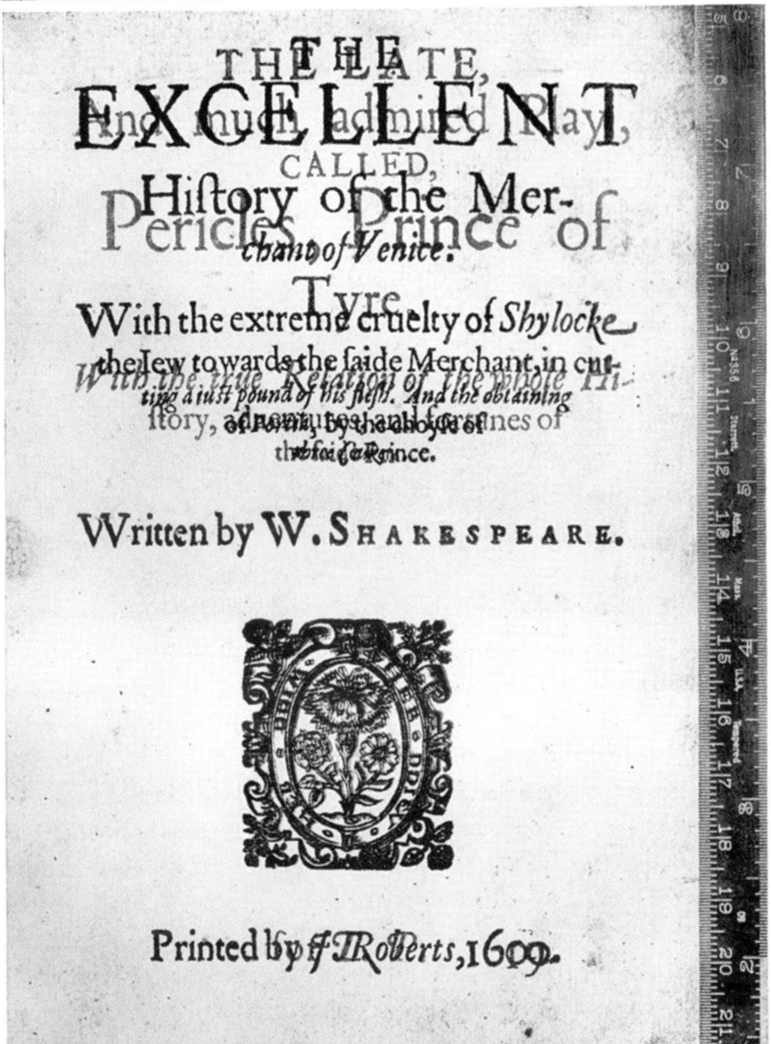

Composite photograph
by John Rea Woolley

PLATE V

Figure 0.5 Composite photograph of the title pages of *Pericles* and *Merchant*, reproduced from William Neidig's essay in *Modern Philology* (1910).

In his landmark article, Greg asked the rhetorical question "What is the literary bearing of these new facts?" and replied, "Practically none."[30] But the answer depends on what we mean by "literary bearing." What Greg had in mind was the establishment of the authoritative texts of Shakespeare's plays, and since none of these plays was an authoritative edition in New Bibliographic terms—that is, none of them was linked immediately to a Shakespeare manuscript—their literary bearing in this sense was negligible. But the "literary bearing" more broadly construed could not have been greater. When thought of as remainders, the Pavier Quartos demonstrated the lack of contemporary appreciation of Shakespeare's works as literature. Now they became the herald of Shakespeare's literary authority. As Rosenbach wrote on the flyleaf of the Gwynn volume before he sold it to Folger, the Pavier Quartos were "the first attempt at a collection of the works of William Shakespeare" (Figure 0.6).[31] Only three years after his death, four years before the First Folio, Shakespeare was already valued so highly that his plays were canonized in a collected volume.

This narrative of fraud and piracy that revealed the Pavier Quartos also propped up the authority of the *second* such collection. There Shakespeare's friends Heminges and Condell famously complain that book buyers were previously deceived with "stolne, and surreptitious copies," perhaps including apocryphal plays in the 1619 collection such as *Yorkshire Tragedy* and *Oldcastle*, as well as the supposedly "bad" quartos of *2* and *3 Henry VI*, *Pericles*, *Merry Wives*, *Henry V*, and *Lear*. As opposed to these "frauds and stealthes of iniurious impostors," the texts in the Folio are genuine products of Shakespeare's hand.[32] In this way, Greg's discovery contributed to the New Bibliographic division of Shakespeare's printed texts into good and bad, authoritative and piratical. In the popular press, and on Wikipedia for example, the Pavier Quartos are often referred to as the "False Folio"—even though they are quartos—precisely because of this dual ideological function as forerunner of and counterpoint to Heminges and Condell's collection.[33]

And this explains why Folger was willing to pay such an extraordinary price for the book. The Gwynn volume testified eloquently to the very beginning of Shakespeare's rise to the literary pantheon; it foresaw, and guaranteed the legitimacy of, the First Folios that Folger was almost maniacally collecting. No wonder he chose Gwynn's book, not one of his numerous copies of the Folio, to hold in his hand in the official portrait that now hangs in the reading room of his library (Figure 0.7).

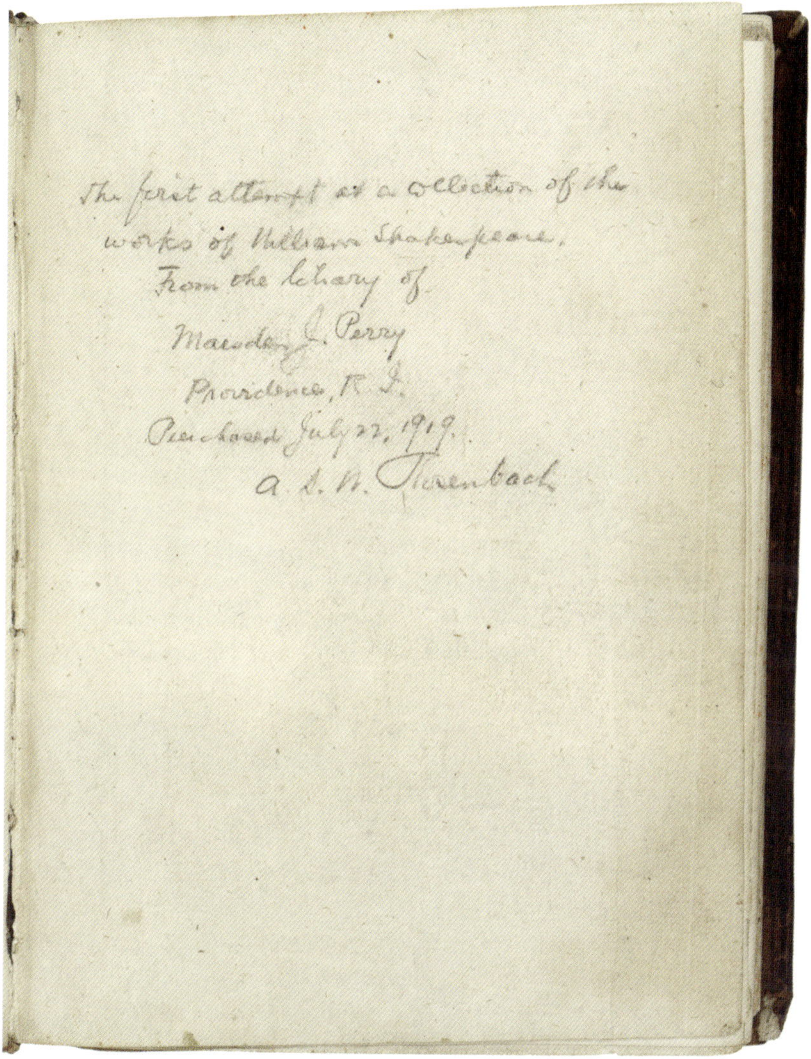

Figure 0.6 A. S. W. Rosenbach's note on the flyleaf of the Edward Gwynn volume. Used by permission of the Folger Shakespeare Library, STC 26101 copy 3.

Figure 0.7 Portrait of Henry Clay Folger by Frank O. Salisbury, oil on canvas, 1927. Used by permission of the Folger Shakespeare Library, FPb57.

Figure 0.8 Volume of Pavier Quartos discovered in 1946, now at the Mary Couts Burnett Library Special Collections Department, Texas Christian University.

In 1946, a second complete set of Pavier Quartos still in an early binding was discovered in the library of Girsby Manor in Lincolnshire (Figure 0.8). The book had been owned by a woman named Hannah Plat in 1755, as attested by an inscription on the last blank leaf of *Yorkshire Tragedy* (Shakespeare Census [hereafter SC] 1745): "Hannah Plat her Book march the 30 writtin by mee James Walker 1755." On the last verso of *Merchant of Venice* (SC 665), the final play in the volume, an earlier owner also signed his or her name alongside a Latin inscription of the date 1674, but this name has been completely obliterated by a later reader.[34] While the current binding dates from the Restoration, probably around the time of the 1674 provenance inscription, the remains of an earlier, repaired binding can be seen where the spine has broken and the underlying sewing is visible. It is clear that the Restoration binding has simply been attached to the book block without altering the order of the plays contained.[35]

Despite this interesting history, however, the reaction to the discovery of Plat's book was considerably more muted than with Gwynn's. No articles were written debating its significance. It was sold quietly on 11 July 1946 by Messrs. Hodgson and Co., Chancery Lane booksellers, for $4,479.59 to the New York collector W. L. Lewis, a price strikingly lower than Folger had paid nearly three decades earlier. The book made its way eventually to Texas Christian University, where it is found today. What accounts for such a decline in interest among scholars and collectors for another "remarkable" early bound set of Pavier Quartos?[36]

Greg's 1908 theory revealed something important about the past, something that none of the great editors and antiquarians of the eighteenth and nineteenth centuries seems to have known. Inscribed on the endpapers of individual copies of the 1619 quartos are notes by earlier collectors, which demonstrate that they were unable to determine the actual date of printing. On a copy of *Oldcastle* at the Clark Library in Los Angeles: "1st Edition / 2d Edition same year omits name of Shakespeare from title" (SC 1446).[37] Below the imprint on a copy of *Dream* that once belonged to Capell and is now at the National Library of Scotland: "1st Edition" (SC 790). An inserted slip in a copy of *Merchant* at the Bodmer Foundation, Geneva, tells us that it is the "Second Edition. same year as the first" (SC 656), while an inscription on another copy, at the Morgan Library, claims it as the "First Edition" (SC 660). On a copy of *King Lear* at Princeton: "Capell, Kemble, & the Cambridge editors, consider that this edition of Lear, without the place of sale in the imprint, is the *first* edition" (SC 511).[38] Even as late as 1911, three years after Greg's essay, the auction catalogue of Henry and Alfred Huth's collection repeatedly asserted that the Pavier Quartos were the true first editions.[39] The new bibliographic techniques that Greg and his colleagues were developing, and their new understanding of the workings of the early modern English book trade, had uncovered a historical fact that could not previously have been known.

But just as it opened up new bibliographic knowledge, Greg's article also began to foreclose it. This simultaneous opening and closing derives from a persistent tension in Greg's method. As Laurie Maguire and Paul Werstine have each persuasively argued in important reassessments of that method, the New Bibliographers' innovative techniques of bibliographic analysis were powerful, but they often jumped too quickly to larger theories that seemed to, but in fact did not necessarily, derive from the provable facts they had discovered.[40] The empirical findings of bibliography are folded into historical and literary-critical narratives that are not themselves subject to scientific proof, but it can be easy for that boundary to blur and for narratives to harden into supposed facts. In this book, I use many of the techniques of New Bibliography to take a new look at the Pavier Quartos, but I try to do so without assuming the conclusions to which the New Bibliographers have led us. In fact, those conclusions have obscured the evidence I will discuss, since the New Bibliographic narrative has been powerful enough to prevent us from properly seeing these books. There is a genre problem that seems almost inherent in bibliographical studies, as Maguire has noted: they tend to take the form of the detective story. "Much of New Bibliography's appeal," she writes, "comes from the narrative charm of the chase," and "Greg presents his material with the delight in factual revelation which characterises Sherlock Holmes."[41] Like Conan Doyle's criminology, bibliography is a method that seeks in the physical attributes of books the clues that can explain how things came to be as they are. This narrative structure impels us toward a solution, an unmasking; our bibliographic evidence pushes us toward a literary conclusion.

The discovery by Greg that these quartos were all printed in 1619 seemed to solve the mystery once and for all, when in fact his Holmesian solution has stopped us from looking for more clues. In recent years, much energy has gone into critiques of early twentieth-century bibliography, its assumptions, and its conclusions, and this work has reshaped our understanding of early modern print culture. And yet, we have often built these critiques on the New Bibliographers' own examination and analysis of the primary documents on which, therefore, both their and our theories rest. Certainly this has been true of the Pavier Quartos: Greg's theory has been revised by a number of excellent scholars who have advanced important new narratives, but all without examining the quartos themselves. What is needed now is a return to the basic bibliographic work of "close looking": reexamining these same materials, but with the advantage of fresh theoretical perspectives, revisionist thinking about the limits of the New Bibliography, and new technologies that allow us quite literally to see things that the New Bibliographers could not.[42]

These new technologies include sophisticated multispectral imaging but also, more mundanely, the commercial airplane. Greg never visited the United States, where Gwynn's copy ended up, although Pollard did make a trip to Providence to see it again in person.[43] Pollard's initial analysis emerged from his brief examination of the Gwynn and Hussey volumes as they crossed his desk, and then later the Garrick copies at the British Museum. Greg's crucial findings derived entirely from his study of the Capell volumes, although by the time of his second essay on the subject he had also examined the Garrick copies, Edmund Malone's copies at the Bodleian Library, and the copies then owned by Alfred Huth (now in the Elizabethan Club at Yale); he never personally saw the Gwynn and Hussey volumes.[44] Far away in the upper Midwestern United States, Neidig made his important contribution entirely from photographs; he seems never to have seen a single copy of these quartos firsthand.[45]

The limited use that these scholars made of extant copies is only underscored by the fact that, not coincidentally, many more copies survive of the 1619 quartos than of virtually any other Shakespeare edition in the period. As Pollard himself noted, their exceptional survival is explainable if some proportion of the copies had been bound between hard covers until the eighteenth century, when, Pollard reasonably presumed, many of these volumes were broken up for separate sale.[46] It was not merely the difficulty of long-distance travel that prevented the New Bibliographers from analyzing more copies of these plays, in other words, since quite a few were near at hand in England. A more ideological barrier was also at work: the New Bibliographic habit of thinking in terms of *editions* rather than individual *copies*. Not until Charlton Hinman's work with numerous copies of the First Folio in the Folger Shakespeare Library—culminating in Hinman's 1963 study *The Printing and Proof-Reading of the First Folio of Shakespeare*—were the advantages to bibliography and book history of this kind of analysis made fully evident. Here Hinman showed that close attention to multiple copies of an edition could reveal how work was divided among various compositors in the printing house, the order of printing the sheets of the book, and important changes to the text made in stop-press corrections.

Since Pollard and Greg were mainly concerned with the questions of when these plays were printed and by whom, whether they were published according to Stationers' Company regulations about the right to copy or in contravention of them, and why the dates and other information in their imprints had been falsified, they apparently saw no need to examine more than a few distinct copies. These questions, after all, properly pertain to entire editions of books. More generally, much of the New Bibliographers' work aimed at better understanding the transmission of the texts of Shakespeare so as to establish the definitive edition of his works, hence Greg's question about "literary bearing." This field Greg defined as "critical bibliography," "the science of the material transmission of literary texts, the investigation of the textual tradition as it is called. . . . It aims at the construction of a calculus for the determination of textual problems."[47] What was the nature of the copy that underlay the edition? What was the correct order of editions of the same title? Which editions were mere reprints of a previous one, and which derived from an independent manuscript? For these questions, too, with the important but only occasional exception of stop-press corrections, it was the edition that mattered, not the copy. The Pavier Quartos, once definitively established as later editions, not firsts, had little to tell editors about Shakespeare's text, since they lacked any independent authority deriving from Shakespeare's hand. The kind of intensive study of multiple copies that Hinman had undertaken with the First Folio was largely irrelevant to the questions the New Bibliographers were asking about the Pavier Quartos.[48]

Finally, the New Bibliographers were mainly concerned with understanding the "processes that leave their mark on the character of the finished book," as Greg wrote in his 1912 address to the Bibliographical Society.[49] Much of what was truly "new" about the New Bibliography was its deeper understanding of early modern typography and paleography, of the workings of printing houses, and of how the Stationers' Company was organized, particularly around the question of copyright. Even "the force of trades-unionism in the sixteenth century" might be considered one of the processes that left "their mark on the character of the finished book."[50] All of these areas of investigation could help to illuminate how the book was produced, and hence whether its text could be trusted or might need to be emended. But the entire field of *reception*, of what happened to printed books after they reached the bookshop, tended to be cordoned off: Greg grudgingly allowed that bookbinding was "a province of bibliography," but he declared bookplates, with their connection to provenance and the afterlife of books, "but a bastard branch of the subject."[51] Any evidence on individual copies that related to their histories after the moment of printing and initial sale was, strictly speaking, irrelevant to the kind of bibliography in which Greg was mainly interested.

For all these reasons, as well as the pragmatic difficulties involved, Greg and his contemporaries were never likely to look at more than a few copies of the Pavier Quartos. It is stunning what they were able to infer from these scant resources. But there are hundreds of other copies that they could not see because they were inaccessible, or that they did not think to examine because of their methodological biases. And since we have generally accepted that they solved the bibliographic mystery, we have not redone their pioneering work, which is now more than a century old. All of the revisionist theories about the Pavier Quartos have therefore been conceived under the same constrained parameters as the New Bibliographers: as much as we have critiqued their theories and conclusions, in a very real sense it has been impossible for us to see what they did not see.

Each copy of an edition is a unique object, with its own bibliographic evidence to offer about its particular history. Of course, not all projects will require looking at so many multiple copies of the same edition. Furthermore, digitization offers some access to copies that cannot be seen in person: current high-resolution "cover-to-cover" imaging far surpasses the old digitized microfilm of copies available through Early English Books Online, and for some research questions this may suffice.[52] But the important bibliographic features I discuss in this book—ghosts, holes, rips and scrapes—are largely imperceptible in digital facsimiles. Where the intensive study of the physical features of multiple copies is truly necessary, collaboration therefore becomes essential. Here the New Bibliographers may have been ahead of us, since the artificial and frequently hierarchical boundaries between scholarship and librarianship, between faculty and curators, had not yet hardened in their day as they too often have in ours. My own understanding of the Pavier Quartos has required this collaboration with librarians, with their deep knowledge of the provenance, curatorial, cataloguing, and conservation histories that have shaped these books into their current forms in the repositories that hold them.

I am not suggesting, in other words, that all scholarship dealing with any particular edition of a text—not even all book historical or bibliographical scholarship—requires detailed, in-person examination of every extant copy. The questions we are asking must guide the methodology we use. Nonetheless, while many copies of an edition will not contain anything too unusual and will look basically like most of the others in that edition, more often than one might think, far more often than I thought, something important turns up. And this evidence relates not simply to the reception of the book, to its history after it was printed and sold, but rather bears directly on the processes that created it. We cannot so easily divide the evidence into *before* and *after*, *production* and *reception*.

Bibliography has traditionally placed far more emphasis on the *before* than the *after*. Or, to put it more precisely: bibliography has traditionally depended on a clear demarcation between *before* and *after*. Part of what I want to suggest here, through an intensive study of one key bibliographic "case," is that we should reconsider this demarcation as we think through the history of books in the longue durée.[53] Elsewhere I have discussed how the "uncanny historicity" of the first quarto of *Hamlet* requires a new way of historicizing that key text in Shakespeare's oeuvre. But this is merely a particularly vivid example of a larger phenomenon. The books that we imagine guarantee our literary historicism often turn out, on closer inspection, to embody multiple temporalities. The physical clues by which we trace the "processes that leave their mark on the character of the finished book" themselves derive from multiple historical moments overlaid onto a single transhistorical object. And the long history of this object affects how we read these clues, making certain aspects visible at some moments and invisible at others. The past seems to be reconfigured by the present, violating the strict chronology that supports the *before* and *after* of traditional bibliographic analysis. Thinking bibliographically must involve not merely *seeing behind* the later historical accretions that intervene between us and the "finished book," although that remains important, but also *thinking through* this long history. The book is a palimpsest: we can use sophisticated tools to read what is written underneath, but if we fail to grapple with how what has been overlaid can rewrite the substrate, we may misread both texts.

What I think of as the "palimpsestic time" embedded in the Shakespeare archive forces a reconsideration of our bibliographic and book historical practice because it violates the coherence of any particular historical "moment." Strictly speaking, it should be said, there is virtually no Shakespeare archive.[54] Archives are produced in the course of running a business, a government office, or some other bureaucratic institution. A rare book library houses the original editions of plays by Shakespeare, an archive might include his will or property deeds; but we have scant archival material related directly to Shakespeare. I use the word "archive" in a loose sense here, because while I am sympathetic to Paul Eggert's complaint that "the term *archive* has been generalized" so much that "it draws into itself nearly everything that wafts by," I think the slippage between the two terms, "library" and "archive," reveals something important about our treatment of Shakespeare's books.[55]

In the words of Vivian Hunter Galbraith, former archivist at the Public Records Office, the crucial distinction of an archive "lies in the organic structure of the records it contains."[56] This organicism was absolutely fundamental to what is often considered the first formal treatment of archival theory, Hilary Jenkinson's 1922 *Manual of Archive Administration*. Jenkinson considered an archive "an organic whole, complete in itself," even if what survives may "represent only fragments of the original body." Jenkinson was heavily influenced by fossil archaeology: the archive, he wrote, enables the "reconstructing and displaying [of] the primitive organism whose remains we are considering."[57]

Because the archive testifies to an organic creature, Jenkinson restricted its contents to documents created in the ordinary course of business of an institution.[58] Crucially, therefore, "archives were not drawn up in the interest or for the information of Posterity." This "impartiality" ensures that they can be used by historians for an objective understanding of history, for a reconstruction of the actual organism as it was when it lived. Historians can thereby be assured that archives are "by their origin free from the suspicion of prejudice in regard to the interests in which we now use them."[59]

It is not that archives are free from bias. They are shot through with it, as Galbraith knew from his work in the PRO, mainly the bureaucratic bias "to deny as far as possible the fact of change and to preserve at all costs the appearance of legality."[60] But the important thing is that this bias is not *our bias*. We can therefore understand and correct for it, whereas we are typically blind to our own biases, or else actively trying to confirm them, as Greg noted in his comment on Pollard's initial theory about the Pavier Quartos. Indeed, read carefully, Greg's remark reveals his own biases as well: "The hypnotic influence that traditionally accepted facts exercise even over the most critical mind . . . prevented Mr. Pollard from suspecting that the ten quartos in question were not merely collected and published in one composite volume *in 1619*" but also printed all together in that year. And yet Pollard never argued in his *Academy* article that Pavier's hypothetical nonce collection had appeared in 1619; rather, he argued that Pavier had brought together these old playbooks (including the ones dated 1619) only in 1622, when he learned that the First Folio was shortly to appear in print. Greg quietly redates Pollard's hypothesis because of his own investment in the year 1619.

Because the archive must be kept as free from bias as possible, Jenkinson goes so far as to insist that the one thing an archivist must absolutely *not* do is to consider the needs of future historians: "The Archivist is not and ought not to be an Historian . . . his duty is to his Archives, independently of any of the Research subjects . . . that make use of Archives for their own ends."[61] In this sense, the archive should be created "by pure chance or at least by considerations which did not include the possible requirements of future Historians."[62]

What makes an archive for these two founding theorists is thus centrally a question of temporality. The future must not impinge upon the present in its attempt to preserve the past. Indeed, the archive ceases to be an archive as soon as one thinks of the future at all—and for that same reason, as soon as one thinks of the past, of posterity, of the very idea of preservation. For preserving the present necessarily involves imagining it as already past, and hence imagining the future uses of the present.

But is such historiographical renunciation possible?[63] Derrida writes that while etymologically *archive* means both "the *commencement* and the *commandment*," it also "*shelters* itself from this memory . . . which comes down to saying also that it forgets it."[64] The archive imagines itself as neutral origin but is constantly undone by its simultaneous involvement in ordering, assigning, and excluding. For Derrida, "archive fever" diagnoses our "compulsive, repetitive, nostalgic desire for the archive, an irrepressible desire to return to the origin, a homesickness, a nostalgia for the return to the most archaic place of absolute commencement."[65] The archive, in this sense, is a back-formation; it is how the present imagines the past as origin—the inversion of Jenkinson's formulation. The archive involves just the sort of temporal boundary crossing that it should forbid. It is not surprising that Derrida turns to the ghost of old Hamlet for his emblem of archive fever: the objects we seek as guarantors of authentic origins stubbornly insist on revealing their ghostly violations of temporal order.

For this reason I (mis)apply the term "archive" to the Shakespearean books that have been intensely collected, curated, and studied over the past centuries. These objects materially embody this same "irrepressible desire to return to the origin," the hope that they can testify to the emergence of Shakespearean drama into print at its commencement. Analytic bibliography has been one of our central tools for reconstructing this emergence, and I do not mean to suggest that this is a naïve or impossible hope. No one is more conscious of the difficulties of reconstructing the past than bibliographers and librarians, and no one is more aware of all the ways in which we have repeatedly violated these archival principles and let an imagined future posterity impinge on the preservation of the past: in gaudy nineteenth-century fine bindings; in the washing and trimming of marginalia; or in the separation of sammelbands into more valuable individual books.

Nonetheless, the sophisticated techniques of bibliography and book history, which can allow us to perceive and account for these later accretions, can mask the stranger, less neatly chronological effects of the centuries of work invested in the Shakespeare archive. The Cambridge librarian Henry Bradshaw, often viewed as a founder of modern analytic bibliography, imagined his work very much along the lines that Jenkinson and Galbraith outline. "The study of palaeotypography," he wrote in 1870, should be treated "as a branch of natural history," which could reveal the past for bibliography just as the fossil record could for biology: "Each press must be looked upon as a *genus*, and each book as a *species*, and our business is to trace the more or less close connexion of the different members of the family according to the characters which they present to our observation."[66] But we have paid less attention to the ways in which our fossil record has been reshaped by the very practices of collecting and archiving that have also preserved it. The Pavier Quartos, I hope to show, are a particularly telling example of the need for a bibliography that attempts simultaneously to return to the moment of origin, to the "processes that leave their mark on the character of the finished book," while questioning the very notion of such an original moment by dwelling in the longue durée, in the book's forever *unfinished* character.

Recent revisionist arguments about the 1619 quartos have focused on the same key questions that the New Bibliographers attempted to resolve. Who was behind the project, and why did he publish these quartos? Who, if anyone, was he trying to deceive with the false imprints? How were the playbooks actually sold in shops, how often as individual playbooks and how often as bound volumes? What is the relationship of these quartos to the First Folio, published four years later?

Greg and Pollard changed their views on these questions, and depending on which statements one quotes, they can be made to stand in for multiple positions. As we have already seen, for instance, Greg initially claimed that Pavier was concerned about accusations of piracy by other stationers, but he later supplemented this view, or replaced it, with the argument that the deception was aimed at the King's Men and the Lord Chamberlain. Pollard likewise admitted that "from the standpoint of the Stationers' Company the volume could hardly be called piratical." The rights to *Lear* belonged to Nathaniel Butter, who appears in the imprint: he had entered and published the first edition of the play in 1608. The rights to *Merry Wives* belonged to Arthur Johnson (likewise in the imprint), who had entered the play by transfer from John Busby and published it in 1602. As Pollard noted, "Johnson and Butter were living members of the Stationers' Company, fully able to protect their rights" if they felt those rights had indeed been infringed. But they did nothing. So perhaps instead Jaggard, who "was connected with the players through his monopoly . . . for printing playbills . . . heard enough plain-speaking [from the King's Men] to frighten him" and alerted Pavier to the danger, leading to the false imprints.[67] Pollard ultimately refuses to decide, concluding only that the deception was designed "to give the volume or set a better chance of passing unquestioned from *either* quarter."[68]

By the time Greg compiled his monumental *Bibliography of English Printed Drama to the Restoration*, he took a similar line: "Pavier had a valid title" to some of the plays; "no one could claim a title to *Pericles*," since it had been published multiple times by stationers other than the one who had entered it; and Pavier "made some private arrangement with Arthur Johnson and Nathaniel Butter, who were both alive and had valid rights in *The Merry Wives of Windsor* and *King Lear*." With *Merchant* and *Dream*, however, Pavier "took the precaution . . . of ascribing the reprints of these plays to [the printer] James Roberts, who was . . . safely dead." But Greg also ascribed the abandonment of the idea of "making a regular collection" to the effect of the Lord Chamberlain's letter to the Stationers' Company.[69]

Greg hedged as well on the question of who was primarily responsible for the project. He always tended to emphasize Pavier above all, but he sometimes suggested more of a collaboration with Jaggard. In a 1924 essay, "The First Folio and Its Publishers," he wrote that the false imprints were a compromise between Pavier, "inclined to be obstinate," and Jaggard, who needed to preserve his relationship with the King's Men, with whom he was already in discussions to print the First Folio. By 1955, on this question too Greg came to no clear conclusion: "Who was the responsible person behind the venture is not on the face of it very clear, and was probably not intended to be," although Greg still refers to the scheme by Pavier's name.[70]

Indeed, the very fact that we have continued to call these quartos the Pavier Quartos has tended to beg some key questions and to reduce the relationships behind the publications to a single agent. On this issue and others, critics have often simplified Pollard and Greg's various claims over the years, making them seem firmer and more clear-cut than they really were, in keeping with a pattern that Maguire documents surrounding New Bibliographical theories of memorial reconstruction.[71] As a result, revisionist scholars have sometimes been arguing as much against an ossified conventional wisdom as against specific claims made by the New Bibliographers. Nonetheless, this conventional wisdom has had real effects on our understanding of the 1619 quartos. In the entry for William Jaggard in the *Dictionary of National Biography*, for instance, Stanley Wells states simply as fact that Pavier was the one who put the collection together: "Jaggard was hired by Pavier (probably in association with Nathaniel Butter and Arthur Johnson)," and "Pavier and his associates . . . persuaded Jaggard to print the remaining plays [after the Lord Chamberlain's order] with false dates."[72] For both the New Bibliographers and those who have followed them, locating the agency for the Pavier

Quartos with Pavier rather than Jaggard has often served to protect the integrity of Shakespeare's Folio texts, also printed by Jaggard, from the corruption associated with the 1619 quartos.[73]

As part of a broader reassessment of New Bibliographical theories about copyright, piracy, and the London book trade, the revisionists have generally downplayed the underhandedness of the scheme. As Gerald Johnson wrote in his influential 1992 essay on Pavier's career, which initiated much of the revisionism around the 1619 quartos, the stationer's "reputation as a pirate seems hard to justify, and a more comprehensive study of his career suggests that it is hardly deserved."[74] To be fair, the established view of Pavier that Johnson describes—"a publisher of 'dubious reputation,' or, more seriously, a 'notorious piratical publisher'"—derives at least as much from scholars writing in the wake of Pollard and Greg as it does from their own work.[75] Still, far more than the New Bibliographers did, Johnson and the revisionists who have followed him stress the presumptively regular workings of the book trade, not always recorded in the Stationers' Company records in the more modern, rationalized, legalistic way that Greg tended to seek. For instance, Johnson considered the publication of *Pericles*, the only one with Pavier's initials in the imprint that the stationer did not have an obvious right to publish, nonetheless not likely to have been disorderly: while the play had been entered in 1608 to Edward Blount (Jaggard's future partner in the First Folio), it had actually been published the following year by Henry Gosson. Gosson had a close relationship with Pavier, later partnering with him to publish ballads. The play was then published by the printer Simon Stafford in 1611. Stafford was still working in London in 1619 and may have come to a private arrangement with Pavier, since in 1626 Pavier's widow entered her transfer of the right to copy in the Stationers' Register in the normal way.[76]

Johnson's revisionist narrative left only two of the plays—*Merchant* and *Dream*—with evidently falsified names in the imprints (though others have false dates), since both are listed as "Printed by J[ames] Roberts, 1600." *Merchant* had been entered by Roberts in 1598 and then transferred by him to Thomas Hayes in 1600, when Roberts printed the first edition for Hayes. On 8 July 1619, Hayes's son Lawrence entered his right to copy the play by transfer from his deceased father. Perhaps Hayes had become aware of the project and was brought in on it at this point. Johnson also wonders whether "Jaggard thought that he had a claim on *The Merchant* since it had been printed by Roberts, whose printing business Jaggard had taken over some ten years earlier." With *Dream* there is no such connection, however; the play had been entered and published by Thomas Fisher in 1600. Fisher disappears from our records in 1602, and despite the occasional claim that the right to a text might become "derelict" and then be claimed by any stationer, Johnson doubts this happened: "Derelict copyrights were usually claimed by the Stationers' Company, which might then allow their reprinting with the payment of royalties to the Company," but there is no record of this having occurred with *Dream*.[77]

Influenced by Johnson, and also by Peter Blayney's critique of New Bibliographical theories of piracy, a consensus has arisen among more recent scholars that any deception cannot have been directed at the Stationers' Company. For one thing, Pavier was a highly placed member of the company, elected to its Court of Assistants on 14 June 1619, only a month or so after the Lord Chamberlain's letter.[78] And while neither William nor Isaac Jaggard ever held office in the company, William's brother John was Under Warden in 1619–20, and William was Printer to the City of London, an important and lucrative position that Isaac assumed after his father's death.[79] Furthermore, as Andrew Murphy writes, "if the falsified dates and casuistically contrived imprints in the 1619 quartos were intended to deceive Pavier's publishing brethren, then the deception was perpetrated with singular ineptitude, since, unlike other examples of counterfeit printing from the period, the Pavier quartos make little enough effort to imitate the title pages of the texts being copied."[80] Instead, David Scott Kastan concludes that the King's Men were the targets: "Most scholars have argued that the intervention from [the Lord Chamberlain] stopped the planned-for collection, but, as printing had already started, Pavier and Jaggard decided to go forward . . . issuing the plays individually, some with falsely dated title pages . . . presumably so they would seem old stock that could safely be sold at Pavier's shop in Ivy Lane."[81] Lukas Erne agrees: "It seems unlikely . . . that the Stationers' Company opposed the printing of the plays or the fake imprints," because "the easily detectable differences between genuine and fake imprints suggest that Pavier made no effort to hide from the publishers of the genuine editions or from the Company at large."[82]

As we have seen, this is less a critique of the New Bibliographers than it has often seemed, since Greg and Pollard acknowledged the problems with any argument that the deception was aimed at fellow stationers. More recent revisionist arguments have gone beyond the debate about precisely who was supposed to be deceived, however, suggesting that there was far less deception involved than we have thought, or perhaps no deception at all.

Sonia Massai argues that Pavier changed his mind about the imagined collected volume, but that his "decision was prompted by an attractive business proposal rather than by the Court order of May 1619." Jaggard was "first inspired by Pavier's projected collection and persuaded the King's Men to invoke the Lord Chamberlain's support to prevent other stationers—and *not* Pavier—from securing previously unpublished plays from their repertory." On this theory, Jaggard "persuaded Pavier to issue his ten Quartos either individually or as a nonce collection, that is, as a volume gathering seemingly older and more recent editions, in order to whet, rather than satisfy, readers' demand for a new collection of Shakespeare's dramatic works."[83] The false imprints are not meant to deceive those who held the rights to these plays: after all, even the title pages of two plays to which Pavier himself owned the rights have false dates, and obviously there was no reason to deceive the stationer in these cases.[84] Rather, these imprints create the impression of a collection put together from scattered old editions—perhaps otherwise hard to obtain in 1619—and thereby foster demand for the new and improved texts of Shakespeare's works soon to be available in the First Folio. In this story, Pavier and Jaggard are in on the scheme together, but so too are the King's Men; neither the Stationers' Company nor the actors are the targets of the deception, which is instead a sophisticated marketing scheme. Only the retail book buyer is tricked.[85]

James J. Marino offers another radical revision of the traditional theory, one that also downplays deception. He sees the publication of the 1619 quartos as part of a battle between the stationers and the actors over divergent ideas of literary property. Unlike most scholars who have discussed the quartos, Marino sees Jaggard as the key agent behind the scheme. Jaggard's inclusion of *Oldcastle* in the group is a crucial clue: "Had this addition been intended as fraud, it would have been remarkably unconvincing, since Jaggard also reprinted the phrase 'acted by the Right honorable the Earl of Nottingham Lord High Admiral of England his Servants,' which clearly identifies the play as belonging not to Shakespeare and his company but to their professional rivals."[86] Such an edition could not have been intended to confuse anyone in the theatrical world. Nor could the quartos have fooled stationers, since Jaggard had only the previous year used the same "HEB DDIEV" printer's device that appears on all but one of the 1619 quartos on his *Catalogue of such English Bookes, as lately haue bene, and now are in Printing for Publication* (1618): "This is a professional industrial publication . . . requiring the cooperation of the entire guild (who had to furnish their information to Jaggard), and with the guild as a primary audience."[87] Rather than truly attempting to deceive anyone, Jaggard is asserting the stationer's expansive understanding of literary property. Since Jaggard's partner Pavier had published the first edition of *Oldcastle*, a play intimately linked to the King's Men's *Henry V*, the publication of both these plays in the 1619 quartos asserted the stationer's customary right to control not only the actual text entered in the Stationers' Register but also any closely related texts that might be perceived to interfere with sales.[88] Hence, adding Shakespeare's name to the 1619 edition of *Oldcastle*, when the first edition in 1600 had been anonymous, "was to assert identity between the play one owned and the play the King's Servants currently performed. Asserting that identity protected the stationer's interest in the work and forestalled attempts to displace one's text with a newer, more 'authentic' version."[89] By contrast, the actors had a vested interest in differentiating Shakespeare's *Henry V* from the *Oldcastle* performed by their rival company. For the stationers, the author's name "affirmed the unity of an intellectual property," whereas the players "deployed writers' names to deny, rather than affirm, any identity between similar texts."[90] The 1619 quartos were "a form of protest . . . to defend the booksellers' notion of their rights."[91]

Cyndia Clegg goes further than even Massai and Marino, providing an extreme example of the revisionist arguments about the Pavier Quartos. She claims that the imprints are not even false, so long as we assume that the date 1608 on *Henry V* was "an honest error," because the other dates all represent the actual year of publication of an earlier edition, and the names in the imprints "properly ascribed ownership" to a stationer who printed or published that earlier edition. The quartos simply represent an effort by the stationers Jaggard, Pavier, Johnson, and Butter to "reaffirm their rights in titles they owned by reprinting them" ahead of the planned First Folio.[92] As a tactic "to exert pressure on the King's Men," the project succeeded: "The King's Men apparently offered their unpublished plays to Jaggard and [his partner Edward] Blount as their share in the project, and Jaggard and Blount provided the titles they owned, including the 'Pavier' quartos."[93] Clegg's theory of the imprints is unique, as far as I am aware: no other scholar of the early English book trade has ever suggested that putting the date and publisher of a previous edition in the imprint was normal practice for a reprint. Nor am I aware of any similar examples: including a date that was not the year of actual printing, or naming a stationer who was not involved in the actual edition on which his or her name appears, was typically associated with subterfuge in the book trade. But Clegg's argument serves to demonstrate how far some recent scholars have gone to deemphasize the trickery that the New Bibliographers found in the Pavier Quartos.

In the ensuing chapters I have occasion to critique various aspects of the major revisionist theories, but I want to stress here that the fresh perspectives they have brought to the subject have prompted my own work. Still, none of them is based on new bibliographic evidence from the quartos themselves. The revisionists have been dependent on Pollard, Greg, and other early twentieth-century scholars even as they have critiqued them. This dependency has made it more difficult to perceive two foundational, and largely unargued, presuppositions about the 1619 quartos that even the revisionists have generally taken for granted. First, with only the occasional recent exception, Pavier has been seen as the key agent behind the project, the "first publisher to envisage and at least partly realize a collection of Shakespeare plays," in the words of Lukas Erne.[94] Second, the 1619 quartos have nearly always been understood first and foremost as, in the words inscribed in the Gwynn volume, "the first attempt at a collection of the works of William Shakespeare." Only occasionally has anyone suggested, as Tara Lyons has recently done, that "Shakespeare's authorship was simply one of many possible organizational frameworks offered to readers purchasing the quartos."[95] As we will see, new bibliographic evidence forces a reassessment of both of these foundational assumptions, while further illuminating all of the key questions that have driven work on the 1619 quartos since the early twentieth century.

Sometimes this new evidence supports the revisionists, sometimes the New Bibliographers, sometimes neither. And sometimes it remains mysterious, provoking new questions rather than any easy answers. This book is based on my personal examination of 289 copies of these quartos, plus an additional fifty-three copies examined for me by others—or 92 percent of the 372 extant copies of which I am aware. When we look again at these books, there is much, much more to see than we knew.

CHAPTER 1

Ghosts

—What is a ghost? Stephen said with tingling energy. One who has faded into impalpability through death, through absence, through change of manners. . . . Who is the ghost from *limbo patrum*, returning to the world that has forgotten him?

—James Joyce, *Ulysses*

The ghost who returns to the world that has forgotten him comes from *limbo patrum*, the space reserved for the patriarchs of the Hebrew Bible, sanctified but living before Christ and hence unable to enter heaven until the harrowing of hell. Punningly, for Joyce, the limbo patrum is the limbo of the father, Stephen Dedalus's father, Hamlet's father, Shakespeare the literary father. The ghost who returns to haunt the Pavier Quartos is the ghost of "Shakespeare," the author function, the principle of collection. Here the author has faded into impalpability through change of manners: we risk misrecognizing this figure and seeing what we already think we know, the author Shakespeare as we understand him after the First Folio and after centuries of collecting, studying, and editing his books and texts.

What is a ghost? A residue of the linseed oil in which lampblack, soot produced by burning oil, is suspended to create printer's ink. Linseed oil that has somehow reacted with a facing page because of the acidity of that adjacent paper.[1] A faint image of the ink imprinted on one page that appears on another page once bound alongside it but that has since been separated from it—in the auction house, in the bookbinder's shop, in the rare book library. A bibliographic ghost returns to the world that has forgotten it to reveal lost collections, lost sammelbands, lost histories.

Jeffrey Todd Knight first brought this kind of bibliographic evidence to wide attention in a brief, groundbreaking article with major ramifications for

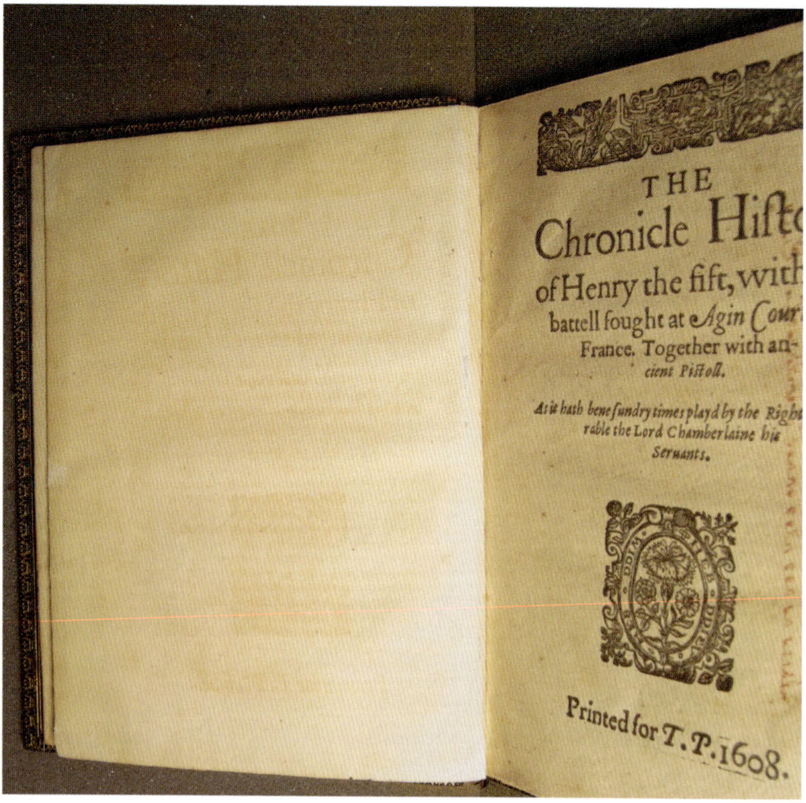

Figure 1.1 Front flyleaf and title page of a copy of *Henry V*, showing ghosting under normal and ultraviolet light. Courtesy of the Kislak Center for Special Collections, Rare Books, and Manuscripts, University of Pennsylvania, PR2812.A1 1619 copy 1.

our study of books.[2] While the meaning of these ghosts is clear, their origins remain mysterious. Ghosts appear on some pages and not others; they sometimes show the impression of formerly adjacent leaves, and often do not, even in cases where we know there was once a neighboring book. The acid content of early paper varied according to the amount of alum added, as a preservative, to the gelatin sizing applied to paper to allow it properly to absorb ink. Because this animal-based gelatin spoiled rapidly, alum was typically added daily to the same batch of sizing made in the paper mill on Monday or Tuesday. Hence paper that was sized later in the week was more acidic than paper sized earlier in the week.[3] The variability of the acidity of paper may help to explain why these ghosts appear only occasionally.

Figure 1.1 (*Continued*)

Paper produced in the ensuing centuries is even more acidic, as more alum was added in the production process, and chemicals involved in the production of wood-pulp paper introduce still higher acidity. Not surprisingly, then, the new endpapers added in the nineteenth century when many Shakespeare quartos were rebound as precious relics have produced ghost images far more frequently and strongly than the early quartos themselves. Ghosts are easiest to see on these endpapers, although the more forceful reaction can paradoxically make it difficult to read the ghostly text itself (Figure 1.1). Those wishing to see a ghost in person should simply look at the Victorian endpapers of early printed books. Once you have seen one, you begin to notice them everywhere—including, more rarely and more intriguingly, on the early pages themselves.

These ghosts can tell us a great deal about how the Pavier Quartos were originally sold in bookshops in 1619. They can also tell us about what happened to them in the years between their initial sale and our encounters with them in libraries today. And they can undo some of the scholarly assumptions about the Pavier Quartos that have helped, retroactively, to determine how these books appear to us today. Along the way, these ghosts, and some other forms of ghostly evidence, will help to build a new census of bound volumes of the 1619 quartos: there were many more of them than we have suspected.

Greg was undoubtedly right that several plays by or attributed to Shakespeare were being sold together in 1619. And the bibliographic evidence that Neidig provided for the order in which the plays were printed is likewise strong, although R. Carter Hailey has slightly modified that order, based on his analysis of the paper stocks used in the printing, suggesting that the first gatherings of *Merry Wives* (including the title page) may have been printed ahead of *Merchant*.[4] (Hailey's theory would explain the seeming anomaly, in the traditional understanding of the order of printing, that *Merry Wives* was correctly dated 1619 *after* the falsification had begun with *Merchant*, dated 1600.) But our belief that the New Bibliographers essentially "solved" the mystery of the printing of these plays, and our consequent neglect of the bibliographic evidence in the quartos themselves, has led us too easily to accept an ideal version of the order in which the plays were bound, above all with *Whole Contention* and *Pericles* beginning the collection, since they have continuous signatures. Indeed, the bibliographical code that Greg and Neidig established has been so powerful that it has often overridden the physical evidence of the books themselves.[5] Despite being the librarian in charge of Capell's collection at Trinity College, Greg could write of the "false order" of the plays in that set, since "it is clear that 'Pericles' ought to follow the 'Contention,'" but in fact *Pericles* appears third in the second volume and *Whole Contention* fourth. In the same breath, however, Greg could add that he believed "the present false order . . . to be original."[6] The ordering of plays in Capell's volume is both true (historically) and false (formally), faithful (unchanged by later collectors) and unfaithful (failing to adhere to its signatures). From the beginning of the modern study of the Pavier Quartos there is this tension between what we might think of as a *prescriptive* and a *descriptive* understanding of the "correct" order of these plays.

The long-standing Folger catalogue record for Gwynn's volume is a perfect example: "Contains The whole contention pts. 1–2 and Pericles. MS. table of contents. Bound with seven other 1619 Shakespeare quartos. . . . Mis-bound: the first five works after STC 26101 are bound between Q4 and chi1."[7] The description of the Gwynn volume both adheres to and obscures its physical appearance. In the *Short-Title Catalogue* (*STC*) and as a Folger shelf mark, STC 26101 refers to the combination of *Whole Contention* and *Pericles*, in which *Whole Contention* ends on signature Q4, and signature chi1 is the title page of *Pericles* (chi or χ being the bibliographer's code for an unsigned internal leaf).[8] The Folger record thus implies that *Whole Contention* and *Pericles* should be bound first in Gwynn's volume, based on their continuous signatures, followed by the seven other plays. But, in fact, the "MS. table of contents" records the true order of binding, in which *Whole Contention* appears first and *Pericles* seventh (Figure 1.2). The disjuncture between the manuscript contents list and the bibliographic code established by Greg and Neidig leads to the note in the catalogue record that claims the Gwynn volume is "mis-bound."

In his essay on the *unheimlich*, or uncanny, Freud writes that "the *unheimlich* is what was once *heimisch,* familiar; the prefix '*un*' . . . is the token of repression."[9] We can say the same of the prefix *mis-* in "mis-bound." On the one hand, the Gwynn copy is prized for its early and authentic binding, which guarantees the unity of the Pavier Quartos as an early modern pre-Folio Shakespeare collection and explains why Henry Folger chose this book to hold in his official portrait. On the other hand, the Gwynn binding is critiqued for failing to conform to modern theories of what it should have been. Modern bibliographic theory here represses the facts of the physical book to make it conform to expectations.

Like many libraries, the Folger catalogues copies of *Pericles* under the heading of *Whole Contention*, since from the perspective of the New Bibliography, *Pericles* is a continuation of the same single book, due to its continuous signatures. This has some strange consequences: the Folger lists sixteen copies of *Whole Contention between the two Famous Houses, Lancaster and Yorke* in its catalogue, but five of these are classified as "imperfect" simply because they do not include *Pericles*, even though nothing is missing from *Whole Contention* itself. Another five are "imperfect" because they are copies of *Pericles* alone, even though that play is not part of the title of the item as listed in the catalogue. A more extreme case: the University of Pennsylvania library catalogue records two copies of *Whole Contention*, but the details

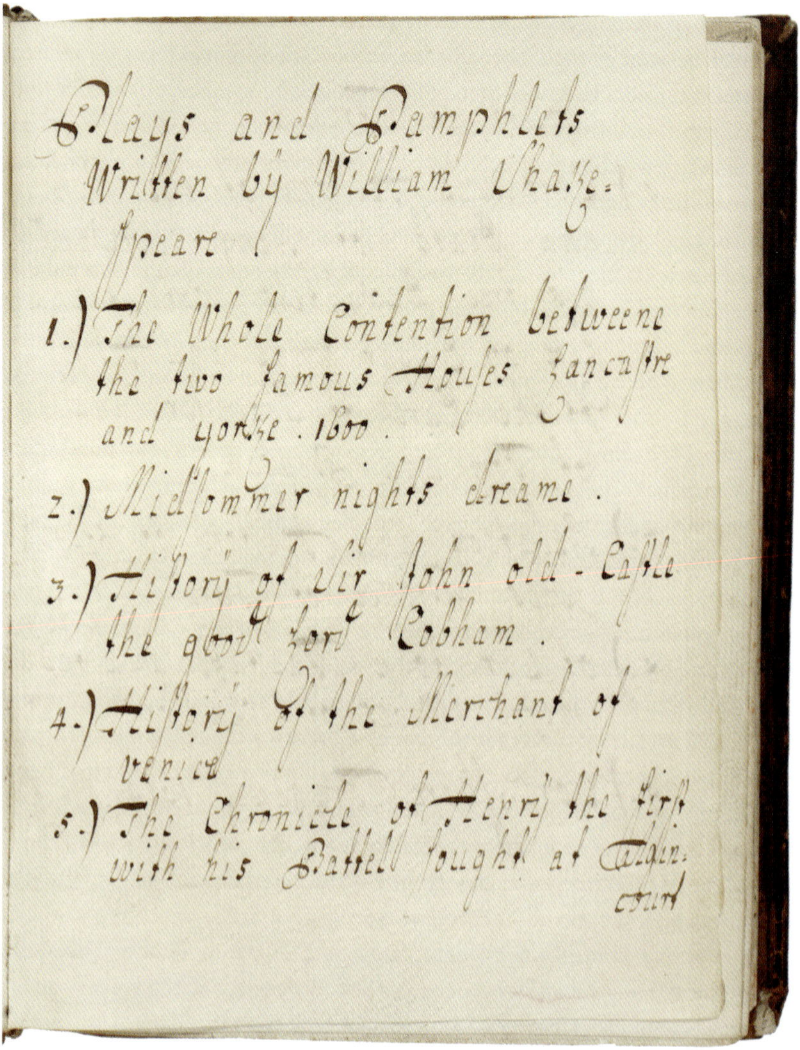
Plays and Pamphlets Written by William Shake-speare

1.) The Whole Contention betweene the two famous Houses Lancastre and Yorke. 1600.

2.) Midsommer nights dreame.

3.) History of Sir John Old-Castle the good Lord Cobham.

4.) History of the Merchant of Venice

5.) The Chronicle of Henry the first with his Battell fought at Agin-court

Figure 1.2 Manuscript table of contents in the Edward Gwynn volume. Used by permission of the Folger Shakespeare Library, STC 26101 copy 3.

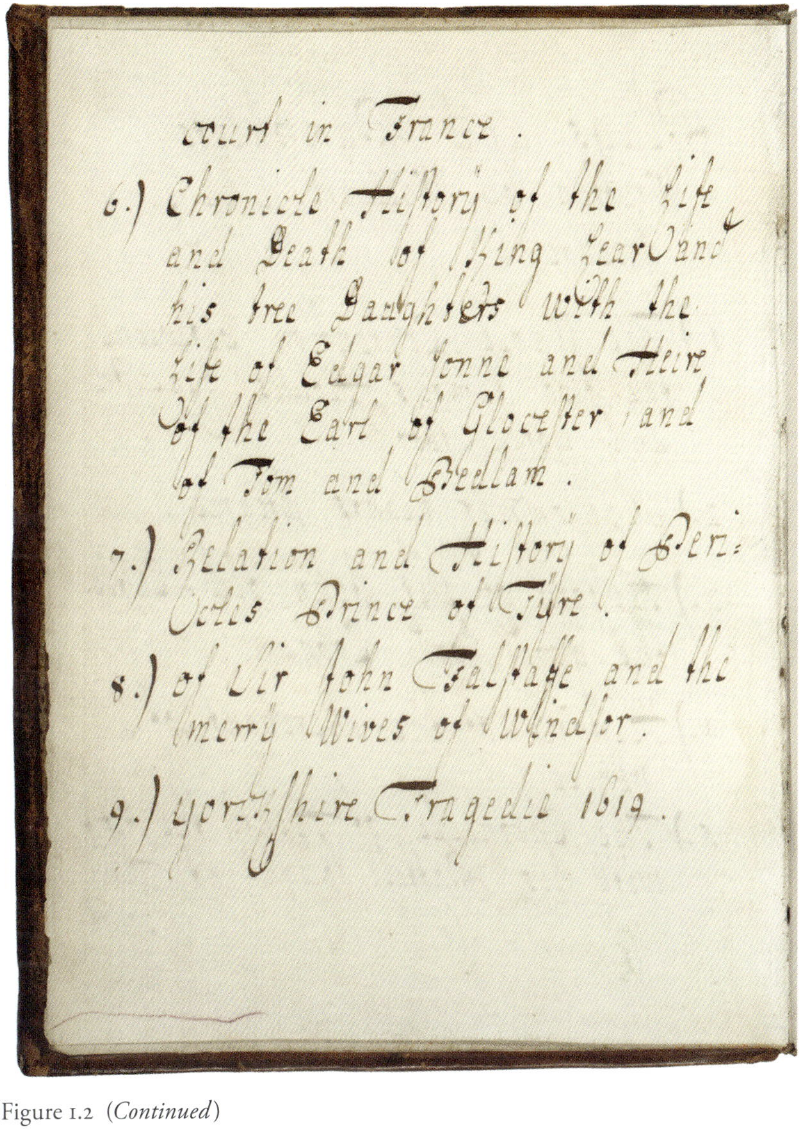
court in France.
6.) Chronicle History of the Life
and Death of King Lear and
his tree Daughters with the
Life of Edgar sonne and Heire
of the Earl of Glocester and
of Tom and Bedlam.
7.) Relation and History of Peri-
cles Prince of Tyre.
8.) of Sir John Falstaffe and the
merry Wives of Windsor.
9.) yorkshire Tragedie 1619.

Figure 1.2 (*Continued*)

reveal that both copies are "imperfect: all before leaf chi1 wanting." If one remembers that "leaf chi1" is the title page of *Pericles*, one can infer (though it does have to be inferred) that in fact the Penn libraries hold no copies of *Whole Contention* at all but rather two copies of *Pericles* only.[10] Penn's apparent copies of *Whole Contention* are ghosts, haunting the catalogue but physically faded into impalpability.

We can learn more about the misbinding of the Gwynn volume, or rather its *binding*, from the Pavier Quartos in the Garrick Collection now at the British Library. It is a testament to the power of the New Bibliographic narrative of the Pavier Quartos that this evidence, which is in fact fairly visible, has apparently never been noticed before. As we have seen, Pollard speculated that Garrick's copies were once bound in a single volume, partly because he was able to pick out "all nine plays from among their fellows simply by their height."[11] Greg noted that the "Garrick copies . . . are all bound separately, but . . . their uniform size . . . points to their having at one time formed parts of a single volume."[12] The Garrick copies are indeed similar in size, although to say they are of "uniform size" is an exaggeration, since by my measurement they range in width from 14.4 cm (*King Lear*) to 15.0 cm (*Dream* and *Merry Wives*); in height, the dimension that Pollard stressed, they are indeed nearly uniform, measuring between 19.1 and 19.3 cm. By itself, however, the nearly uniform size of the quartos cannot tell us as much as Greg and Pollard assumed, because they all were trimmed during multiple rebindings and indeed were almost certainly trimmed by none other than Edward Capell while he was cataloguing the collection for Garrick, precisely in order to give them a "uniform size."

Capell was a close friend of Garrick's, and the great actor engaged the Shakespeare editor to put his collection into some order.[13] Capell designed an unusual system for doing so. The books were arranged by size and bound into volumes of six to eight plays. Each volume was given a Roman numeral and categorized with other volumes of similar size, within a centimeter or so, under the same letter. Thus Garrick's Pavier Quartos were all catalogued in the E series, although they were not all in the same volume: *Whole Contention* and *Pericles* were consecutive in E.II; *Yorkshire Tragedy* and *Oldcastle* were in E.VI; *Merchant*, E.V; *Merry Wives*, E.III; *Lear*, E.IV; *Henry V*, E.I; *Dream*, E.VII. The problem with inferring too much from the similar sizes of the quartos is that, as the collection's bibliographer, George Kahrl, notes, "One centimetre is a small distinction to make between volumes, and the binder, putting together the plays according to the contents list provided by Capell[,] . . . may have had to trim leaves to fit the correct sequence."[14] We cannot assume, in other words, that the books had quite such similar measurements before Capell had them rebound into the volumes for Garrick.

Capell's manipulation of the plays raises another caveat: we cannot assume that *Whole Contention* and *Pericles* had always been consecutive. While they are currently bound in a single volume, that binding dates only from the 1840s, when the plays were removed from Capell's sammelbands and bound individually for better conservation. In Garrick's day, as noted above, they appeared consecutively as the second and third items in E.II, preceded by *Albion's Triumph* and followed by several nondramatic romances.[15] But even this may tell us less than it appears, because Capell had already noticed—indeed, may have been the first to notice—the continuous signatures that link the plays together bibliographically. In a footnote to *Whole Contention* in the Garrick catalogue, he wrote that, despite the lack of a date in the imprint, the playbook "was certainly printed in 1619, along with a Pericles . . . for the signatures are continued through both plays; This ending with Q, and the Pericles beginning with R."[16] Similarly, on the title page of his own copy of *Whole Contention*, he wrote that the play, though undated in the imprint, was printed in "1619.—at the same time with the Pericles that follows [i.e., that should follow]; as appears by the continuation of the signatures."[17] When he rebound his own copies of the Pavier Quartos into the two volumes now at Trinity College, Capell evidently declined to put *Whole Contention* and *Pericles* into their "correct" order, despite noting their continuous signatures, since there they appear in "reversed" sequence. But we cannot know whether he did so for Garrick.

In Capell's numerical catalogue for Garrick, in fact, the two playbooks are widely separated, with *Whole Contention* appearing as number 531 and *Pericles* as 472. This might well imply that the two were not in fact consecutive when Capell initially catalogued them, although his numbering system is highly idiosyncratic and has resisted attempts at explanation.[18] Nonetheless, the fact that Capell was aware of the continuous signatures certainly raises the possibility that he was the one responsible for binding the two playbooks consecutively, and that prior to his attentions they had not been bound together in Garrick's collection. Despite Pollard and Greg's hopes, neither the relatively uniform size of the playbooks nor the fact that *Whole Contention* and *Pericles* are now bound together in a single volume, and were bound consecutively (along with other titles) in Garrick's own day, can establish whether they ever formed part of a bound volume of the 1619 quartos. But there is material evidence that can: ghosts.

On the last verso of the Garrick *Merchant* (SC 644) can clearly be seen the ghost image of some lettering, in reverse (Figure 1.3).[19] Enough can be discerned to make certain that this is the title page of the Pavier Quarto of *Oldcastle*. The arrangement of letters, line breaks, and the capital *L* in "Life" essentially precludes any other text. In a mirrored and color-altered image, the ghost becomes more substantial (Figure 1.4). Because these ghosts are created when adjacent leaves are bound together for a significant period of time, we can be sure that Garrick's copy of *Merchant* used to be bound immediately preceding a copy of *Oldcastle*. Was this copy of *Oldcastle* the Garrick copy? It is impossible to say, although it seems probable, since the copies of these plays had likely traveled together for a while even before Garrick acquired them.

Garrick's "Collection of Old Plays," as it was widely known, derived from a number of sources, most prominently the Harleian Collection owned by Robert Harley (1661–1724) and his son Edward (1689–1741), the first and second Earls of Oxford, which in turn included items previously owned by Humphrey Dyson (1582–1633), who had likely seen many of the plays when they were first performed. The Harleian Collection was sold to the bookseller Thomas Osborne in the early 1740s, after it was catalogued by Samuel Johnson, and many of the plays were then purchased by Robert Dodsley, who used them when compiling his *Select Collection of Old Plays* in 1745–46.[20] Dodsley's *Old Plays* consisted of sixty-one plays in twelve volumes, although the complete Harleian Collection included, Dodsley wrote, "between 6 and 700" plays. Garrick seems to have bought the entire collection, or the majority of it, but we cannot be sure; he certainly acquired a number of copies as well from the sale of the Shakespeare editor Lewis Theobald's estate in 1744 and 1747, since the initials "L.T." appear on some of the plays in the collection.[21] The provenance of many of the more than one thousand plays in the collection cannot now be traced, however, and among these, unfortunately, are the Pavier Quartos.[22] Still, the common provenance of so many of the plays in Garrick's collection suggests that these too had passed from one owner to the next as a group since the seventeenth century.

Regardless of whether the Garrick *Merchant* had once been bound preceding the Garrick *Oldcastle*, we know from this ghost that it had been part of a bound volume containing at least some of the Pavier Quartos. Likewise,

Figure 1.3 Ghost on the last verso of David Garrick's copy of *Merchant*. © The British Library Library Board, C.34.k.23.

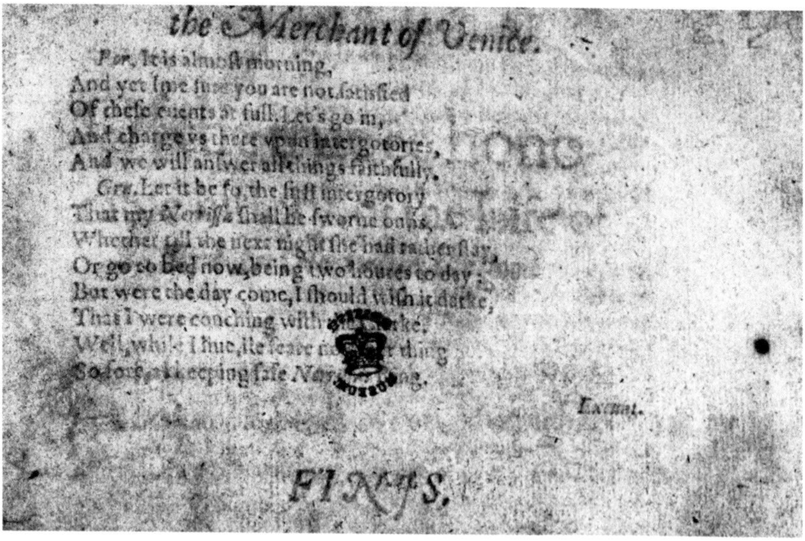

Figure 1.4 Color-altered and mirrored image of the ghost on the Garrick *Merchant*. © The British Library Library Board, C.34.k.23.

the last verso of the Garrick *Lear* (SC 487) shows, very faintly, the reverse image of the date "1608" in the same typeface that Jaggard used to print the Pavier Quartos: the numerals 1 and 0 that rise to x-height, the 8 that descends well below the baseline, and the sharply overhanging ascender on the numeral 6 (Figure 1.5).[23] The only Pavier Quarto that could possibly have produced this ghost image is *Henry V*, since only this play and *Lear* itself have "1608" in the imprint, and only on *Henry V* is the date positioned in the correct place to produce this ghost. (And no other *STC* book printed in 1608 fits with the evidence.)

In neither case can these ghosts have emerged when the plays were bound in Garrick's sammelbands, since we know from Capell's flyleaves that none of these plays were in the same volume. In Garrick's day, *Lear* was followed by Shirley's *The Gamester* in E.IV; *Merchant* was followed by *The Unfortunate Usurper* in E.V; *Oldcastle* followed Fletcher's *Wit Without Money* in E.VI; and *Henry V* followed Massinger's *Duke of Milan* in E.I. And while it is conceivable that Garrick himself, or Capell, disbound a volume of Pavier Quartos, it seems more likely that these plays were no longer bound consecutively when Garrick acquired them.[24] In other words, the evidence of these ghost images points to a volume of Pavier Quartos bound in the early seventeenth century

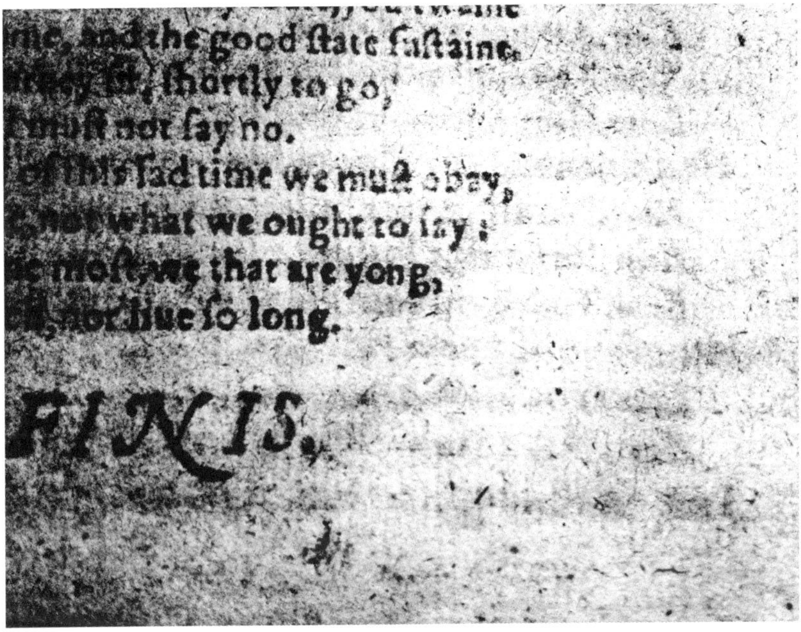

Figure 1.5 Ghost of "1608," just to the right of FINIS, in color-altered and mirrored image of the last verso of David Garrick's copy of *Lear* (C.34.k.19). © The British Library Board, C.34.k.19.

but later broken up into individual playbooks. Again, we cannot be certain that this volume contained all of, or exclusively, the Garrick copies of these plays, but that is the most likely explanation.[25]

These quartos were examined closely by Pollard and Greg when they were investigating the Pavier Quartos, and yet they give no indication of having seen these ghosts. Perhaps this kind of bibliographic evidence was simply unknown to them—I have found no reference to ghost images like these in scholarship from the early to mid-twentieth century. Had Pollard and Greg noticed the ghosts, presumably they would have discussed them, since they would have supported their inference that the Garrick copies once formed part of a bound volume. Ghost images are easy to miss, but under the kind of close scrutiny habitual to a bibliographer as brilliant as Greg, they are apparent enough. The fact that they have remained hidden in relatively plain sight all this time suggests that ingrained habits of thinking have created a scholarly blind spot. For us, as I have suggested, this blind spot results from the belief that the New Bibliographers essentially solved the bibliographic mystery of the printing of the Pavier Quartos, even if (as revisionist book historians have argued) they did not put that evidence into the proper historical narrative. For the New Bibliographers, this blind spot resulted from their tendency to ignore evidence of the circulation of books after the sheets left the press, as they trained their analyses on print production. I linger on this point to stress that it takes no remarkable skill to discern these ghosts. I have been struck during the course of my research by how frequently I have found them. In about a third of all the libraries I visited, a ghost was lurking among the Pavier Quartos. These ghosts are everywhere in our books, and they offer a major new piece of bibliographic evidence for how books circulated and were read before they took the physical form in which we now encounter them.

The Boston Public Library (BPL) also owns a copy of each of the Pavier Quartos, individually bound. On the last verso of *Pericles* (SC 1008), the ghost of "Mr William Shakespeare" himself appears, from the title page of *Lear* (Figure 1.6).[26] I have also found a ghost image on a copy of *Oldcastle* at the Elizabethan Club at Yale (SC 1453), which shows that *Henry V* once followed it. The same combination of *Oldcastle* and the ghost of *Henry V* turns up at Princeton (SC 1441). Meanwhile the copy of *Oldcastle* now at the Victoria and Albert National Art Library (SC 1450) used to be followed by *Whole Contention*. Another ghost appears on the copy of *Dream* at the Harry Ransom Center in Texas (SC 803), showing that it was once bound ahead of *Merchant*. And two more ghosts are found at the Folger: the ghost of *Oldcastle* on a copy of *Lear* (SC 496), and the ghost of *Yorkshire Tragedy* on a copy of *Henry V* (SC 325).[27]

Each of the ghosts I have discussed appears on the final verso of the play, and hence all are of title pages; in my experience, this is where ghost images tend to appear most frequently in early books. Sometimes internal leaves produce ghosts, although it is a puzzle why they do not do so more often (which would render books somewhat hard to read). Perhaps title pages are more likely to leave ghost images both because they use larger letters and because the relative lack of type on the page, and hence the increased pressure exerted by the printing press on each character, somehow makes them particularly liable to react with the facing page. But it may simply be that ghosts are more easily seen on final versos, which are often either entirely or partially blank. On the title pages of copies of *Merry Wives* at the Folger (SC 728) and the Martin Bodmer Foundation in Geneva (SC 731), for example, I could not be certain that what I was seeing was indeed a ghost (presumably of the last

Figure 1.6 Ghost on Boston Public Library copy of *Pericles*, G.126.28.

verso of the text that once preceded it): it was too difficult to make out, a very light ghost if one at all, and obscured by the text of the title page itself.[28] In other words, readers wishing to hunt for ghosts should pay close attention to the final verso, but they should not restrict their search to that page.

Other kinds of ghostly evidence can alert us to more lost volumes of Pavier Quartos. Here we are concerned not with direct physical evidence like a ghost image but with secondary evidence that is nonetheless highly suggestive of previous bindings. For example, sometime before 1799 when Eton College acquired its copy of *Pericles* (SC 1013), a previous owner wrote on the last verso the motto "Lux post tenebras," which happens to be the motto on the printer's device used only on *Dream* among the Pavier Quartos (Figure 1.7).[29] It seems likely that the title page of *Dream* was once bound immediately after *Pericles,* so that as the book lay open, the reader was staring at the printer's device on the recto and copying its motto onto this verso. Another piece of secondhand evidence can be found in an old library catalogue at the University of Virginia: a set of Pavier Quartos donated in 1853 and once owned by Thomas Randolph, governor of Virginia and son-in-law of President Jefferson. This set likely burned in the fire that destroyed much of the library in 1895, but the old catalogue includes the order in which the plays were bound (Figure 1.8). It is unclear whether Randolph's book was still in an early binding like the Gwynn and Plat copies, or whether, like the Hussey and Capell copies, it had been rebound in later years.[30] Yet another now lost copy can be found in the 1786 sales catalogue of the estate of John Henderson. This auction included three consecutive lots that almost certainly reveal a Pavier collection that had been broken into three volumes, each likely still in the original sequence in which they were bound (Figure 1.9).[31]

A book at the Newberry Library provides a more palpable body to parallel the ghostly copy in the Henderson auction catalogue. And yet it too has been hiding in plain sight, because, as in the examples of *Whole Contention* and *Pericles* discussed above, cataloguing practices have obscured

Figure 1.7 Eton College copy of *Pericles*, with manuscript motto taken from the printer's device on *Dream*. Reproduced by permission of the Provost and Fellows of Eton College, Sal.4.30(2).

our understanding of its true nature. This small volume containing copies of *Merry Wives* (SC 736), *Oldcastle* (SC 1435), and *Whole Contention* (SC 1705) is described in the catalogue record as a later collector's sammelband, a "made-up volume . . . put together probably in the 18th or 19th century."[32] The assumption that this is a "made-up volume" derives from the blue paper wrapper currently stitched around the plays (Figure 1.10). This simple binding does date to a later period; perhaps it was done by the William Henderson who signed the title page of *Merry Wives*. But there would have been little reason for a collector in the eighteenth or nineteenth century to have chosen to bind these three particular plays together in a sammelband, since, as we have seen, no one in either century had any idea that they had in fact been printed at the same time and formed part of a group, beyond the fact that they all have Shakespeare's name on the title page. The coincidence of these three Pavier Quartos just happening to be bound together by a later collector, solely on the basis of their common authorial attribution, seemed too far-fetched to me, and fortunately the Newberry librarian, Jill Gage, and conservator, Lesa

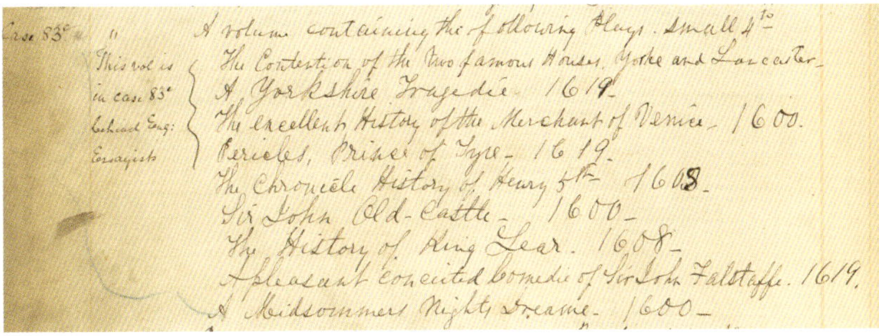
Case 83
This vol is in case 83 Cabinet Eng: Essayists
A volume containing the following Plays. Small 4to
The Contention of the two famous Houses, Yorke and Lancaster.
A Yorkshire Tragedie 1619.
The excellent History of the Merchant of Venice 1600.
Pericles, Prince of Tyre 1619.
The Chronicle History of Henry 5th 1608.
Sir John Old-Castle 1600.
The History of King Lear. 1608.
A pleasant conceited Comedie of Sir John Falstaffe. 1619.
A Midsommer Nights Dreame. 1600.

Figure 1.8 Nineteenth-century University of Virginia library catalogue listing of Pavier Quartos. From the University of Virginia Archives, Albert and Shirley Small Special Collections Library, RG-12/12/1.119, page 414.

Dowd, generously agreed to peek under the blue paper wrapper to look for evidence of previous binding.[33]

On the spine underneath the wrapper are the residues of an earlier sewn binding, a more careful and labor-intensive binding than the simple wrapper holding it together in its current form (Figure 1.11). Three leather thongs provided the sewing stations to which the gatherings were attached, and, Dowd reports, "there is old glue on the spine [and] a small remnant of leather between the second and third thongs," the remains of the earlier binding. The three thongs have been cut at the ends, "likely when taken out of an original binding," indicating that these plays were at some point removed from a larger grouping.[34] Almost certainly these are the remains of a single volume of Pavier Quartos that was later broken into smaller groupings, probably for sale at auction, just like the one in John Henderson's estate (although not actually that one, since the order of plays differs).

What the Newberry Library volume represents, then, is something far rarer than its catalogue record suggests: the most extensive surviving bound volume of Pavier Quartos after the Gwynn, Capell, and Plat copies. Why was it mistaken for a more ordinary, later sammelband? Again, I suspect the New Bibliographic narrative has caused us to take for granted an "ideal copy" of the bound collection, in which *Whole Contention* and *Pericles* should appear bound together at the start. In the Newberry volume, *Whole Contention* appears "out of order," and for this reason, I think, it was long taken to be a later collector's "made-up volume." Once catalogued as such, it became unavailable as evidence that could reveal anything about the original sale of the Pavier Quartos, since it now seemed to testify only to a later collector's

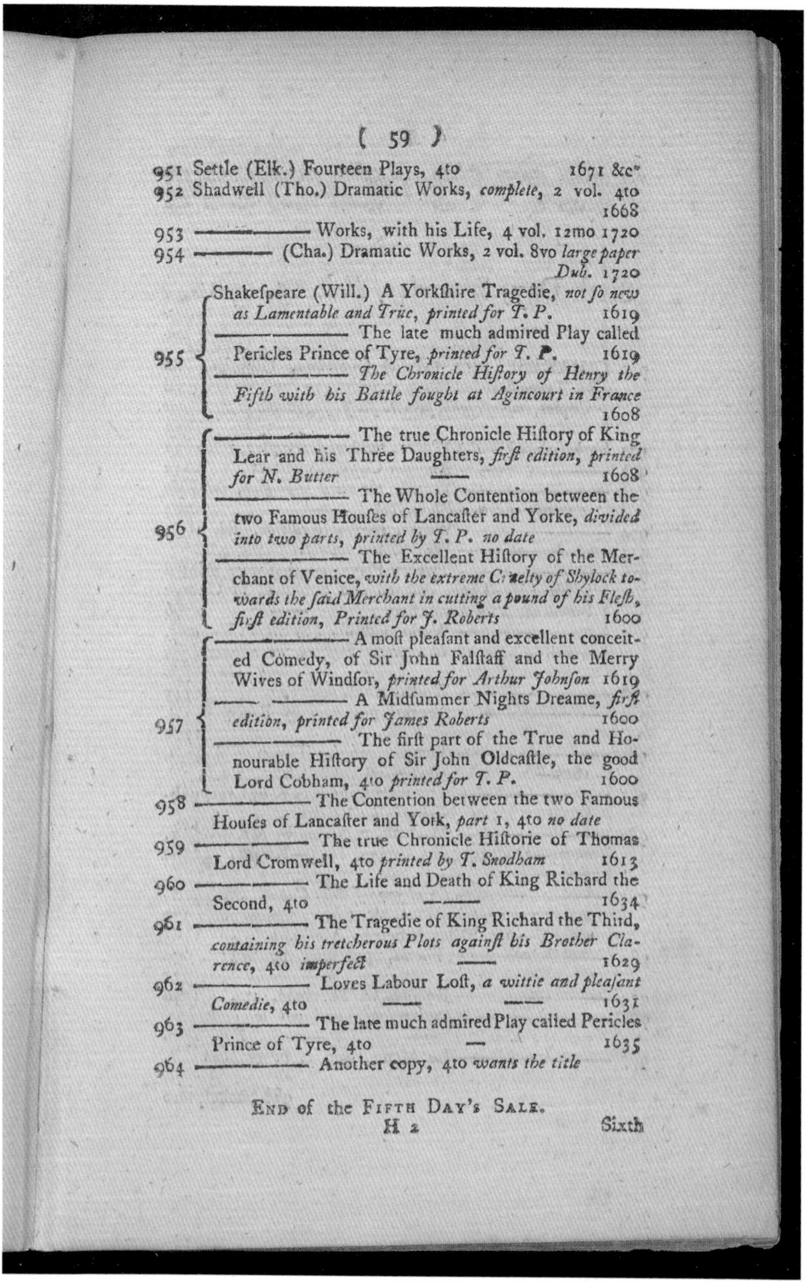

(59)

951 Settle (Elk.) Fourteen Plays, 4to 1671 &c.

952 Shadwell (Tho.) Dramatic Works, *complete*, 2 vol. 4to 1668

953 ——— Works, with his Life, 4 vol. 12mo 1720

954 ——— (Cha.) Dramatic Works, 2 vol. 8vo *large paper Dub.* 1720

955 Shakeſpeare (Will.) A Yorkſhire Tragedie, *not ſo new as Lamentable and True, printed for T. P.* 1619
——— The late much admired Play called Pericles Prince of Tyre, *printed for T. P.* 1619
——— *The Chronicle Hiſtory of Henry the Fifth with his Battle fought at Agincourt in France* 1608

956 ——— The true Chronicle Hiſtory of King Lear and his Three Daughters, *firſt edition, printed for N. Butter* —— 1608
——— The Whole Contention between the two Famous Houſes of Lancaſter and Yorke, *divided into two parts, printed by T. P. no date*
——— The Excellent Hiſtory of the Merchant of Venice, *with the extreme Cruelty of Shylock towards the ſaid Merchant in cutting a pound of his Fleſh, firſt edition, Printed for J. Roberts* 1600

957 ——— A moſt pleaſant and excellent conceited Comedy, of Sir John Falſtaff and the Merry Wives of Windſor, *printed for Arthur Johnſon* 1619
——— A Midſummer Nights Dreame, *firſt edition, printed for James Roberts* 1600
——— The firſt part of the True and Honourable Hiſtory of Sir John Oldcaſtle, the good Lord Cobham, 4to *printed for T. P.* 1600

958 ——— The Contention between the two Famous Houſes of Lancaſter and York, *part* 1, 4to *no date*

959 ——— The true Chronicle Hiſtorie of Thomas Lord Cromwell, 4to *printed by T. Snodham* 1613

960 ——— The Life and Death of King Richard the Second, 4to —— 1634

961 ——— The Tragedie of King Richard the Third, *containing his tretcherous Plots againſt his Brother Clarence*, 4to *imperfect* —— 1629

962 ——— Loves Labour Loſt, *a wittie and pleaſant Comedie*, 4to —— —— 1631

963 ——— The late much admired Play called Pericles Prince of Tyre, 4to — 1635

964 ——— Another copy, 4to *wants the title*

End of the Fifth Day's Sale.

H 2 Sixth

Figure 1.9 Listing of Pavier Quartos in the *Catalogue of the Library of John Henderson* (1786), page 59. Beinecke Rare Book and Manuscript Library, Yale University, X348.E29 1786/2/20.

Figure 1.10 Volume containing three Pavier Quartos, with added blue wrapper, at the Newberry Library, Chicago, Vault Case 4A 956.

Figure 1.11 The Newberry Library volume with the spine opened, revealing previous binding.

whims. To read the evidence of this volume back into the situation in 1619 would thus be anachronistic. But in fact it is later scholarship and curatorial practices that anachronistically created this anachronism. To understand how this book came to be the way it is, to understand it bibliographically, we need to think across the longue durée of its full history.

All of this ghostly evidence adds to our census of bound volumes of the 1619 quartos—I have mentioned evidence for sixteen such sets to this point, but more are to come—and already reveals something important: the Pavier

Quartos were less uniform than they have seemed to be since the New Bibliographic narrative of their printing, interruption, and fraudulent imprints has become orthodoxy. These copies differ dramatically in their order of binding. In other words, seventeenth-century booksellers and collectors do not seem to have read and understood twentieth-century bibliography, or indeed to have had any conception of "the" Pavier Quartos as a singular and stable collected volume.[35]

Nowhere can the power of the New Bibliographic narrative be seen so clearly as in a volume of all the Pavier Quartos once owned by Thomas Goodman (c. 1668–1738), who was appointed royal physician to William and Mary in 1690.[36] Goodman's library was auctioned in March 1739, following his death a few months earlier, and while we do not know its purchaser, the volume must have passed relatively quickly into the hands of Mary Orlebar (1730–1821).[37] Sometime before 8 May 1763, Orlebar gave the book to Bishop Thomas Percy (1729–1811), because on that date, Percy recorded a memorandum on its front flyleaf:

> NB. Miss Orlebars made me a present of this book with a view that I shd. give it to my friend Mr. Garmer, who was collecting Quarto Editions of Shakespeare plays. I accordingly sent it dow[n] [t]o him at Cambridge, but whe[n] [h]e came to examine the volume he found *tha*t he was already possessed of every play in it except King Lear, which he therefore took out, & sent me back the Volume. ~~This being the case I think I ought to return the book to Miss Orlebars againe~~. May 8. 1763. T. P.[38]

At some point after Mr. Garmer returned the book to him—and after he did not, in fact, return the book to Orlebar—Percy removed two other plays from the volume. One of these was *Yorkshire Tragedy*. The other is far more interesting.

On the verso of the flyleaf where Percy wrote his memo—now part of a volume including only *Whole Contention* (SC 1691) and *Pericles* (SC 1018)—is a striking table of contents (Figure 1.12). First in this list is Thomas Heywood's *Woman Killed with Kindness*, a play that was clearly attributed to Heywood on the title page of every early edition.[39] Note that, again, "The contention of the Houses of York and Lancaster" and *Pericles* are not consecutive in this list. So how does this copy of *Whole Contention* come to be bound with *Pericles* today at the Folger, along with this flyleaf, which must instead have preceded Heywood's *Woman Killed* when Orlebar owned the

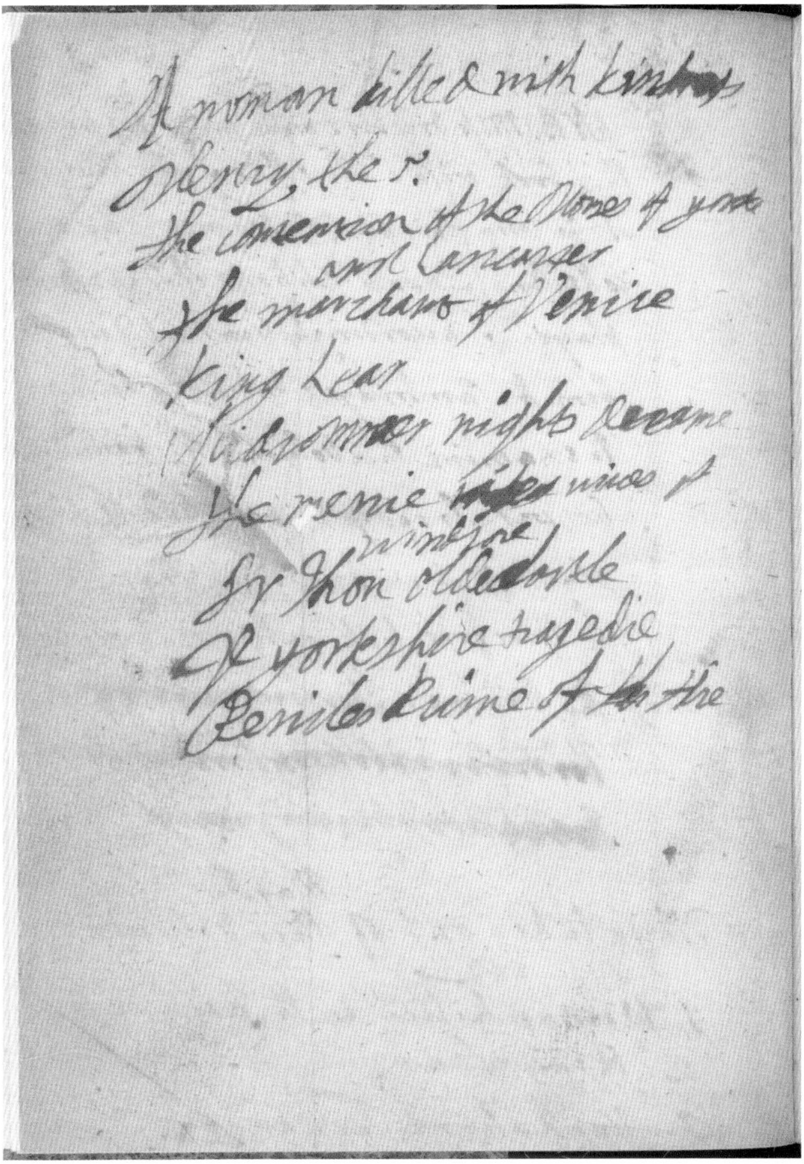

Figure 1.12 Manuscript table of contents, including *Woman Killed with Kindness*, bound in the Thomas Goodman-Mary Orlebar volume of Pavier Quartos. Used by permission of the Folger Shakespeare Library, STC 26101 copy 2.

book and gave it to Percy? And what is Heywood's play doing in this list in the first place?

When Folger bought the copy, the remaining plays were in a binding dating to around 1850, still in the same order as listed on the flyleaf.[40] In 1963, however, the Folger curator Giles Dawson disbound the collection, rebinding five plays as individual volumes and binding *Whole Contention* and *Pericles* together according to their continuous signatures. In other words, only in 1963 did these seventeenth-century copies of *Whole Contention* and *Pericles* correspond to the early twentieth-century bibliographic description of their ideal state.[41]

Dawson rebound the plays individually (except for these two) because, he wrote in a typescript note, while the "1850 binding was perfectly sound and satisfactory," nonetheless "the extreme tenderness of many of the leaves caused by the use of the volume, at some time after 1850, for the pressing of botanical specimens and the resulting mildew" suggested the need for better conservation. He was no doubt encouraged in this decision by his belief that the original order of binding was unimportant for a historical understanding of Shakespeare's plays: "The presence of the non-Pavier *Woman Killed* pretty well guarantees that the original collector had no special plan in view and therefore that the arrangement in Miss Orlebars's volume was hit or miss."[42]

Dawson makes two linked claims here that helped to justify the rebinding: first, Heywood's *Woman Killed* is a "non-Pavier" play; and, second, the order in which the plays appear on the manuscript contents list is "hit or miss." Both claims ultimately derive from the New Bibliographical theory of the Pavier Quartos. Significantly, at the beginning of this typescript note, Dawson lists the plays involved according to the traditional New Bibliographic order, the order of printing that Neidig had been able to deduce: "These three plays were, when H. C. Folger acquired them, bound together with *Merchant* (22298), *M. Wives* (22300), *Midsummer* (22303), *Henry V* (22291), and *Oldcastle* (18796), all being Pavier quartos of 1619." In other words, when a consummate bibliographer like Dawson thought of the Pavier Quartos, he quite naturally and unconsciously thought of them as following this order, and he therefore saw an order of binding that differed as indicating that "the original collector had no special plan in view"—especially because of the inclusion of "the non-Pavier *Woman Killed*." Dawson's adherence to the New Bibliographic theory of the Pavier Quartos then had serious material effects on this book, resulting in the loss of its 1850 binding and any evidence it may have contained, the separation of these plays from each other, and a long-lasting confusion over the history of binding these plays that the Folger's senior cataloguer Erin Blake has only recently sorted out. Again we see the retroactive transformation of the physical appearance of these books, which allows the evidence to fit, anachronistically, with later bibliographic theory.

A lot rests on that phrase "the non-Pavier *Woman Killed*." It is a phrase that happens to be false. In 2010, Jeffrey Todd Knight found another instance in which a bound book of Pavier Quartos had apparently included the very same non-Shakespearean play that was once included in the Goodman-Orlebar volume. On the blank final verso of the Huntington Library's copy of *Henry V* (SC 334), Knight reported, there appears a faint ghost image: "A search of texts contemporary with Pavier's reveals that the image is in fact the title page of Thomas Heywood's play, *A Woman Kilde with Kindnesse* (1617), which must have been bound with *Henry V* for some time in order to leave such a visible mark."[43] This discovery was the clue that sent me looking for ghost images in other copies of the Pavier Quartos. If Knight's essay had not alerted me to this fascinating piece of bibliographical evidence for previous binding, the numerous other ghosts I have discussed in this chapter would likely have remained invisible—which should remind us how much bibliographical evidence still waits to emerge under the right circumstances and caution us against drawing firm conclusions too quickly.[44]

As Knight argues, the Huntington ghost, together with the Orlebar table of contents (and, I would add, the Goodman catalogue listing), suggests that "the series was not necessarily Shakespearean." But Knight concludes that the "textual combination is likely the work of readers," a book buyer's sammelband, suggesting "how early owners, enabled by the built-in flexibility of printed products like the Pavier quartos, could make books . . . both inside and outside prescribed schemes of organization."[45] Other scholars have followed Knight's lead: Lukas Erne writes that the presence of *Woman Killed* in the Goodman-Orlebar volume is "an eloquent reminder that the composition of such bound volumes was typically determined not by the playbooks' publishers or booksellers but by their owners, who could choose to constitute their bound volumes as they pleased."[46] Here even these excellent scholars accept too quickly the New Bibliographic theory of the Pavier Quartos (not surprisingly, as they had not seen all of the evidence that we now have). In fact, there is compelling evidence that Heywood's play was bound with Shakespeare's works not by readers but by a stationer; it was not added to the series later but formed part of it from the start, offered for sale with the 1619 Shakespeare quartos and possibly with other plays altogether.

This first attempt at a collected Shakespeare was not quite as Shakespearean as we have thought.

In 1774, the bookseller Benjamin White published *A Catalogue of Several Libraries and Collections of Books*, which listed works that he had lately purchased and was offering for sale from his shop at Horace's Head in Fleet Street.[47] Number 6785 in this voluminous list includes ten items bound together, beginning with *Dream*, running through all of the traditional Pavier Quartos, and ending with the 1617 edition of *Woman Killed* (Figure 1.13). Here we have a third instance in which the "the non-Pavier" Heywood play turns up in a bound collection of Pavier Quartos. Obviously this cannot be coincidence: the odds of three different later readers all independently choosing to bind the same Heywood play in a sammelband with the Pavier Quartos are minuscule. We have not been able to see this fact because, after the New Bibliography, we have regarded Heywood's play as a priori "non-Pavier," since, as A. S. W. Rosenbach wrote on the flyleaf of the Gwynn volume, the Pavier Quartos must be "the first attempt at a collection of the works of William Shakespeare." Heywood is not Shakespeare, therefore *Woman Killed* is not part of the Pavier Quartos.

Even before the New Bibliographic discovery of the Pavier Quartos, the practices of collectors and curators in the centuries following the initial sale of these books had enforced this separation. In Garrick's "Collection of Old Plays," for instance, *Woman Killed* was in the E range, like all the other Pavier Quartos; in volume E.IV, it stood alongside the Pavier *Lear* and five non-Shakespeare plays. Was this copy of *Woman Killed* originally found in a bound volume of Pavier Quartos, as the ghosts on Garrick's copies suggest once existed? Did Garrick's copy mix Heywood with Shakespeare as we know the Goodman-Orlebar copy, the Benjamin White copy, and the copy indicated by the ghost image at the Huntington Library all did? I have found no evidence that can tell us the answer, although it is entirely possible that such evidence exists and will turn up. Finding that evidence, however, has been made harder by the differential treatment of the Garrick copies in the intervening years. When the British Museum rebound and recatalogued its books in the 1840s, the most valuable books in the Garrick collection, including of course the Shakespeare plays, were "bound in full morocco and put into glass cases; these were given shelf marks in the C.34 range. The rest were half-bound and were given marks in the 643 and 644 sequences."[48] Not surprisingly, today the Garrick copy of *Woman Killed* has the shelf mark 644.e.33 (Figure 1.14). Centuries of collecting, cataloguing, and bibliographical theoriz-

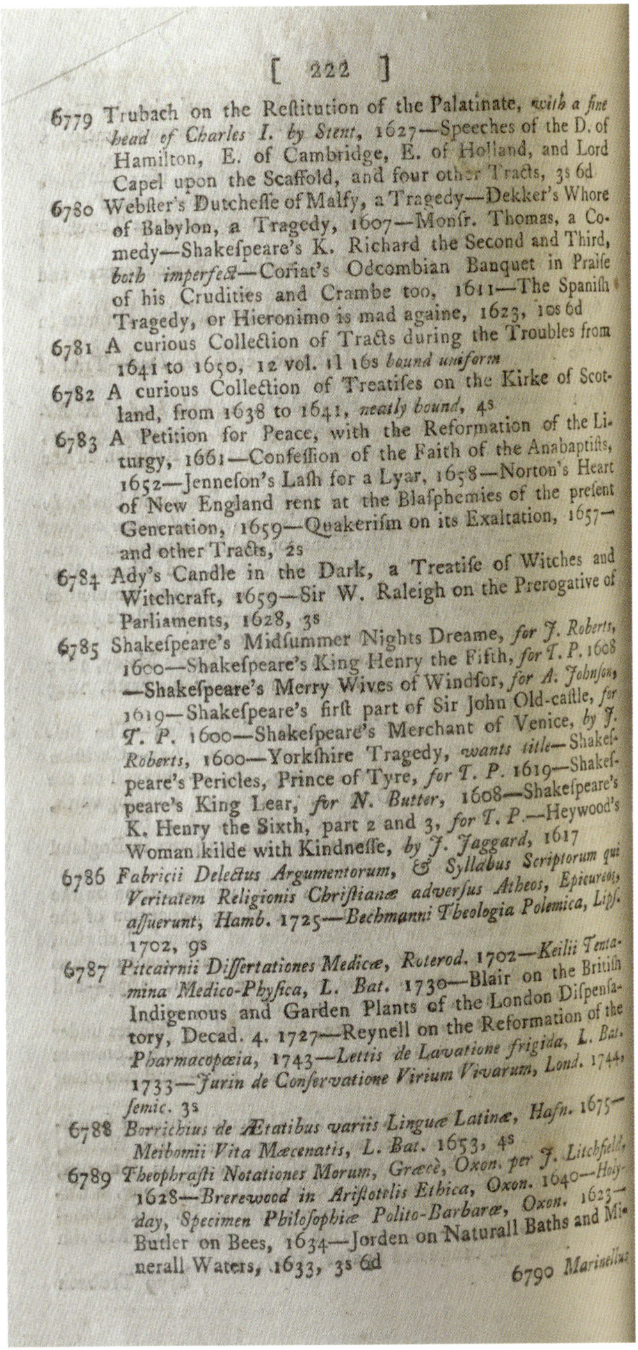

[222]

6779 Trubach on the Restitution of the Palatinate, *with a fine head of Charles I. by Stent*, 1627—Speeches of the D. of Hamilton, E. of Cambridge, E. of Holland, and Lord Capel upon the Scaffold, and four other Tracts, 3s 6d

6780 Webster's Dutchesse of Malfy, a Tragedy—Dekker's Whore of Babylon, a Tragedy, 1607—Monsr. Thomas, a Comedy—Shakespeare's K. Richard the Second and Third, *both imperfect*—Coriat's Odcombian Banquet in Praise of his Crudities and Crambe too, 1611—The Spanish Tragedy, or Hieronimo is mad againe, 1623, 10s 6d

6781 A curious Collection of Tracts during the Troubles from 1641 to 1650, 12 vol. 1l 16s *bound uniform*

6782 A curious Collection of Treatises on the Kirke of Scotland, from 1638 to 1641, *neatly bound*, 4s

6783 A Petition for Peace, with the Reformation of the Liturgy, 1661—Confession of the Faith of the Anabaptists, 1652—Jenneson's Lash for a Lyar, 1658—Norton's Heart of New England rent at the Blasphemies of the present Generation, 1659—Quakerism on its Exaltation, 1657—and other Tracts, 2s

6784 Ady's Candle in the Dark, a Treatise of Witches and Witchcraft, 1659—Sir W. Raleigh on the Prerogative of Parliaments, 1628, 3s

6785 Shakespeare's Midsummer Nights Dreame, *for J. Roberts*, 1600—Shakespeare's King Henry the Fifth, *for T. P.* 1608—Shakespeare's Merry Wives of Windsor, *for A. Johnson*, 1619—Shakespeare's first part of Sir John Old-castle, *for T. P.* 1600—Shakespeare's Merchant of Venice, *by J. Roberts*, 1600—Yorkshire Tragedy, *wants title*—Shakespeare's Pericles, Prince of Tyre, *for T. P.* 1619—Shakespeare's King Lear, *for N. Butter*, 1608—Shakespeare's K. Henry the Sixth, part 2 and 3, *for T. P.*—Heywood's Woman kilde with Kindnesse, *by J. Jaggard*, 1617

6786 *Fabricii Delectus Argumentorum, & Syllabus Scriptorum qui Veritatem Religionis Christianæ adversus Atheos, Epicureos, assuerunt, Hamb.* 1725—*Bechmanni Theologia Polemica, Lips.* 1702, 9s

6787 *Pitcairnii Dissertationes Medicæ, Roterod.* 1702—*Keilii Tentamina Medico-Physica, L. Bat.* 1730—Blair on the British Indigenous and Garden Plants of the London Dispensatory, Decad. 4. 1727—Reynell on the Reformation of the *Pharmacopœia*, 1743—*Lettis de Lavatione frigida, L. Bat.* 1733—*Jurin de Conservatione Virium Vivarum, Lond.* 1744, *femic.* 3s

6788 *Borrichius de Ætatibus variis Linguæ Latinæ, Hafn.* 1675—*Meibomii Vita Mæcenatis, L. Bat.* 1653, 4s

6789 *Theophrasti Notationes Morum, Græcè, Oxon. per J. Litchfield*, 1628—*Brerewood in Aristotelis Ethica, Oxon.* 1640—Holyday, *Specimen Philosophiæ Polito-Barbaræ, Oxon.* 1623—Butler on Bees, 1634—Jorden on Naturall Baths and Minerall Waters, 1633, 3s 6d

6790 *Marinellus*

Figure 1.13 Listing of Pavier Quartos, including *Woman Killed*, in Benjamin White's *Catalogue of Several Libraries and Collections of Books* (1774), page 222. Courtesy of the Rare Book Department, Free Library of Philadelphia, LC25.42 no. 1.

Figure 1.14 The difference in the treatment of *Woman Killed* and the traditional Shakespearean Pavier Quartos can be seen in the bindings of the Garrick copies at the British Library. © The British Library Board, C.34.k23; C.34.k.27; C.34.k.14; 644.e.33.

ing have made Heywood's play seem far distant from Shakespeare's quartos, such that its appearance in a manuscript table of contents or as a ghostly image on a blank final verso can now appear to us only as a "hit or miss" assemblage. And because New Bibliographic theory focused our attention on the "processes that leave their mark on the character of the finished book," rather than on the long history of processes that have left their marks on the always unfinished book, we have been blind to the effects of these later transformations.[49]

I have one more ghost to summon now, one that reveals this blindness right at the beginnings of our story. The very copies that set W. W. Greg on the path to his "revolutionary hypothesis" contain significant evidence that neither he nor any of his New Bibliographic colleagues were able to see. On the last verso of *Henry V* in Capell's set (SC 319), there is another, very faint ghost image of the title page of *Woman Killed* (Figure 1.15).[50] Greg was as careful a bibliographer as anyone before or since; he examined these quartos

Figure 1.15 Color-altered and mirrored image of the ghost on the last verso of *Henry V* in Capell's collection. By permission of the Master and Fellows of Trinity College, Cambridge, Capell Q.12[2].

more closely than anyone before or since; he described and catalogued them in his role as librarian of Trinity College, Cambridge. And yet the ghost of Heywood's play in this volume simply could not be seen. This blindness resulted partly from the ideological presuppositions of the New Bibliographers (their interest in discovering the prehistory of Shakespearean authorship as canonized in the First Folio); partly from the limits of bibliography at the time (this ghost is difficult to perceive and highly unlikely to be noticed on an otherwise blank page unless one is looking for this kind of evidence, of which no bibliographer at the time seems to have been aware); and partly from the prior history of collecting, curating, and canonizing Shakespeare in the late seventeenth and eighteenth centuries, which had already made Heywood's play seem out of place and led to its removal. Since we have not gone back to reexamine the books in detail, we have inherited that blindness.[51]

As noted above, Capell was aware that *Pericles* "should" have followed *Whole Contention*, "as appears by the continuation of the signatures." From this evidence, we can infer (as did Greg) that Capell probably did not reorder the plays when he rebound them, since had he done so he almost certainly would have placed *Whole Contention* immediately before *Pericles*.[52] Capell was far less interventionist than many contemporary collectors: he "never by any chance touched the edges" of his books, according to Greg, and since all the plays in his two-volume set of Pavier Quartos have the same green edge treatment, they likely came into his possession in that way. In fact, the boards of the current binding are somewhat too large for the book block, suggesting that Capell wanted to ensure that no trimming was necessary when they were rebound. Other volumes in his collection bind together plays with various edge treatments (such as gilding or coloring), while most collectors in the eighteenth and nineteenth centuries found such diversity aesthetically displeasing and would have eliminated it in rebinding.[53] Greg concludes: "I imagine that the plays when [Capell] acquired them were in a single volume, and that he divided them into two for convenience of handling; he is unlikely to have made any other change."[54]

But it is almost certain that he did. There is a key piece of evidence on the blank verso of *Henry V* with the ghost of *Woman Killed*. A large water stain on that page is not matched by anything on the facing recto, the title page of *Pericles*, making clear that the current arrangement postdates this water damage (Figure 1.16). The copy of *Woman Killed* that once was bound in Capell's set of Pavier Quartos should therefore exhibit two telltale signs, green edge treatment and a water stain mirroring this one. Just such a copy is now at the Bodleian as part of the Edmond Malone collection. It bears the same dark green edge treatment as Capell's two volumes.[55] A water stain appears throughout the book, strongest in the middle, and it appears on the title page as the exact twin of the one on Capell's *Henry V*. On the last verso of *Woman Killed*, however, the stain runs only along the lower part of the outer margin, and this stain is indeed matched on the title page of Capell's *Pericles*. Finally, Capell's typical mark of ownership—the initials "EC" in red—appears on the title page (Figure 1.17).[56]

We can thus be fairly sure that when Capell bought his Pavier Quarto volume, *Woman Killed* was included. In its current two-volume form, the plays are numbered consecutively in the top-right corner of the title page, restarting at 1 in each volume, and so this numbering must have been done after the removal of *Woman Killed*, in preparation for the rebinding or after it was done. Because Heywood's play must have seemed out of place to him, Capell probably removed it when the original volume was in the bindery, writing his initials on the title page now that it was a separate item not bound securely between his usual personalized covers.[57] But if the play

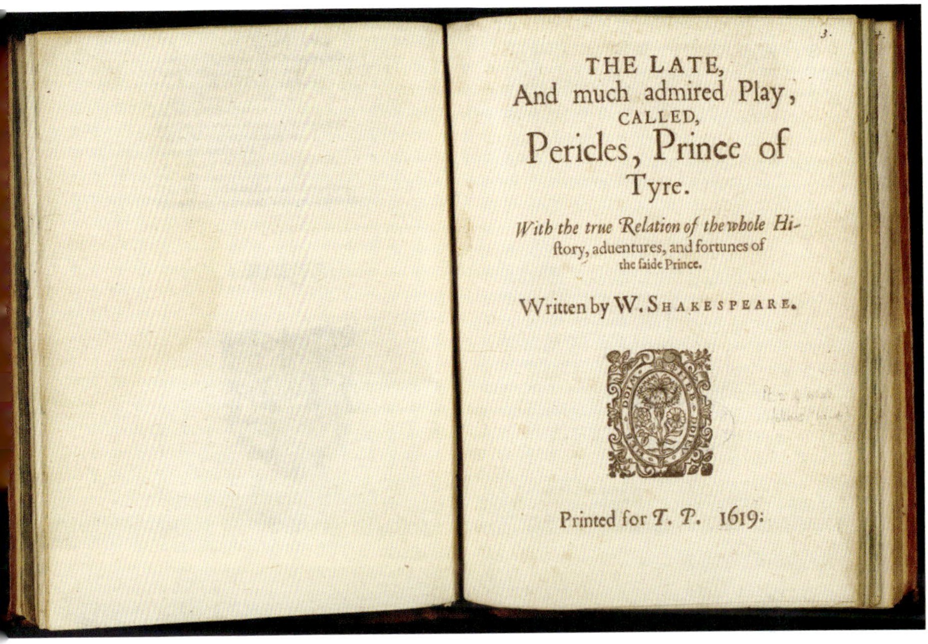

Figure 1.16 Page opening showing water stain on the last page of *Henry V* but not the title page of *Pericles* in Capell's volume. By permission of the Master and Fellows of Trinity College, Cambridge, Capell Q.12[2–3].

seemed an intruder in the set, Capell nonetheless might have gleaned an important piece of information from its presence there. Next to the printer's device on the title page of *Whole Contention* (SC 1682), Capell wrote: "The Device of Isaac Jaggard see, the last Play." By the "last" play, Capell must mean the "preceding" play, since *Whole Contention* is itself the final play in the volume; his note therefore must point to *Pericles*. But nothing about the title page of that play—nor, for that matter, those of *Yorkshire Tragedy* and *Merry Wives*, which are also dated 1619 and also bear Jaggard's device—would have told Capell that the device was Jaggard's, since that name does not appear on any of them. The only play in his volume—or *formerly* in his volume—that could have told him this information was *Woman Killed*, with the same printer's device and the imprint "LONDON, Printed by Isaac Iaggard, 1617."

Capell's decision to remove Heywood's play mirrors Greg's inability, a century and a half later, to see the ghost of that play on the last verso of Capell's *Henry V*. Neither of the scholars, preeminent bibliographers and editors though they were, could imagine that Heywood's play might belong in this

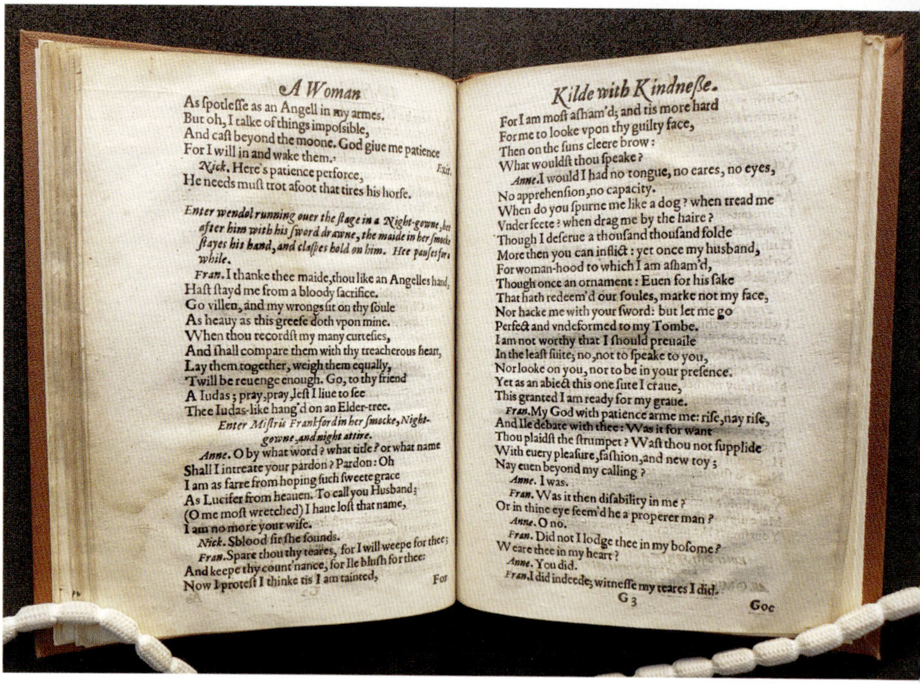

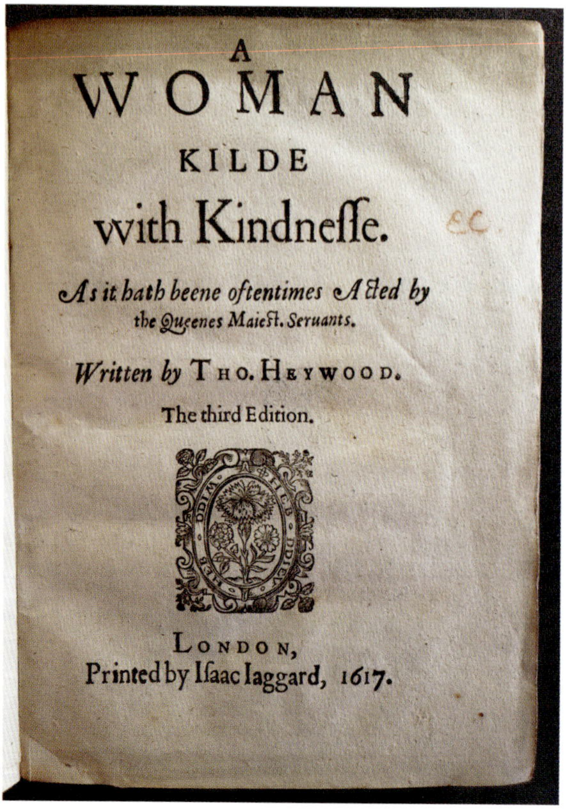

Figure 1.17 Water stain in the middle of Capell's copy of *Woman Killed* (sigs. G2v–G3r), and (less visibly in this photograph) on its title page, which bears Capell's initials. Bodleian Library, University of Oxford, Mal. 182(2).

grouping.[58] Greg too was under the "hypnotic influence that traditionally accepted facts exercise even over the most critical mind," even as he gently critiqued Pollard for being unable to shake that influence. For Pollard, the traditionally accepted facts were the dates listed in the imprints of the Pavier Quartos, which had always been taken to indicate the actual date of printing. For Greg, the traditionally accepted fact was that the Pavier Quartos were an exclusively Shakespearean collection. Even had he noticed this ghost, he no doubt would have explained it as a later accretion, an odd exception of some kind, much as Knight explained the similar ghost he found on the Huntington copy of *Henry V.*

This same traditionally accepted fact, as I have stressed, played an important role in how copies of the Pavier Quartos appear to us today in the British Library, the Folger Shakespeare Library, and elsewhere. Indeed, Benjamin White's catalogue itself testifies to the impossibility, already in 1774, of seeing how *Woman Killed* might fit into such a grouping. There the volume of Pavier Quartos is listed under the category of *Miscellaneous Tracts* in quarto. On the same page is listed, for example, a volume including John Webster's *Duchess of Malfi* (undated), Thomas Dekker's *Whore of Babylon* (1607), *Monsieur Thomas* (undated, but only published in 1639), Shakespeare's *Richard II* and *Richard III* (both undated), and *The Spanish Tragedy* (1623), along with Thomas Coryate's nondramatic *Coryats Crambe* and *Odcombian banquet* (both 1611). This is clearly a reader's sammelband, bundling texts published at least twenty-two years apart, and miscellaneous by genre (tragedy and comedy), form (drama, prose, and poetry), and author. In White's catalogue, the volume of Pavier Quartos looks similar, and no doubt to White and many of his customers it looked similar. But it is *not* the same kind of volume, since we can be sure that *Woman Killed with Kindness* was issued as part of the collection initially, not later gathered with the others by a reader. We have mistaken the appearance of the collection for the processes that led to that very appearance. Our error is itself part of the story of the creation of the Pavier Quartos.

Before continuing that story, and thinking further about why Heywood's *Woman Killed* came to be included in some of these volumes, we need to reckon with a simple, but important, fact that this chapter has established: many more bound volumes of the quartos were sold from bookshops in 1619 than we previously imagined. We now know of nineteen volumes of these plays that either still exist or are well attested by documentary or bibliographic evidence (see Appendix A).[59] And if we imagine press runs for these playbooks in the range of seven hundred to eight hundred copies, or about twenty times the number of copies that are extant today, we can see that there must have been many more than nineteen bound volumes actually sold. Bound sets seem to have made up a decent proportion of the total run, certainly far more than most recent critics have suspected. (This is true even if we reasonably conclude, as Pollard did, that copies once bound between boards would survive disproportionately to those sold individually.) The bound volumes that we can reconstruct show extreme variation in their order of binding: in the case of the nine sets where we know a sequence of at least three plays (EG, HP, EC, N, EH, TG-MO, JH, BW, TR), there is no similarity at all in the order. And, contrary to how they have consistently been treated by scholars and curators, *Whole Contention* and *Pericles* are never found consecutively (see Appendix B). When Pollard speculated, based on only three examples, that "*Pericles* was separated from *The Whole Contention*" deliberately, as part of the obfuscation, he was more right than he could have known.[60]

The sheer number of bound or once bound volumes in this census urges us to be more cautious about assuming that the collection was an "abortive scheme," "abandoned" after intervention from the King's Men "forestalled" it and led to its "collapse."[61] When Pollard writes that "to give the volume or set a better chance of passing unquestioned . . . it would be well to destroy all evidence of its having been intended as a collected edition," we need to remember that the primary "evidence of its having been intended as a collected edition" would have been all those bound volumes that were circulating in the book trade in 1619 and after.[62] It cannot be quite right to say, as Pollard does, that the "plays were sold singly, and . . . some purchasers bought sets unbound and bound them at their own pleasure."[63] The frequency with which these quartos were bound together in a single volume—often with *Woman Killed* included—indicates that, while clearly customers could have purchased any one of the plays individually, the plays were promoted as a set. Aaron T. Pratt is correct that "there is no evidence that copies were offered ready bound" and that "the one contemporary binding we know of . . . looks to have been custom," since it has Gwynn's name tooled on the cover.[64] But the new evidence of bound volumes of the 1619 quartos—and if evidence survives to indicate nineteen, surely many more once existed—strongly implies that Pavier, Jaggard, and possibly other stationers were regularly offering these plays for sale from their shops *as a collection*. Perhaps some of these sets included only some of the plays, a group of three or five or six: with the ghost evidence we cannot be sure, but the eight volumes for which we have more complete information included all of the traditional Pavier Quartos, and three of those eight included *Woman Killed* as well. Whether the stationers kept on hand one or two ready-bound volumes or customers instead commissioned their binding when they purchased them, the existence of so many bound sets can only be explained if the manner of their sale was not left quite so open and flexible as we have imagined.

Indeed, one intriguing bit of evidence in the Plat set now at Texas Christian University suggests that, at least in this particular instance, the plays included were imagined right from the start as a collection, never considered for individual sale. The last verso of a number of plays in the Plat volume shows a ghost of the title page of the following play, which is exactly what we would expect to find in such a collection.[65] But the ghost on the last verso of *Yorkshire Tragedy* (SC 1745), signature D3v, is more unusual: the title page of *Yorkshire Tragedy* itself. How did this odd auto-ghosting occur? For some reason, about which I speculate below, Jaggard printed the *Yorkshire Tragedy* title page on the final sheet of the edition, as signature D4r; the title page would then be cut out of that gathering and glued in at the beginning like a cancel. (The same process was followed with *Pericles*, in which the title page was also printed on the final leaf, as signature 2B2r; see Table 0.1.) When the sheets of *Yorkshire Tragedy* came off the press and were collated and folded to create the quarto, in other words, the title page was touching the blank verso of D3, in position to create this ghost. At this point what seems to have happened is that the entire Plat volume was put together, in folded sheets, and then beaten or pressed by the binder in preparation for sewing. Only following this pressing, which helps to create a more compact block of sheets, would the binder cut out the title pages of *Yorkshire Tragedy* and *Pericles* and glue them into proper position. Apparently, in this case, the pressure exerted by beating and pressing was enough to create this ghost, even though the pages would not have been adjacent for more than a day or so at most. What this tells us is that this copy of *Yorkshire Tragedy* was never considered as a candidate for individual sale, only as part of this larger bound collection. Regarded in this way, the ghost of the *Yorkshire Tragedy* title page on its own last verso offers us the earliest material evidence we have—earlier even than the Gwynn binding—that the Pavier Quartos were imagined in the printing house and in the bookshop as a collection.[66] They were marketed and sold to readers as a set for binding together, even as they were also available for individual sale. We have not fully reckoned with that fact in our theories of the Pavier Quartos.

Indeed, creating a group of quartos that could be sold as a bound set must have been the main intention even after the publishers began to place false imprints on the title pages of the plays printed later in the series. As David Scott Kastan writes, "Most scholars have argued that the intervention from on high stopped the planned-for collection, but, as printing had already started, Pavier and Jaggard decided to go forward" so that they could stand a chance of recouping their investment in the playbooks.[67] But since type for most of the plays would not yet have been set when the publishers decided to falsify the imprints—and presumably when "the intervention from on high" prompted this decision—it cannot be the case that the false imprints were imagined as a way to salvage their financial investment.[68] Why would they have gone ahead with printing these plays at all, rather than simply scrap the idea, if they wanted to save money? They could have continued to sell copies of the plays they *had* already printed—*Whole Contention, Pericles, Yorkshire Tragedy*, and perhaps *Merry Wives*—in order to recoup their investment in those plays, but they had as yet made no real investment at all in printing the others.

Furthermore, the particular plays that they chose to print were hardly the best sellers among Shakespeare's works. The publishers would have had little reason to expect a rapid sale of them as individual plays. Only *Pericles* would have seemed like a steady seller in 1619, having previously been published in three editions (1609, 1609, 1611). The others were all more than a decade old, and most of them nearly twenty years old. None had been published more than twice before, and most only in a single edition. None of the most popular history plays—*1 Henry IV* (1598, 1598, 1599, 1604, 1608, 1613), *Richard II* (1597, 1598, 1598, 1608, 1615), *Richard III* (1597, 1598, 1602, 1605, 1612)—appears in the group. Nor do popular tragedies like *Hamlet* (1603, 1604, 1611), *Romeo and Juliet* (1597, 1599, 1609), and *Titus Andronicus* (1594, 1600, 1611). Nathaniel Butter owned the rights to *The London Prodigal*, just as he owned the rights to *Lear*, and its title page claims the play was "By *William Shakespeare*," just as the title pages of *Oldcastle* and *Yorkshire Tragedy* do. Yet it was not included. Neither was *Titus Andronicus*, even though in 1619 the rights to that play were owned by Pavier himself.[69] Clearly the publishers exercised some real discretion over their selection of plays. They seem to have chosen plays that were older, somewhat forgotten, which they could package together for a new readership after Shakespeare's death, as a kind of "rediscovered masterpieces." But these were hardly the most obvious choices if Pavier and Jaggard were looking to pirate some Shakespeare plays to sell individually as a way to recoup their now endangered investment in a collection.

What the false imprints tell us, therefore, is that the emphasis was first and foremost on the collection itself. The publishers wanted to preserve their investment precisely in the collection as a form, and they needed to find a way to print enough plays to do so. No doubt plenty of individual copies were also sold—and this flexibility would have helped to make the investment a viable one, as Sonia Massai, Tara Lyons, and others have argued—but those sales helped to support the primary goal of issuing a bound set.[70] When John Jowett writes that Pavier's "initial plan to issue a collection of plays in a single volume . . . evolved into more diversified forms of publication," therefore, he gets the causation backward: the more diversified ways of selling the books (individually or all together) were designed precisely to enable Pavier and Jaggard to issue a collection of plays in a single volume.[71]

The use of James Roberts's name in the imprints of both *Merchant* and *Dream* suggests that, at least initially, these two plays were published without the agreement of the stationers who owned the rights to them. But if the overall goal was to bring out a bound collection—so much so that considerable financial risk was taken in printing falsified editions of a number of these plays even after the Lord Chamberlain's order in May 1619—this supports what many scholars have argued, namely, that the deception involved cannot primarily have been aimed at stationers who felt their rights to *Merchant* or *Dream* had been violated. After all, the right to copy takes no notice of whether a text is printed individually or in collection, and even plays to which Pavier himself owned the rights (*Henry V* and *Oldcastle*) had their imprints falsified. If Pavier and Jaggard needed to deceive someone so that they could continue to produce their bound volume of plays, therefore, the intended dupes must have had a vested interest in the collection per se. The obvious candidates are the King's Men, of course. But perhaps the target was also Edward Blount, the primary stationer along with Jaggard who would be, and may already have become, involved in the First Folio project. Was Jaggard double-crossing his future partner on the Folio, trying to profit from two very different, but competing, forms of Shakespeare collection? We do not know exactly when the Folio project was begun in earnest, nor when Blount or Jaggard became involved, but it is at least possible that Jaggard felt the 1619 collection, *as* a collection, needed to be hidden from Blount at this stage.

This emphasis on the collection may therefore seem to support Marino's argument that the Pavier Quartos were "some London Stationers' response to the King's Men's aggressive business strategies and to the ways the King's Men deployed Shakespeare's name to secure their property claims."[72] The problem is that this battle over the name of Shakespeare does not fully explain the Pavier Quartos. For one thing, it is not quite clear how the false imprints work in Marino's argument: if they are meant to deceive the King's Men, then how could Jaggard's assertion of literary property actually work, since no one would know about it? And most important of all, the inclusion of *Woman Killed with Kindness* in a good proportion of the bound volumes, with "*Written by* THO. HEYWOOD" on the title page, makes clear that the collection was not in any simple way an assertion of the stationers' right "to define [the] nascent canon" of Shakespeare's works.[73]

The strangeness, to our modern eyes anyway, of finding Heywood's play repeatedly bound up with the Pavier Quartos likewise poses a challenge to the other most important recent revisionist theory of the quartos. Massai's narrative involves a coordinated effort on the part of Pavier, Jaggard, and the King's Men to create a "pre-publicity stunt" for the First Folio by offering readers a volume that appeared to be "the scattered remains of a recently deceased playwright."[74] As a marketing strategy or stunt, the publication of a group of plays running to 326 leaves in quarto seems fairly risky; this is a very long book, representing a considerable investment if it mainly functioned as pre-publicity for another, longer book to be published four years later.[75] And it is hard to see the frequent inclusion of Heywood's *Woman Killed* as in any way contributing to this marketing strategy. How could Heywood's play help to "whet . . . readers' demand for a new collection of Shakespeare's dramatic works"?[76] The presence of *Woman Killed* indicates a further attempt to disguise exactly what this collection was, but not simply to make it seem to retail book buyers like "the scattered remains" of *The Works of William Shakespeare.*

Rosenbach's inscription describing the Gwynn volume as "the first attempt at a collection of the works of William Shakespeare" derives from Pollard, Greg, and Neidig's work. Our own acceptance of this claim has guided our investigations of the Pavier Quartos ever since. Many more bound sets of this collection of plays appeared in bookshops in 1619 than we have suspected, but they were not simply Shakespearean. In four cases that we now know of, Heywood's play appeared between their covers, nearly a quarter of the total in my ongoing census, and nearly half of those for which we know the full contents. Since only a fraction of the total press run of these quartos still survives to yield evidence of previous binding, no doubt many more bound sets than nineteen, and many more than four including *Woman Killed*, were sold from London bookshops in 1619 and the years following. Chapter 2 expands on this discovery, confirming that *Woman Killed* was included quite frequently in the collection, a fact that points us toward some answers, but also toward some further questions.

CHAPTER 2

Holes

> No Stationer . . . shall from hensforthe, Binde, Sell, Utter, or putt to Sale . . . Any booke in any volume whatsoeuer whiche is or shalbe bored or prycked thoroughe with Bodkyn, Alle, needle, or other instrument, and stitched with thryd, slyp of leather, or other suche devise . . . conteyninge any greater number of sheetes then is hereafter expressed.
>
> —Stationers' Company Liber A

Our census of bound volumes of the 1619 quartos has already established that these plays were sold as a set more frequently than we have thought, suggesting that a collection per se was the main goal, and that Heywood's *Woman Killed* was sometimes bound up with the plays usually considered part of the group. The bibliographic evidence in this chapter, tiny holes that are often buried deep in the gutters of ornate nineteenth-century bindings, can add to the story. Most playbooks in the period, like most short pamphlets of all genres, were not sold bound but rather simply stab-stitched (Figure 2.1).[1] As Aaron T. Pratt explains, in this process a book's "quires are not individually sewn onto cords or other supports as they would be if traditionally bound; instead, to hold the quires together, a single piece of thread travels through the . . . assembled quires at three points, from front to back and back to front, near the gutter edge."[2] Some basic protection for the text could be provided by wrapping some paper around the volume before stab-stitching, or by composing the text with a blank initial and closing leaf, but often the title page and final leaf served as the only "cover" for the book.

Stab-stitching saved time and materials compared to a traditional binding, reducing costs to publishers and customers. Pratt estimates that "the additional cost for a binding would appear to have doubled or even tripled

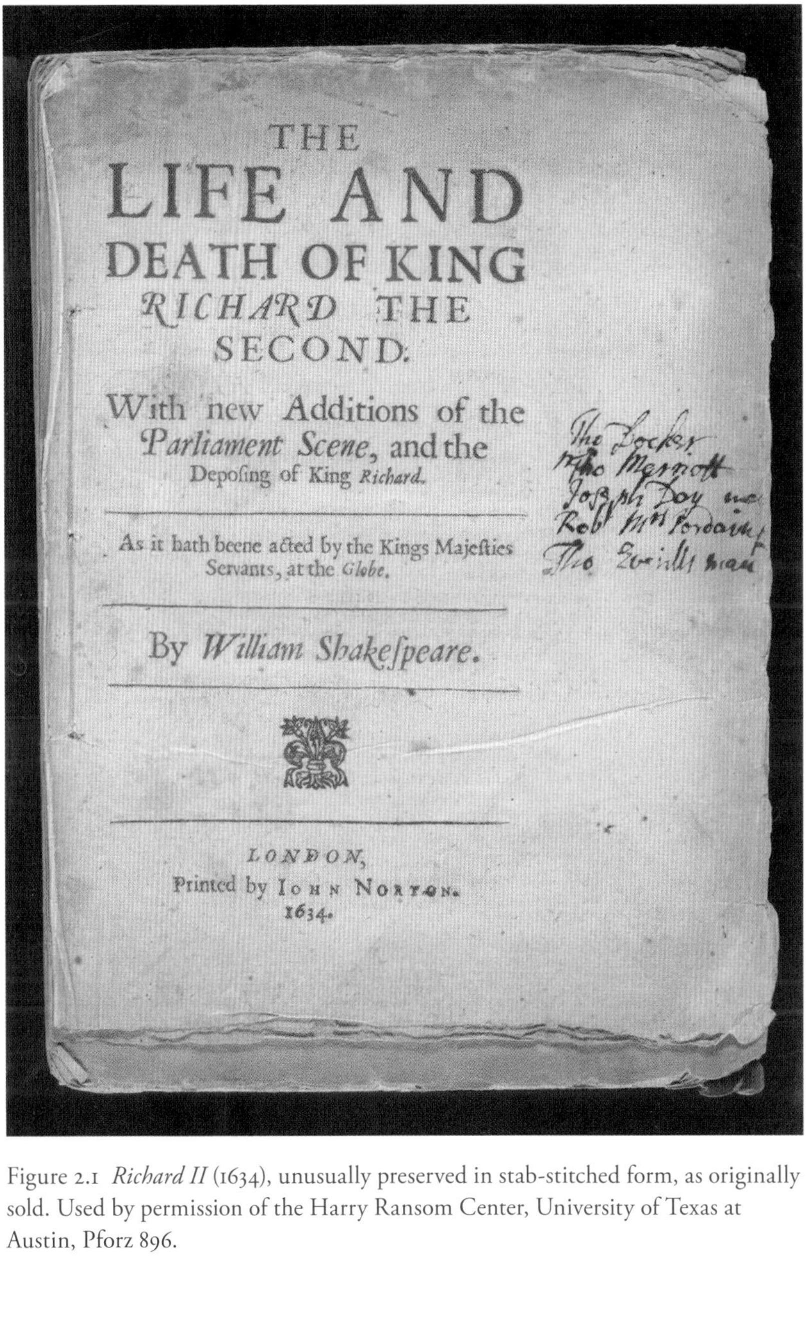

Figure 2.1 *Richard II* (1634), unusually preserved in stab-stitched form, as originally sold. Used by permission of the Harry Ransom Center, University of Texas at Austin, Pforz 896.

the total retail price of a quarto playbook," so it is not surprising that many customers waited until they had six or eight or ten pamphlets before having them bound into a single volume. Binding a single playbook would have seemed absurd in the seventeenth century, whereas the individually bound quarto is precisely the form in which we now typically encounter Shakespeare's early editions.[3]

Longer books, meanwhile, were generally bound at the time of initial sale—although Pratt shows that occasionally even very long books of a hundred leaves or more could be stab-stitched.[4] Booksellers probably stocked some longer books prebound "on spec," while always being ready to procure a binding to the customer's specifications once the book was purchased.[5] In a sewn binding, the thread "passes in and out through the spine fold of each quire, looping around (or passing over) supports that lace into the book's covers." Sewing holes "appear only in the folds," whereas in stab-stitching, "in order for the thread to secure the papers on all sides amply, the holes must stand somewhat in from the spine edge."[6] Books originally sold bound, therefore, have no stab-stitch holes, as in the University of Pennsylvania copies of Seneca's *Ten Tragedies* printed in 1581 (224 leaves) and John Lyly's *Six Court Comedies* printed in 1632 (318 leaves).[7]

There were thus two fundamentally different ways of getting books ready for sale, two types of books that readers purchased at stationers' shops, and—importantly—two different kinds of material traces left in the books. If a book has stab-stitch holes, it was almost certainly originally sold as a single unbound text, although it might initially have been stab-stitched but then bound together with other texts for retail sale, or possibly stab-stitched along with one or two other texts. If a book lacks these stab-stitch holes, we can be reasonably sure that it was originally sold as part of a bound volume.

Since the late eighteenth century, Shakespeare's playbooks have been treated as precious relics, and the repeated material transformations of these books in the hands of collectors, auction houses, and libraries have made their stab-stitch holes more difficult to see. Indeed, the most prized books today are the least likely to be found still in the form in which they were originally sold, as Pratt explains: "A significant number of early owners took playbooks they purchased in stab-stitched copies and had them bound together into composite volumes. Eighteenth- and nineteenth-century owners who were keen to 'update' their playbooks then broke these composite volumes back into individual copies, repackaging them in new bindings that turned them into singular, precious, luxury objects. These later owners also

Figure 2.2 Small holes provide evidence of previous stab-stitching in a copy of *Rape of Lucrece* (1594). Used by permission of the Folger Shakespeare Library, STC 22345 copy 1, sigs. B4v–C1r.

gave dedicated bindings to playbooks that had remained in a stab-stitched form, obscuring their past or erasing it entirely."[8] The plays we read today in rare book libraries represent only the current stage of a long historical process that has changed, and often obscured, the material forms they took in the past. Nonetheless, it is still usually possible to discern the stab-stitch holes if one looks closely, and they provide an important piece of bibliographic evidence for how a book was first sold (Figure 2.2).[9]

It is very rare to find an individual playbook that does not have stab-stitch holes. The reasons are simple: "stab-stitching does not correlate with anything other than length"; the median length of playbooks was thirty-eight leaves; and books of this length were almost always sold stabbed.[10] In his study of more than eighteen hundred quartos listed in the *STC*, Pratt found that 85 percent of books that are forty leaves or shorter show evidence of stab-stitching. And since he counts only cases where the presence or absence of holes can be established fairly certainly, his figures no doubt understate the real frequency of stab-stitching, "possibly by as much as ten percent or more."[11] Even among books ranging from eighty-one to ninety-six leaves, 65 percent contain stab-stitch holes. Indeed, stab-stitching was such an effective, cheap, and popular method of preparing books for sale that in 1586 the bookbinders, who saw decreased demand for their sewn bindings, successfully pressured the Stationers' Company to adopt regulations stating that all books over a certain length had to be traditionally bound, not stab-stitched.[12]

With the exception of the very short *Yorkshire Tragedy* (sixteen leaves), and the longer *Whole Contention* (sixty-four leaves), the Pavier Quartos are all close to the median length of playbooks: *Pericles*, thirty-four leaves; *Merry*

Wives, twenty-eight; *Merchant*, forty; *Henry V*, twenty-eight; *Oldcastle*, forty; *Dream*, thirty-two; *Lear*, forty-four; *Woman Killed*, thirty-six. Based on Pratt's study, probably more than 90 percent of pamphlets around this length left the bookshops stab-stitched, and we would therefore expect to find holes in the vast majority of copies of the Pavier Quartos. But we do not.

Excluding copies in which any evidence of stab-stitching would have been destroyed—for example, by mounting each leaf individually onto larger pages—I have looked for stab-stitch holes in 265 copies of the traditional Pavier Quartos.[13] In only 39 percent of these copies could I find evidence of stab-stitching, a rate well under half that of other surviving books of comparable length.[14] As in Pratt's study, this figure likely understates the actual rate of stab-stitching, since one can never definitively establish the *lack* of holes. Still, if we use Pratt's rough estimate of a 10 or 15 percent undercount, something like half of the extant copies of the 1619 quartos seem to have initially been sold as part of a bound volume. The evidence of stab-stitch holes, or the lack thereof, thus underscores the evidence presented in Chapter 1: many more Pavier Quartos than we have generally assumed were circulating in bound volumes in 1619 and the years following.

As mentioned above, copies that were once included in a bound set probably survive disproportionately compared to those that were sold individually, and so we cannot simply extrapolate from the extant copies to assume that half of all the copies printed were originally sold in collection. Nonetheless, it is clear that a sizable number were. This was not a project abandoned midstream in favor of individual sale, nor was it merely left up to customers whether to purchase an individual play, or to bind a few of them together, or to purchase the whole group. These plays were being sold as a set—apparently as an entire set, although possibly also in groupings of several but not all of the plays. They were presented to potential customers as a group and issued from bookshops in that form—probably in many cases already bound.[15]

Most of the copies included in my census of bound volumes do not have stab-stitch holes, suggesting they were either sold ready-bound or were bound up upon sale. The Gwynn, Capell, and Plat volumes show no holes in any of the plays; neither do any of the surviving copies that formed part of the Goodman-Orlebar set (SC 331, 652, 727, 785, 1018, 1425, 1691). The Bodleian copy of *Woman Killed* that Capell removed from his set of Pavier Quartos does not have stab-stitch holes, and neither do four of the plays that were once in the Hussey volume and are now at the Folger (SC 1686), the Shakespeare Birthplace Trust (SC 663, 513), and Harvard (SC 1736).[16] But the copies with ghost images suggest that not every bound volume of Pavier Quartos was made up exclusively of plays that had never been stab-stitched. Some "ghosted" copies show no evidence of holes: the Folger *Henry V* (SC 325), the Huntington *Henry V* (SC 334), the Ransom Center *Dream* (SC 803), and the Princeton *Oldcastle* (SC 1441). Likewise, there are no holes in the Eton *Pericles* with "Lux post tenebras" written on its last verso (SC 1013). But the BPL *Pericles* (SC 1008), the Garrick *Merchant* (SC 644) and *Lear* (SC 487) at the British Library, the Elizabethan Club *Oldcastle* (SC 1453), and the Folger *Lear* (SC 496) do contain stab-stitch holes. And yet we know that these copies, like the others with ghosts, once were bound alongside another of the 1619 quartos. It is possible that they were purchased individually, stab-stitched, and only later bound up in a reader's sammelband with at least one other play in the group. But given all the other evidence of bound Pavier Quarto volumes, it is more likely that these copies had already been stab-stitched in the bookshop for one reason or another, before they were incorporated into a bound volume at the time of retail sale. Perhaps they had been stab-stitched so as to be available for browsing more easily, or perhaps they had been made ready for individual sale before being inserted into a bound set.[17] The presence of stab-stitch holes, as discussed above, does not *preclude* sale as a bound volume; but the genuine absence of these holes almost always indicates it.[18]

The survival rates of these plays tell the same story. Pollard noted that many more copies survive of the Pavier Quartos than of other Shakespeare plays, "as would naturally be the case if they had been preserved in volumes until the eighteenth century."[19] The plays traditionally included in the group survive in an average of thirty-eight copies (based on current knowledge). This compares with an average of twelve copies for editions of Shakespeare plays published in the previous decade (1608–18) and twenty-four for those published in the 1620s and 1630s.[20] The greater survival of the Pavier Quartos compared to other Shakespeare editions must derive from the fact that they were frequently packaged together in a large bound volume of 326 leaves, or 362 leaves if *Woman Killed* was included.[21] Longer books survive in significantly greater numbers than shorter books, even though many customers routinely bound into sammelbands the pamphlets they had initially purchased stab-stitched.[22] In other words, even Shakespeare plays that were initially sold stab-stitched but were likely to have been bound together with other texts later in their lives do not survive as well as the Pavier Quartos. This is another indication that many Pavier Quartos were offered from bookshops specifically as bound collections, not merely left up to individual book buyers to purchase as a group or not.

The only other individual professional play from the Shakespearean period that turns up repeatedly without stab-stitch holes is the 1617 edition of Heywood's *Woman Killed with Kindness.* Strikingly, of the twenty-six copies of this edition that I have examined or that someone has examined for me, nine show no evidence of stab-stitch holes.[23] This rate of stab-stitching (65 percent) is well below the norm, although it is also higher than the rates for the plays traditionally included in the group. Again this evidence confirms what we saw in the previous chapter: a significant number of the bound volumes of Pavier Quartos originally included *Woman Killed*, but not all of them did. Some proportion of the press run of the 1617 *Woman Killed* must have already been sold stab-stitched in the two years before the publication of the Pavier Quartos. And because stationers generally exchanged batches of new books with each other in order to stock their shops with a variety of titles, even quite a few unsold copies of *Woman Killed* would not have still been in the publisher's warehouse in 1619. Nonetheless, since a third of the extant copies of Heywood's play lack stab-stitch holes, and since it was included in almost a quarter of the bound volumes in my census, clearly many book buyers had a set of Pavier Quartos with *Woman Killed* in it.[24]

Heywood's presence in the collection clarifies the agency behind it: the Pavier Quartos are not as much Pavier's as we have thought. While his initials do appear on five of the Shakespearean title pages, two others have such false imprints that Pavier's involvement has been merely an assumption. Meanwhile, as discussed above, both Nathaniel Butter and Arthur Johnson were alive and well in 1619, and there is no reason to doubt their involvement in the project. This fact has been pointed out repeatedly, including by both Pollard and Greg themselves.[25] And yet the recurring emphasis on Pavier as the key agent behind the scheme, not to mention that his name is conventionally given to the collection itself, seems always to push us back to seeing the imprints featuring the names of Butter and Johnson as "misleading" and a "serious falsification," with Pavier having somehow infringed on their rights.[26] If Pavier published what we call the Pavier Quartos, then the appearance of these other stationers' names on these title pages, and the lack of Pavier's, can only seem deceptive.

Like our library catalogues (discussed in Chapter 1), our most important reference work has helped to enshrine the conventional wisdom about the

1619 quartos. The notion that Pavier was the true "publisher" of all these plays is thoroughly embedded in the *Short-Title Catalogue*. The *STC* lists the imprints for *Merchant* (STC 22297) and *Dream* (STC 22303) as "*J. Roberts* [*W. Jaggard f. T. Pavier*,] 1600 [1619.]," and for *Merry Wives* (STC 22300) as "[*W. Jaggard*] *f. A. Johnson* [i.e. *T. Pavier*,] 1619." In all three cases, the STC takes the involvement of Pavier for granted and displaces the agency behind the project from Jaggard to him. The entry for *Merry Wives* simply assumes the fraudulent nature of the imprint, claiming that Johnson played no role in its publication. It is not clear why the *STC* does not do the same for *Lear* (STC 22293), which it lists as: "[*W. Jaggard*] *f. N. Butter*, 1608 [1619.]"[27] The situation with *Lear* is exactly the same as with *Merry Wives*, since the first edition of each had been published by the stationer who is listed as the publisher in the imprint of the 1619 quarto. The inconsistency between these two entries shows that the conventional wisdom about the "Pavier" quartos—that they are all "Pavier's"—rests on a series of unarticulated and largely unexamined assumptions.

In fact the only people we know for certain were involved in *all* of the playbooks were the printers.[28] Their centrality to the project is confirmed by the frequent presence of Heywood's play in these bound volumes. Benjamin White's 1774 sales catalogue gives us a clue in its description of the final play in the collection: "Heywood's Woman kilde with Kindnesse, *by I. Iaggard*, 1617."[29] Heywood's play was printed and published by Isaac Jaggard, in the same shop where the 1619 quartos were printed. *Woman Killed* was the only professional play that either of the Jaggards had solely published to date, although William had copublished the 1607 first edition of the play.[30] What seems to have happened, then, is that the Jaggards bound up some remaining copies of their two-year-old edition of Heywood's play with the Shakespeare dramas that they were publishing with the help of Pavier, Butter, and Johnson. Possibly Lawrence Hayes, whose father had published the first edition of *Merchant* and who entered it in the Stationers' Register on 8 July 1619, was also brought into the consortium, since, like Butter and Johnson, he left no evidence of any objection to the publication.

Jaggard's centrality may explain why only the initials "T.P." appear on the title pages associated with Pavier. Note that these initials are also on *Pericles*, which is correctly dated 1619, and so they do not seem to have been part of any attempted deception. Pavier used his initials in imprints very rarely: excluding the 1619 quartos themselves, only 13.5 percent of his imprints fail to include his full last name. Of the twenty-five that list only his initials, eight are ballads, where the use of initials was fairly conventional, given the limited space available on the page. If we exclude these items, Pavier listed his initials alone on less than 10 percent of his imprints. But of all publications that are described in the imprint as merely "sold by" Pavier, a full 40 percent include only his initials.[31] The use of initials may therefore simply indicate his junior partnership in the venture; perhaps we should think of these play quartos, too, as having been "sold by" T.P. rather than truly printed "for" him. With the Jaggards as the unifying figures, and three or four booksellers gathered to participate in the project, they might be better imagined as the "Jaggard Quartos," emphasizing the main publishing agents. I therefore use that term henceforward, as one way to break the "hypnotic influence" of the "Pavier Quartos," although "Jaggard Quartos" too is a shorthand formulation that elides some of the agency behind the collection.[32]

Jaggard was not trying to smuggle his edition of *Woman Killed* into the Shakespearean collection without customers noticing, since the play appears first in the table of contents in the Goodman-Orlebar volume. Neither Thomas Goodman nor Mary Orlebar seems to have balked at the fact that a Heywood play led off this volume, and book buyers in the early seventeenth century must not have done so either, given how often it appeared in the collection.[33] To us—after a century of work on the "Pavier Quartos," after three centuries of Shakespearean canonization, and after the sammelband has lost the cultural centrality it had in the early modern period—such a combination looks decidedly strange. As discussed in the previous chapter, this strangeness has been part of the reason we have not previously seen the evidence of Heywood's inclusion. How, then, can we explain Jaggard's decision to include it, which must have depended on his informed belief that customers would not find its presence as strange as we have?

It is not that early modern Londoners were used to seeing books like this in the stalls around St. Paul's. Publishers had long organized their collections of drama and other kinds of texts by author.[34] Among publisher-issued collections of professional drama, the Jaggard Quartos are unique in featuring multiple non-collaborating authors. The inclusion of Heywood's *Woman Killed* makes the Jaggard Quartos categorically different from the 1647 Beaumont and Fletcher folio, for instance, since those playwrights had come to be considered almost a single entity, well-known collaborators who worked in harmony. Likewise, collaborative plays were certainly included in the Shakespeare folio, and the Beaumont and Fletcher folio includes work by Philip Massinger and others, but these collaborations are unmarked. The Shakespeare folio claims to be entirely Shakespeare's work, and the Beaumont and Fletcher folio entirely Beaumont and Fletcher's, despite the fact that Massinger's role in writing some of those plays was widely known and acknowledged elsewhere.[35] But Heywood's appearance in the Jaggard Quartos is not collaborative; it is miscellaneous. The Jaggard Quartos have long been understood as "the first attempt at a collection of the works of William Shakespeare," and they do seem to have originated in 1619 as a solely "Shakespearean" collection, at least in terms of attribution if not actual authorship. But by the time the project hit the bookstalls, when sold with *Woman Killed* included, they turned out to be the only publisher's collection of professional drama to bind together the plays of one playwright (or playwrighting partnership) with a play explicitly advertised as by someone else entirely.

The other notably unusual feature of this collection, its highly variable binding order, is related to this miscellaneity. In extant copies of the landmark folio drama collections of the period—Jonson (1616), Shakespeare (1623), Beaumont and Fletcher (1647)—the contents almost always appear in the same order, despite the sometimes duplicative or erroneous signatures and catchwords in these books, and despite the fact that, as very large jobs, they were printed over long stretches of time, with numerous states of individual sheets, and, in the case of the Beaumont and Fletcher folio, in multiple print shops.[36] The presence of a table of contents in each of these folios surely helped to guide the binder even when the signatures could be confusing. And importantly, the structure of the sheets in these folios does not align with the structure of the plays they contain: plays end and begin in the middle of gatherings, and so rearranging them would have caused immediate and obvious problems. While the Shakespeare First Folio could later be rebound in three volumes of comedies, histories, and tragedies—as in the copy in the library at Mount Stuart on the Scottish Isle of Bute—the plays could not be easily shuffled as in the Jaggard Quartos.

Some other, nondramatic collections show publishers taking care to ensure that they were bound in the desired order. A very large collection of *The Sermons of Mr Henry Smith, Gathered into One Volume* (1657) includes multiple sections, each with its own run of signatures; the pagination is continuous across the first two sections but then restarts with each subsequent section. The final page of the book is "A Direction for the Binders. The Order in which this Volume is to be Bound," listing the component sections in proper order.[37] While no such instructions appear in any of the folio drama collections, this "direction" demonstrates that binding order could be an important consideration for publishers.

Drama collections in smaller formats were more variable than these large folio books, precisely because the underlying sheet structure generally did not prevent reordering. These were sometimes "nonce collections" compiled from copies of previously printed editions, but there were also newly printed collections made up of plays meant to be sold both as part of the set and individually. Since the Jaggard Quartos are only the second collection of professional drama of any real size, after the Jonson folio, comparisons to these other collections may be somewhat misleading. Such comparisons risk creating a false teleology, importing conclusions drawn from later decades back to a period when the conventions of such volumes were still in flux.[38] With that caveat in mind, however, we can see that the use of a separate title page for each play in the Jaggard Quartos (with the exception of *The Second Part of the Contention*, which has only a head title) was not unusual: Jonson's folio had included them, and later collections of drama by Brome, Lyly, Marston, Shirley, Massinger, and others did so as well.[39] The lack of continuous signatures across all of the Jaggard Quartos was less common, but by no means unique: the registers for Lyly's 1632 *Six Court Comedies* (in duodecimo), Marston's 1633 *Works* (octavo), and Massinger's 1655 *Three New Plays* (octavo) were all continuous; but Shirley's 1653 *Six New Playes* (octavo) restarts its signatures with each play, and the registers for Brome's two different octavo collections of *Five New Playes* (1653, 1659) are only partly continuous.[40]

A comparison of extant copies of the Lyly (1632), Shirley (1653), and Brome (1653) collections reveals how binding order could vary depending on the signals sent to the binder by the printed sheets. In the absence of the kind of direct instructions provided at the end of *The Sermons of Mr Henry Smith*, the binder could nonetheless gather important information from the book itself. Most crucial, of course, were the signatures: it was second nature to a binder to collate sheets into the proper register before binding. With its continuous register throughout, Lyly's *Six Court Comedies* gave the binder instructions about "The Order in which this Volume is to be Bound" every bit as explicit as the note at the end of Smith's sermons. Not surprisingly, therefore, all of the thirty-two extant copies that I have surveyed are currently bound in the "correct" order according to signatures.[41]

If the signatures were not consecutive, or if they were erroneous or otherwise confusing, the binder could look to a general title page for guidance.

These title pages often listed the contents, presumably in the intended order of binding. The title page of Brome's 1653 collection did so, and that collection also used continuous signatures for its first three plays (*A Mad Couple Well Matched*, *The Novella*, and *The Court Beggar*), although the final two plays (*The City Wit*, *The Damoiselle*) each have their own run of signatures.[42] Brome's collection is virtually always found now in the "correct" binding order according to the title-page listing (twenty-four copies surveyed), but one copy at the Folger (B4870 copy 2) reveals that it sent slightly weaker signals to the binder than did Lyly's. In this copy the last two plays, those with separate registers, are bound at the front of the book, immediately after the general title page (sig. A1) and before the preliminary matter (sigs. A2–5). On the title page, someone has added numerals next to the list of plays to indicate their actual order of binding, in what looks like an early hand (Figure 2.3).

The combination of a partly continuous register with a title-page listing resulted in nearly all copies of Brome's collection being "correctly" bound today. But the lack of continuous signatures in two plays seems to have left them open to wandering in the Folger copy. Shirley's collection of the same year also included a title-page listing of contents, but the plays do not share continuous signatures. This latter fact seems to have made a real difference, since extant copies of Shirley's collection are far more variable than Brome's. Of the thirty-one extant copies surveyed, five are bound in orders different from the listing on the title page, and these orders often differ from each other as well. The title page lists the plays as follows: *The Brothers, The Sisters, The Doubtful Heir, The Imposture, The Cardinal,* and *The Court Secret*. But copies now at Duke and Haverford reverse the order of the last two plays. A copy at the British Library binds the plays: *Cardinal, Sisters, Doubtful Heir, Court Secret, Brothers, Imposture*. The copy at the University of Pennsylvania is different from all of these: *Cardinal, Brothers, Sisters, Doubtful Heir, Court Secret, Imposture*. And the copy at the Morgan Library differs yet again: *Brothers, Cardinal, Imposture, Doubtful Heir, Sisters, Court Secret*.[43] The situation with Shirley's plays begins to look more like that of the Jaggard Quartos. Nonetheless, more than eight in ten copies of *Six New Playes* are now bound in the "correct" order, thanks to the title-page listing of contents.

The importance of this title-page listing is demonstrated by the odd case of the second volume of Ben Jonson's *Workes*, printed in folio in 1631 but reissued in 1640 with a new general title page. That general title page

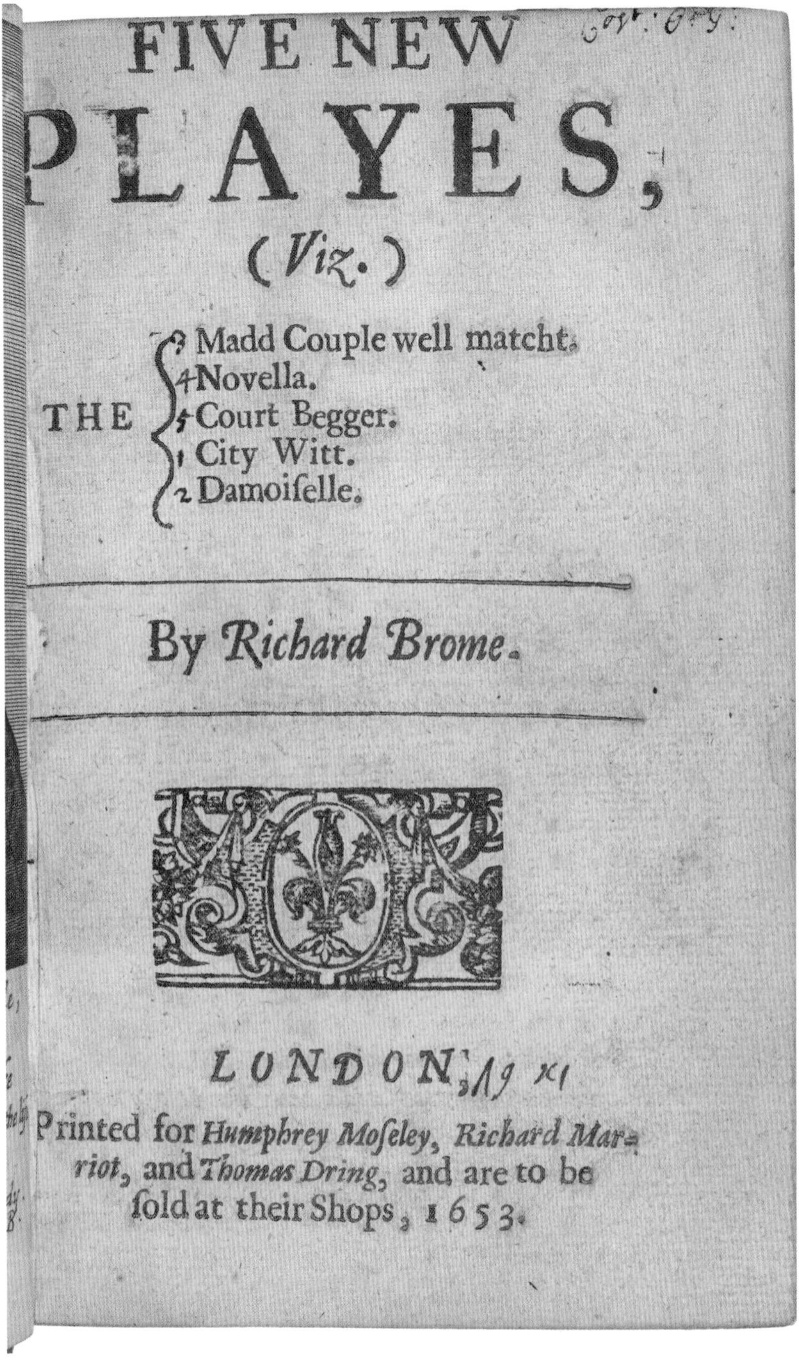

FIVE NEW

PLAYES,

(*Viz.*)

THE

- Madd Couple well matcht.
- Novella.
- Court Begger.
- City Witt.
- Damoiselle.

By *Richard Brome*.

LONDON,

Printed for *Humphrey Moseley*, *Richard Marriot*, and *Thomas Dring*, and are to be sold at their Shops, 1653.

Figure 2.3 Title page of Richard Brome's *Five New Playes* (1653), listing the plays but not in the order they are actually bound. Used by permission of the Folger Shakespeare Library, B4870 copy 2.

reversed the order of the second and third plays as dictated by the signatures, which run continuously from *Bartholomew Fair* to *The Devil is an Ass* to *The Staple of News*. As a result, "two-thirds of the [extant] copies . . . follow the title page and [bind] *Staple* before *Devil*."[44] Here the title page seems to have overridden the register, although since *Staple of News* just happens to begin with signature Aa after the printers had already run through the alphabet once, and since after the Bb gathering the printers dropped the doubled letter and simply continued with C, the register may have been confusing to the binder. By contrast, we have seen with the small-format drama collections that the guidance offered by a title-page listing of contents seems often to have been less effective than the register of signatures in enforcing a particular binding order.

Of course, both the register and the title-page listing of contents offer information to more recent binders as well. Copies that were initially "mis"-bound may have been set to rights in the ensuing centuries, as we have seen with the Goodman-Orlebar copies of *Whole Contention* and *Pericles* at the Folger. Both collectors and libraries have rebound these copies over the years; standards of taste and institutional protocols for many years favored the "correcting" of binding errors. We cannot be certain, therefore, that a copy currently found in the "correct" order has always been that way, but the same is true for all of the collections I discuss here, which mitigates this methodological problem for my purposes. And if a book is currently bound in the "incorrect" order, we can be more sure that it has always been that way, since it is highly unlikely a collector or library would have transformed a "correct" order to an "incorrect" one during rebinding.

Furthermore, numerous copies of the Shirley collection bound according to the title-page contents make clear that they are not retrospective rebindings. A copy at the University of Illinois, for example, is in a modern binding, but it inadvertently binds only the last gathering of *The Brothers* in the wrong place; a modern rebinding that "fixed" the order of plays would presumably have corrected this as well, and so the current binding order probably reflects the early one.[45] The copy at the National Library of Scotland is in title-page order but with the conjugate leaves C2 and C7 of *The Sisters* and *The Court Secret* transposed.[46] Again, this error would likely have been corrected in a modern rebinding designed to fix an earlier "misbinding." Other copies are in very early bindings and have not been rebound since the seventeenth century. We can therefore conclude that while some copies of the Shirley collection may well have been "fixed" over the years so that they follow the title-page order, that process does not account for the entirety of the evidence as it has come down to us today.

It is clear from these examples that while small-format collections could be bound in variable order, more frequently than the landmark folios that have dominated our understanding of drama collections, they are nonetheless generally found today in the "correct" order. The examples of Shirley's *Six New Playes* and Brome's *Five New Playes* demonstrate both that the lack of continuous signatures could allow plays to wander through the volume, but also that the order in which plays were listed on the title page influenced binders even when the signatures offered no guidance. The Shirley collection is more variable than a collection with continuous signatures like Lyly's, or with mainly continuous signatures like Brome's, but it is far less variable than the Jaggard Quartos.

While scholars since Pollard and Greg have always considered highly significant the decision to abandon the continuous signatures after *Pericles*, therefore, another decision about the collection may have been equally important. As mentioned above, both *Pericles* and *Yorkshire Tragedy* feature an odd method of setting the title page: in each case, it was printed as part of the final gathering of the play, then cut from that sheet and inserted at the beginning as a cancel. This is uncommon and far from best practice: indeed, it is why these two plays are often missing their title pages today, as the cancel page lacks the structural integrity that the folds of a gathering provide. Carter Hailey speculates that this process was undertaken to ensure that Jaggard's "HEB DDIEV" printer's device was available for the other title pages, as printing was quasi-concurrent.[47] But it may also indicate that Jaggard still expected to print a general title page when he began composing the text of *Yorkshire Tragedy*, and the divisional title pages for both that play and *Pericles* were an afterthought once he decided not to do so. The lack of a date in the imprint for *Whole Contention* likewise suggests that a general title page with the date 1619 in the imprint was considered before being ultimately abandoned.[48] A general title page for the Jaggard Quartos that listed the contents of the collection, or a preliminary half sheet that included the title page and some kind of table of contents, would have ensured much more consistency in binding, as we have seen, even without continuous signatures. But it would also, of course, have made clear the publishers' involvement. The lack of a general title page, the variable order of binding, the various (falsified) dates, and the abandonment of continuous signatures form a mutually reinforcing nexus that must have signaled the unusual nature of this collection.

When we situate the Jaggard Quartos among these comparable collections, what remains strikingly exceptional is the absence of copies with *Whole Contention* and *Pericles* bound consecutively. The Jaggard Quartos offer a stark contrast to Brome's 1653 collection, in which the only copy now bound in a variant order moves precisely those two plays without continuous signatures. If continuous signatures tended to ensure uniformity of binding order for collections, why do the only two plays signed continuously in the Jaggard Quartos never appear together? For a professional binder, *not* binding *Whole Contention* and *Pericles* in sequence would actually have been harder than doing so. Binding according to the run of signatures was a deeply ingrained professional habit, which would likely have required specific instructions to override. In other words, Jaggard must have given some kind of "Direction to the Binder" to keep these plays apart, despite their continuous signatures. This "Direction" need not have been explicit, although it may have been. Simply delivering the printed sheets to the binder already gathered with these two plays separated would have done the trick. Likewise, when selling or exchanging batches of books in sheets with other booksellers, Jaggard must have somehow ensured that *Whole Contention* and *Pericles* would not end up bound in sequence in any sets sold by them either.[49]

Why might readers in 1619 not have been put off by this separation of plays sharing continuous signatures, or by the extremely variable order of binding, or by the inclusion of Heywood's *Woman Killed*? Because while this kind of collection was unprecedented when published by a stationer, it was a common sight in readers' own libraries. In other words, copies of this highly unstandardized collection—with variable ordering, variable plays included, and various imprint dates stretching across nineteen years—must have *looked* like readers' sammelbands. That they were not is demonstrated by the lack of stab-stitch holes in so many copies: the individual plays in readers' sammelbands inevitably contain the stab-stitch holes that reveal how they were originally purchased before the reader bound them together.[50] They may also have looked like the kind of assemblage of both new and older copies that could sometimes be purchased in bookshops—although at least for the ones we know about, such as the volumes of John Boys's religious texts put together in the late 1610s that Aaron Pratt has studied, such nonce collections were always organized by a single author.[51]

All of these factors suggest that, contrary to recent revisionist arguments, Jaggard was in fact attempting to deceive someone. He did so by manipulating the set precisely to imply that it was not a typical publisher-issued collection. The next chapter argues that this deception extended beyond the "processes that leave their mark on the character of the finished book" to include post-printing manipulations of copies.[52] Unlike the false imprints and (to a lesser extent) the variable order of the plays, this evidence played no role in the New Bibliographers' arguments, and hence it has gone unnoticed by more recent scholars as well.

CHAPTER 3

Rips and Scrapes

> Magic or other secret means are not involved. How often I hear, "The tear is not visible at all; one wire line just continues into the next. How do you do it?" When I explain that it is really only the little knife that does it all, almost nobody wants to believe me, and yet it is the truth!
>
> —Max Schweidler, *The Restoration of Engravings, Drawings, Books, and Other Works on Paper*

Another aspect of the Jaggard Quartos that everyone, including the revisionists, has taken for granted is that the title pages divide into two camps: accurate imprints with the date 1619 (or the "accurate enough" imprint on the undated *Whole Contention*), followed by fraudulent imprints backdated to 1600 or 1608. This divide is absolutely fundamental to the story that has been told since Greg's "On Certain False Dates in Shakespeare Quartos." And so long as we concern ourselves only with the "processes that leave their mark on the character of the finished book," it is true enough.[1] But copies of the three plays dated 1619 now held at the Boston Public Library—*Pericles* (SC 1008), *Yorkshire Tragedy* (SC 1722), and *Merry Wives of Windsor* (SC 716)—show that these two camps were not so neatly distinguished (Figure 3.1).[2] In fact, it is easy to turn an accurate imprint into a less-than-truthful one.

At a glance, all seems normal here. But these title pages have a secret. The paper has been torn and extremely skillfully repaired. The tear line is still visible, although at first it may be mistaken for a water stain. When viewed with transmitted light, however, the difference in paper stock becomes apparent, even though great care was taken to disguise the repair, going so far as to match the chain lines and wire lines of the papers (Figure 3.2). In each

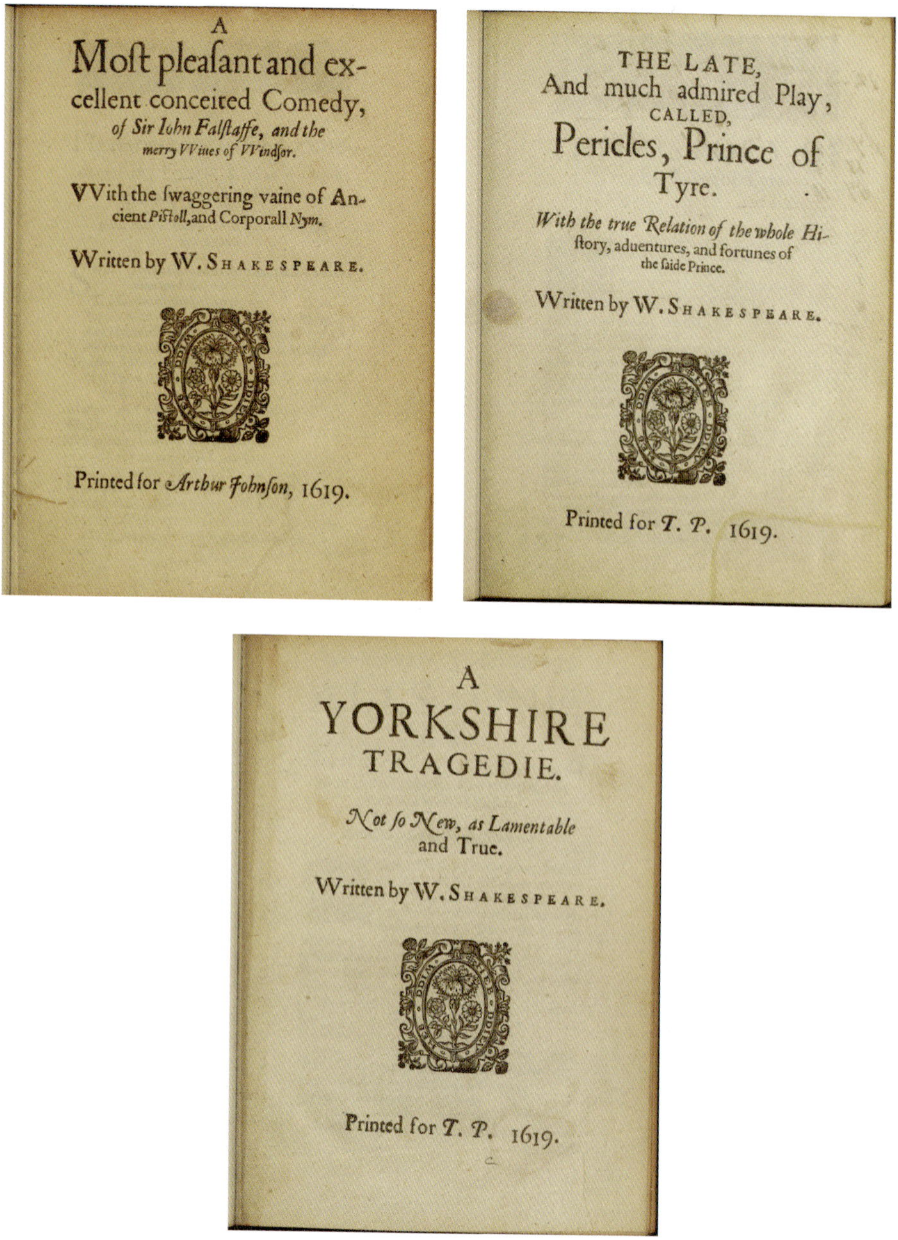

A
Most pleasant and excellent conceited Comedy, of Sir Iohn Falstaffe, and the merry VVives of VVindsor.
VVith the swaggering vaine of Ancient Pistoll, and Corporall Nym.
Written by W. SHAKESPEARE.
Printed for Arthur Iohnson, 1619.

THE LATE, And much admired Play, CALLED, Pericles, Prince of Tyre.
With the true Relation of the whole History, aduentures, and fortunes of the saide Prince.
Written by W. SHAKESPEARE.
Printed for T. P. 1619.

A
YORKSHIRE TRAGEDIE.
Not so New, as Lamentable and True.
Written by W. SHAKESPEARE.
Printed for T. P. 1619.

Figure 3.1 Title pages of *Pericles, Yorkshire Tragedy,* and *Merry Wives* at the Boston Public Library, G.176.28, G.176.57, G.176.20.

Figure 3.2 Backlit image of the title page of the BPL *Merry Wives*: the repair is expertly done, matching the chain lines and wire lines of the paper.

case, the paper was ripped precisely around the date 1619. Indeed, on the *Yorkshire Tragedy* title page this may not be a rip at all: the hole was punched carefully into the paper without ever reaching the margins (Figure 3.3). And in each case the date visible now is not actually printed onto the page. It is written in pen facsimile as part of a later repair. Despite the great technical skill of the facsimilist, we can see on the verso that the date does not bite into the paper the way metal type does under the force of the printing press (Figure 3.4). Under a microscope, ink that is imprinted is lighter in the interior of each character, as the pressure of the printing press squeezed the ink toward the borders of the type, a phenomenon known as "ink squash." Ink written onto the page, as in these cases, is more uniformly distributed (Figure 3.5).

These repairs were not intended to deceive anyone, even though they attempt to reproduce exactly the appearance of the original printed imprint. Rather, they are part of the standard arsenal of techniques that late eighteenth- and nineteenth-century book collectors and dealers had at their disposal for enhancing the aesthetic appeal of old and frequently damaged books.[3] Scattered throughout catalogues and auction records of the period are books described as expertly "mended" or with various leaves in "perfect" facsimile. What distinguishes the repairs on these Jaggard Quartos is how

Figure 3.3 Close-up of the repair to the BPL *Yorkshire Tragedy*, with backlighting.

Figure 3.4 Verso of the title page of the BPL *Yorkshire Tragedy*, under raking light, showing that the ink does not bite into the page.

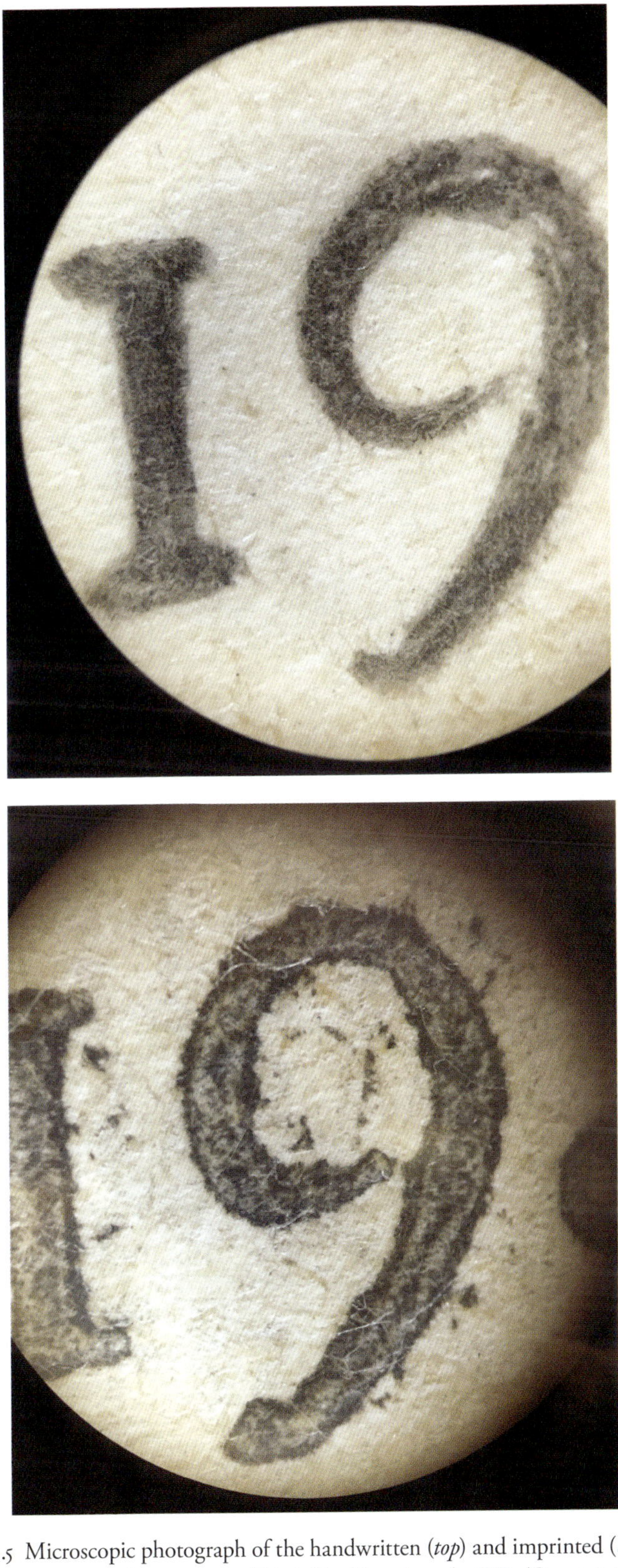

Figure 3.5 Microscopic photograph of the handwritten (*top*) and imprinted (*bottom*) date in the imprints of two copies of *Yorkshire Tragedy* at the BPL (G.176.58, G.176.57).

localized they are around the date, while the rest of the title page remains in excellent condition. Typically these pen facsimiles replace whole leaves or the entire margin of a page that had been excessively trimmed during a rebinding. Henrietta Bartlett's 1939 *Census of Shakespeare's Plays in Quarto* lists thirty-two copies with a complete facsimile title leaf, for example, and forty with at least one interior facsimile leaf, far more frequent than any kind of partial restoration.

With the expert help of curator Jay Moschella, who alerted me to these facsimile dates and guided me through the relevant archives, I have been able to trace much of the provenance of these three repaired Jaggard Quartos. They came to the BPL as part of the collection of Thomas Pennant Barton, the first great American collector of Shakespeare, and Barton acquired them all from his usual London book dealer, Thomas Rodd. Rodd seems to have come into a good number of Jaggard Quartos in the early 1840s, since his 1845 catalogue advertises no fewer than ten copies, and possibly an eleventh if his *Lear* was the Jaggard Quarto and not the actual first edition of 1608.[4] In December 1846, Rodd wrote to Barton: "I have this day addressed to you via Liverpool, a Box containing the articles in the list inclosed." Among the items in the box were these copies of *Yorkshire Tragedy* and *Merry Wives*, and Rodd made no attempt to hide the repairs, highlighting the skill with which they had been done: "The copies of the Yorkshire Tragedy & the Merry Wives have titles repaired, the date of each being filled in by fac simile. This is however so admirably done that it would be impossible even for a practised eye to detect it: still it would be dishonourable to neglect making it known to you, as I now do, and leave you at the same time at liberty to take or reject as you think proper."[5] About two years later, Barton acquired the *Pericles* from Rodd, again fully aware that the "*date* is supplied in fac-simile."[6]

The correspondence between Barton and Rodd allows us to date the repairs with some precision. They are skillful enough that they cannot have been made much earlier than the beginning of the nineteenth century: older techniques for repairing paper could not achieve these effects.[7] And they were already made when Barton bought them in the late 1840s. Given that date range, and given the skill on display, the pen work was probably done by the master facsimilist John Harris (1791–1873), who did this kind of work from around 1815 until he went blind in 1856.[8] If the repairs are not his, they must be by one of the other contemporary "clever manipulators of the same class," but, as an early account in the *Times Literary Supplement* reported, "it may be questioned if any of them possessed the almost startling skill of John Harris."[9]

Harris described his process in a report to the jurors of the Great Exhibition of 1851. First, he would trace a copy of the desired page "in a soft ink," then "transfer the same to a thin paper, and . . . re-transfer on to the intended leaf." He thereby "produced an outline lettered page, which, by being gone over carefully and imitating the original, produced the desired leaf."[10] (The same process could be applied to only a portion of a page, as in the Jaggard Quarto imprints.) Harris's work for the British Museum was "so perfectly done," according to one contemporary account, "that, after a few years, he has himself been puzzled to distinguish his own work from the original, so perfect has the fac-simile been, both in paper and typography." Indeed, this fact led the principal librarian Anthony Panizzi to order "that in future all additions made to a book in fac-simile should be marked as being so in a note at the bottom of the page, to prevent the possibility of subsequent librarians being imposed upon."[11]

Equally impressive on these title pages is the paper repair, with its matching chain and wire lines. While the border between the two papers is readily visible now, it may well have been less perceptible at the time because such repairs tend to age unpredictably.[12] In his *Essai sur la restauration des anciennes estampes et des livres rares* (1846), the first substantial European manual of paper repair, Alfred Bonnardot stresses the importance of finding paper identical to the original and of keeping a "supply of old papers of all kinds from every period, taken from sacrificed old books or the margins of bad prints."[13] Taking care to select a piece identical in color, in the amount of sizing, and in "les vergeures" or the chain and wire lines, the restorer applies glue to the moistened margins of the tear. Then the new piece of paper, also wet, is secured into place by running a knife across the border of the blend. A thin cloth is used to soak up excess moisture, and the paper is placed in the press. This final step, pressing the papers together, would likely have required working on a book in sheets, not in the binding. "I have seen," Bonnardot relates, "holes so expertly filled that one could scarcely perceive the precise border of the patch. The edges of the hole, as well as those of the patch, were thinned with the scraper and adjusted with such precision, that all the serrations were entangled one inside the other without leaving any trace of the join." He adds that some restorers do not wet the papers first, which is "more expeditious, but also less perfect," leaving "the connecting lines a little raw," and "the added piece can hardly be concealed."[14] Perhaps the BPL copies were repaired with this "dry" technique, leaving the blend line apparent. But the "vergeures" were handled perfectly, continuing seamlessly across the blend line.[15]

We know that Thomas Barton was an admirer of John Harris's work, thanks to an entry in the wish list of Shakespeare "Folios or Portions of them" that he sent to another London bookseller: "*A Fac-Simile of Harris much wanted*—Title page, or Verses (or both)."[16] Barton's copies of the 1611 *Titus Andronicus* and the undated (c. 1625) *Hamlet* include a Harris facsimile title page, and both of these were purchased from Rodd.[17] Barton's collection also included copies of Shakespeare's autographs done by Harris and then published by Rodd, and a portrait of Rodd himself "drawn from the face after death and finished from recollection by J. Harris."[18]

Rodd clearly had an ongoing relationship with Harris to do this kind of work, and the bookseller also once handled two other Jaggard Quartos with precisely the same kind of tear and repair: a *Merchant of Venice* now in the Library of Birmingham (SC 641) and a *Henry V* now at the University of Akron (SC 346).[19] On both of these copies, just as on the BPL copies, the title page has been torn around the date only, and the date is written in pen facsimile, not printed (Figure 3.6 and Figure 3.7). But Rodd never seems to have owned another Jaggard Quarto with this same kind of facsimile work around the date: a copy of *King Lear* now at the Senate House Library of the University of London (SC 512) that is repaired so perfectly that it is almost impossible to discern (Figure 3.8). Indeed, while this copy is described in Henrietta Bartlett's 1939 *Census* as having the "date and one word of imprint in facsimile," I initially wondered if Bartlett might have made an uncharacteristic mistake here. But there is a clear provenance history indicating this facsimile repair going back to the 1846 Sotheby's auction of the collection of William Holgate ("*red morocco, gilt leaves, imprint repaired*"), where it was purchased by the bookseller William Pickering, and further inspection confirmed the paper repair and pen facsimile.[20] This repair is far more expert than the others, particularly in the blending of the papers.[21]

And there are more: ghostly evidence of two other copies. A *Dream* listed in a Quaritch catalogue from 1894, but currently unlocatable, is described as having "the bottom corner of the title mended, so that it has been necessary to supply the numeral of the date"; and a 1919 auction catalogue from the Henkels auction house in Philadelphia lists an *Oldcastle* with the "date and small portion of imprint in facsimile."[22] The only play among the traditional Jaggard Quartos for which I can find no evidence of a tear-and-repair copy is *Whole Contention*. And, perhaps not coincidentally, *Whole Contention* is also the only Jaggard Quarto with no date at all in the imprint.

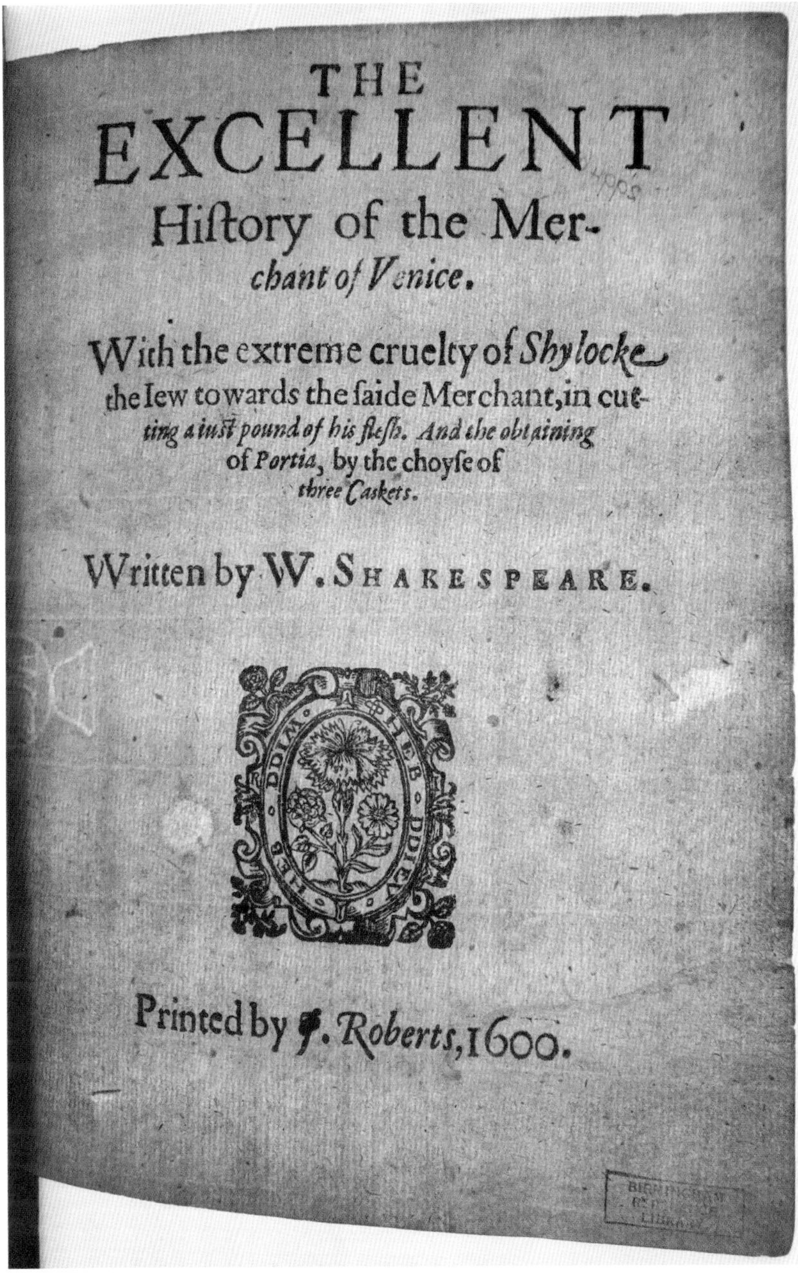

THE
EXCELLENT
Hiſtory of the Mer-
chant of Venice.

With the extreme cruelty of *Shylocke*
the Iew towards the ſaide Merchant, in cut-
ting a iuſt pound of his fleſh. And the obtaining
of *Portia*, by the choyſe of
three Caskets.

Written by W. SHAKESPEARE.

Printed by *J. Roberts*, 1600.

Figure 3.6 The tear-and-repair copy of *Merchant of Venice* at the Library of Birmingham (S336.16).

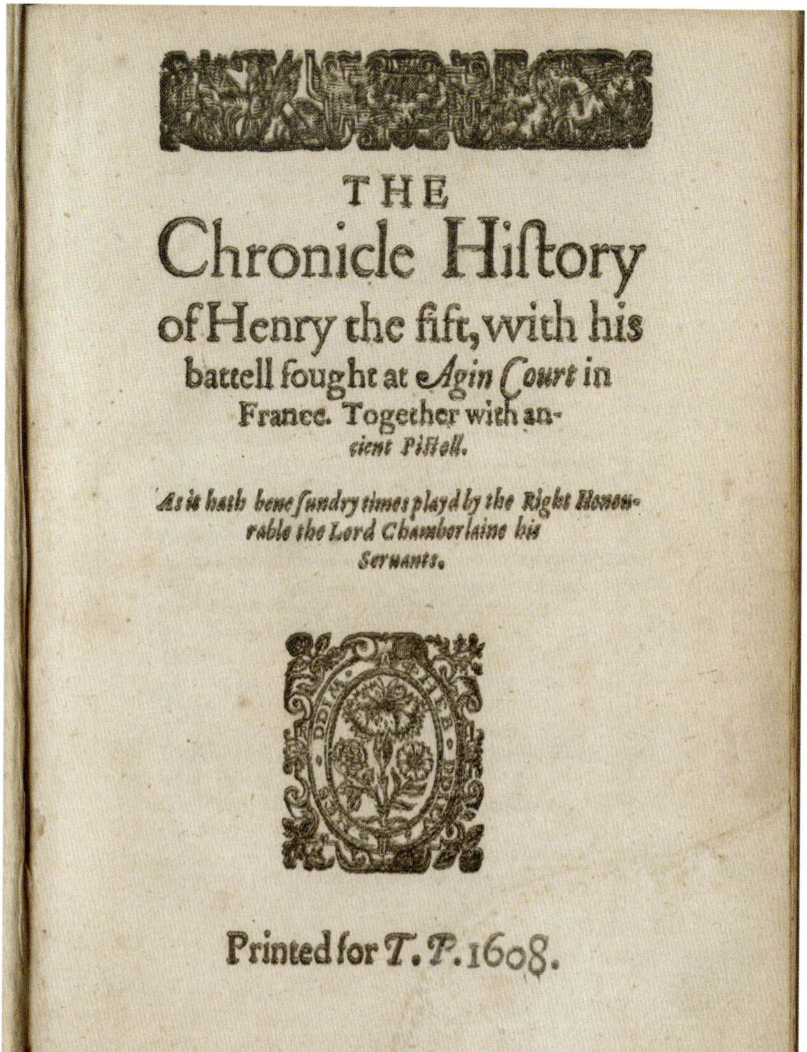

THE

Chronicle Hiſtory

of Henry the fift, with his battell fought at *Agin Court* in France. Together with ancient *Piſtell.*

As it hath bene ſundry times playd by the Right Honourable the Lord Chamberlaine his Seruants.

Printed for *T. P.* 1608.

Figure 3.7 The tear-and-repair copy of *Henry V* at the University of Akron Library (Rare Vault PR2812.A1 1619).

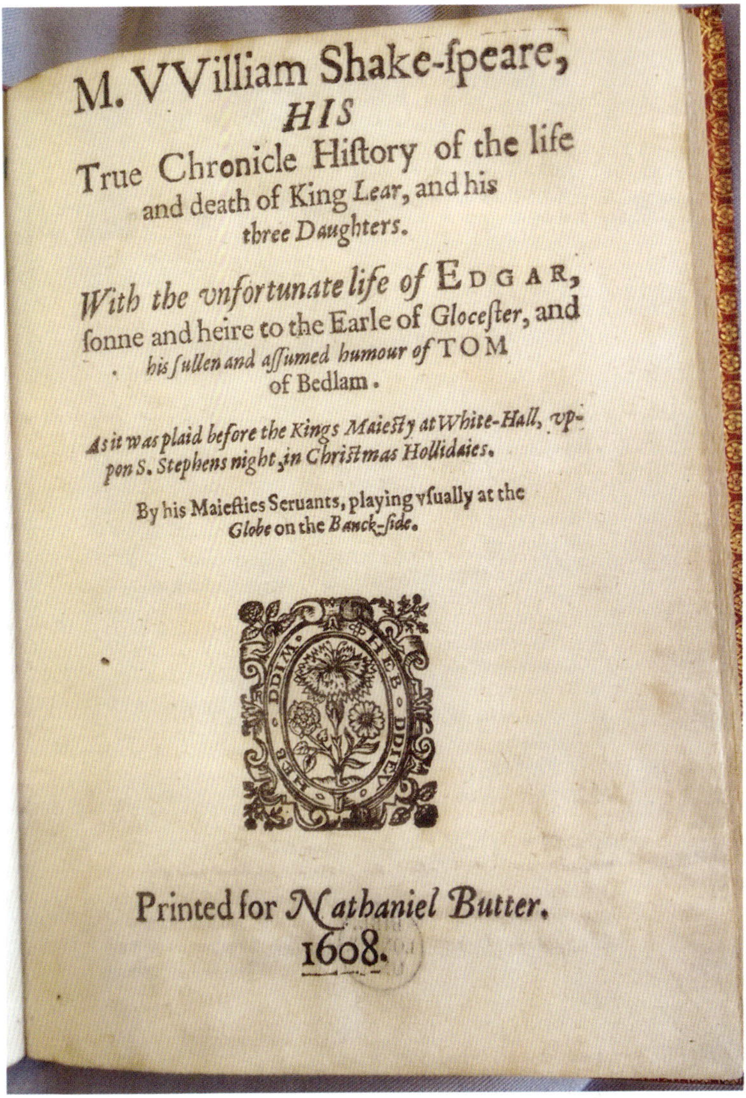

Figure 3.8 The title page of the Senate House Library copy of *King Lear* under normal lighting, and a detail of the imprint portion of the verso with backlighting ([S.L.] I [Shakespeare—1608] (S)).

The 1846 Holgate auction included not only the Senate House *Lear* but also the tear-and-repair copies of *Oldcastle* ("*red morocco, imprint repaired*") and *Pericles* ("*red mor. date repaired*"), and possibly the *Merchant of Venice* ("*blue morocco, gilt leaves, some leaves mended*").[23] In the same auction were Jaggard Quartos of *Whole Contention*, *Yorkshire Tragedy*, *Merry Wives*, *Henry V*, and *Dream*, although without any indication of repairs to the title page or imprint.[24] In other words, Holgate owned one copy of each of the traditional Jaggard Quartos, and he also owned the 1617 *Woman Killed*, "unbound," which was purchased by Rodd, according to the annotated catalogue.[25]

There is evidence, therefore, that at least some of these repaired Jaggard Quartos had traveled together, already repaired, for some time prior to Rodd's sale to Barton.[26] The three plays at the BPL, the Birmingham *Merchant*, and the Senate House *Lear* were all bound by Charles Lewis (1786–1836), the most fashionable London bookbinder of the early nineteenth century. So too was the now lost *Oldcastle*, according to the record of its auction in New York on 15 January 1926, where it is described as "full red morocco, gilt, gilt edges, by C. Lewis."[27] Perhaps the binder Lewis rather than the bookseller Rodd is the key link in the chain here. Booksellers and binders alike often kept damaged books or fragments, "so-called hospital copies that could be cannibalized in order to make up perfect examples," and Lewis no doubt had good examples of early paper on hand to use in blended repairs of this kind.[28] But the binder of the Akron *Henry V* is unknown, as is the binder of the unlocatable *Dream*, although Lewis may have been responsible for its "green morocco extra, gilt edges" (as described by Quaritch) if it is the same copy as the one sold in the auction of George Smith's collection at Sotheby's in 1867 and described as a "fine copy in green morocco extra, g[ilt] e[dges] by C. Lewis."[29]

Finally, we can trace a number of Jaggard Quartos, including the Akron *Henry V*, back even earlier to the collector John Bellingham Inglis (1780–1870), whose collection was sold at Sotheby's in 1826, following his declaration of bankruptcy three years earlier. The Akron *Henry V* is still in Inglis's signature binding "with an acorn in each angle of the gilt framework on the sides."[30] Bartlett lists only four other copies with Inglis provenance in her 1939 *Census*, none of them Jaggard Quartos, but this is because she can identify Inglis's copies only when they remain in his "acorn" binding. The Inglis auction catalogue in fact lists fourteen copies of plays covered by Bartlett's *Census*, and no doubt many of these were rebound later. As in the Holgate auction, one copy of every traditional Jaggard Quarto was sold (although not

Woman Killed).[31] Of these, Rodd purchased all but the *Pericles*, *Merry Wives*, and *Oldcastle*. The catalogue gives no indications of condition, such as these title-page repairs, but we know from its binding that Inglis's *Henry V* was the tear-and-repair copy, and some of the other tear-and-repair copies may well have come from Inglis.[32]

It may ultimately prove impossible to trace the source of these repairs, but whether they were done for Inglis, Holgate, Lewis, or Rodd, or some combination of them and others, they clearly date from the early part of the 1800s. While such repairs could conceivably have been done without taking apart the book, as Bonnardot describes them they were far more likely to have been done during a rebinding, when the book was in sheets. The Lewis bindings have gilt edges, and there is no perceptible difference in the gilt between the original sheets and the patch, again suggesting that the repair was done before binding.[33] We can conclude, therefore, that the *Henry V* was probably repaired by 1826, the date of the Inglis auction, and the others before 1836, when Charles Lewis died.

There is tantalizingly suggestive evidence, though, that some if not all of these copies traveled together even before that time, whether as yet repaired or not, and even that they once coexisted in a single volume of Jaggard Quartos.[34] These playbooks are remarkably similar in size. The Birmingham *Merchant*, BPL *Merry Wives*, and BPL *Pericles* all measure 18.6 × 14 cm for the binding, and representative leaves are very similar as well (18 × 13.2–13.5 cm). The Senate House *Lear* is almost precisely the same, at 18.5 × 13.8 cm for the binding and 18.1 × 13.1 cm for a representative leaf. Such measurements, especially when made at different times and in different places, are not precise, and measuring leaf width is particularly difficult due to the curve at the gutter. We can therefore consider these all to be functionally the same size. Indeed, the *Lear* and the *Merchant* were listed by Bartlett in 1939 as having identical measurements, at 7⅛ × 5¼ inches; and the Henkels auction record lists the lost *Oldcastle* as having precisely those same dimensions. The Akron *Henry* is somewhat smaller in the binding, at 18.1 × 13.5 cm, but virtually identical in leaf size, at 17.9 × 13.5 cm.[35] The disparity in this copy is particularly intriguing, given that it is the only one we do not know was bound by Lewis and that it was likely bound at a different time. And yet the leaves share measurements strikingly similar to those of all the others; the boards are simply trimmed much closer to the book block. Since it was common for composite volumes to be broken up and individually rebound prior to sale, it is conceivable that Inglis at one point owned a complete set of Jaggard Quartos bound together. The copies for sale at his auction may represent this disassembled volume, with *Henry V* having been earlier bound for Inglis in his favorite binding, while the others were rebound by Lewis in more standard bindings in preparation for the auction. It is possible, in other words, that these tear-and-repair copies point us toward a complete bound set of Jaggard Quartos that had each been defaced in some way around the date in the imprint, except for the significantly undated *Whole Contention*.

These title pages represent a particularly vivid example of the need to think about Shakespearean bibliography across the longue durée. The analytic tools of bibliography can help us to understand how these title pages came to be the way they are, revealing their paper blends and pen facsimiles, and we can trace their provenance to attempt to determine who was responsible for their current appearance. But whatever we do, we cannot see "behind" these repairs to how they would have appeared to readers from 1619 through the early nineteenth century. These repairs have destroyed any earlier evidence that might have illuminated that question for us, but they have at the same time preserved these copies, which otherwise might not have been considered worthy of inclusion in nineteenth-century collections and might therefore have disappeared altogether.[36] The repairs preserve even as they efface, allow us to see even as they obscure.

The crucial fact to remember is that the current appearance of these books results from a nineteenth-century repair process, but that repair itself resulted from something about these title pages that happened to them earlier. Whatever that something was, it is perceivable now only in its ghostly form as the impetus for repair. Of course, title pages are highly subject to wear and tear, and I suppose it is theoretically possible that all of these title pages were accidentally damaged in the same way, necessitating their similar repair. But I doubt it. The repairs are all localized to the imprint, and the punched hole in the BPL *Yorkshire Tragedy* makes evident that whatever the pen facsimile and paper blending are repairing, it had to do specifically with the date.

Furthermore, the repaired corners of these title pages look nothing like the kind of accidental damage we often find on the margins of early books, as in the copy of the Jaggard Quarto of *Merry Wives* at the Folger (SC 726), in which the missing date has also been supplied in ink, in this case wrongly as 1618 (Figure 3.9).[37] Here the paper is degraded, eaten away, just as we often find in poorly preserved early modern books. Or consider the unusual copy

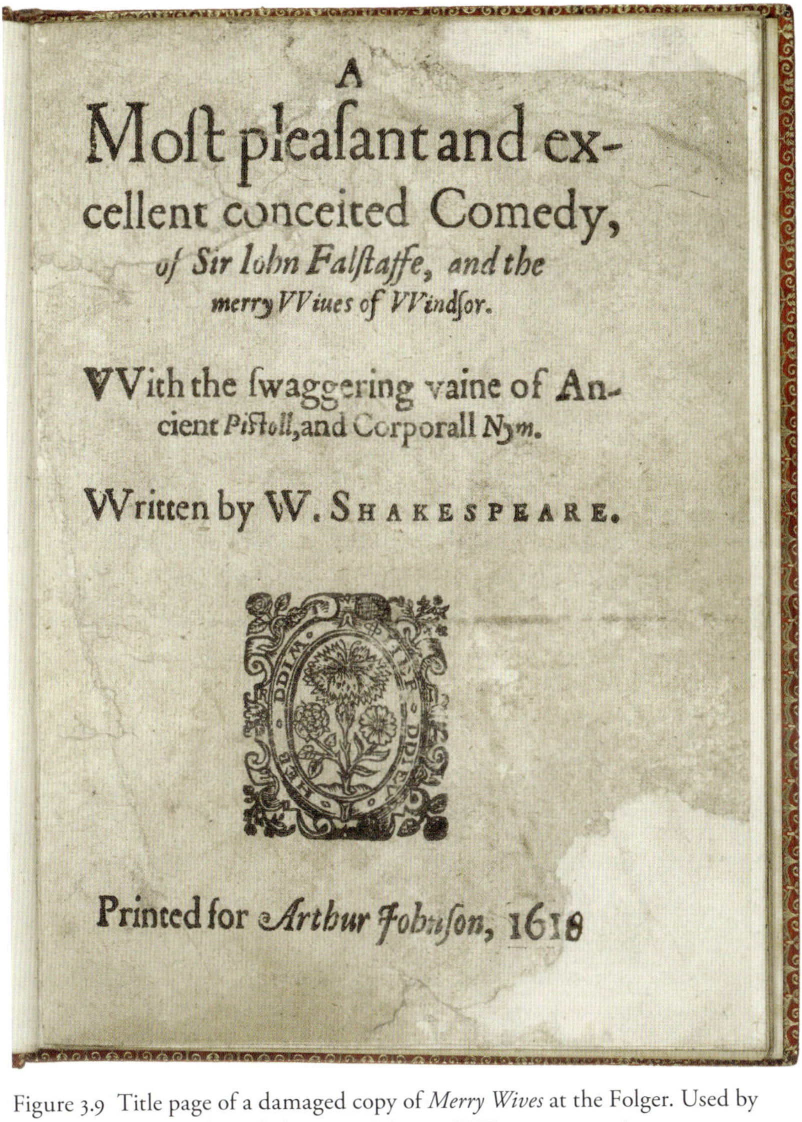

Figure 3.9 Title page of a damaged copy of *Merry Wives* at the Folger. Used by permission of the Folger Shakespeare Library, STC 22300 copy 6.

of the 1639 edition of *1 Henry IV* at the Folger (SC 265), with a title page from the 1622 edition inserted in place of its original missing one. The inserted title page has been mended at the bottom, where the last line of the imprint, including the date, had been lost, probably when the book was over-trimmed during binding (Figure 3.10). This line was then supplied in a professional pen facsimile (far better than the "1618" *Merry Wives*).[38] This copy of *1 Henry IV* fully conforms to the norm for such repairs: the entire last line of the imprint was lost, not merely the date; the margin line between the two papers is jagged, where the paper had further degraded, not neatly cut.

Another comparison: the copy of the first part of Thomas Heywood's *If You Know Not Me, You Know Nobody* (1613) at the Elizabethan Club at Yale. Like the Folger *1 Henry IV*, it has been repaired inaccurately—possibly in an attempt to increase the value of the book, although possibly just by accident (Figure 3.11). Here the date of the first edition, 1605, has been written in pen facsimile, along with a good portion of the imprint and part of the woodcut of Queen Elizabeth. (Unlike these two cases, the repairs on the Jaggard Quartos cannot have been done to deceive book buyers into believing they were earlier and hence more valuable editions, because they always restore the correct imprint date.) The repair was likely done by Francis Bedford, who worked under Charles Lewis and inherited his shop, and who gave the copy its current binding.[39] Not surprisingly, given Bedford's connection to Lewis, the technique here is very similar to that used for the tear-and-repair copies, but again, the damage that this repair seeks to undo was not localized to the date alone. The top outer corner is also repaired, indicating that the title page had been damaged more generally. The only copy of the Jaggard Quartos that we might want to reconsider in light of these comparisons is the Senate House *King Lear*, in which possibly the entire imprint is pen facsimile and on new paper. The repair on that copy is so expert that it is very hard to perceive, so I cannot be absolutely certain that it should be included in the same category as the others. If the entire imprint has indeed been restored, then it appears somewhat more analogous to the Folger *1 Henry IV* or the Elizabethan Club *1 If You Know Not Me* than to the other tear-and-repair copies of Jaggard Quartos.

Nonetheless, these comparisons make clear that something very different must have happened to the Jaggard Quartos, something specifically to do with the dates in their imprints. And among copies of Shakespeare's plays, this kind of repair clusters around the Jaggard Quartos to an extent that cannot be coincidental. Whereas we know of eight such copies of Jaggard Quartos alone,

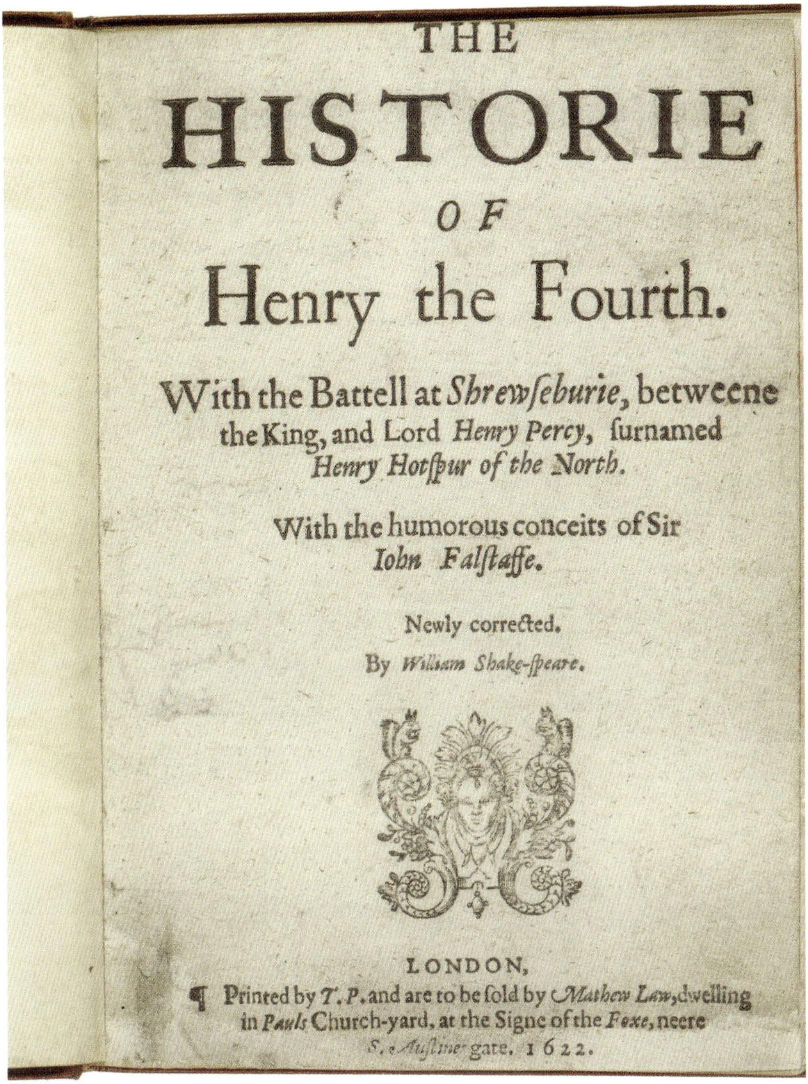

THE

HISTORIE

OF

Henry the Fourth.

With the Battell at *Shrewsburie*, betweene the King, and Lord *Henry Percy*, surnamed *Henry Hotspur of the North.*

With the humorous conceits of Sir *Iohn Falstaffe.*

Newly corrected.

By *William Shake-speare.*

LONDON,

¶ Printed by *T. P.* and are to be sold by *Mathew Law*, dwelling in *Pauls* Church-yard, at the Signe of the *Foxe*, neere *S. Austine*-gate. 1622.

Figure 3.10 Title page of a sophisticated copy of *1 Henry IV* (1622/1639) at the Folger, under normal lighting, and a detail of the imprint portion of the verso with backlighting. Used by permission of the Folger Shakespeare Library, STC 22287 copy 5.

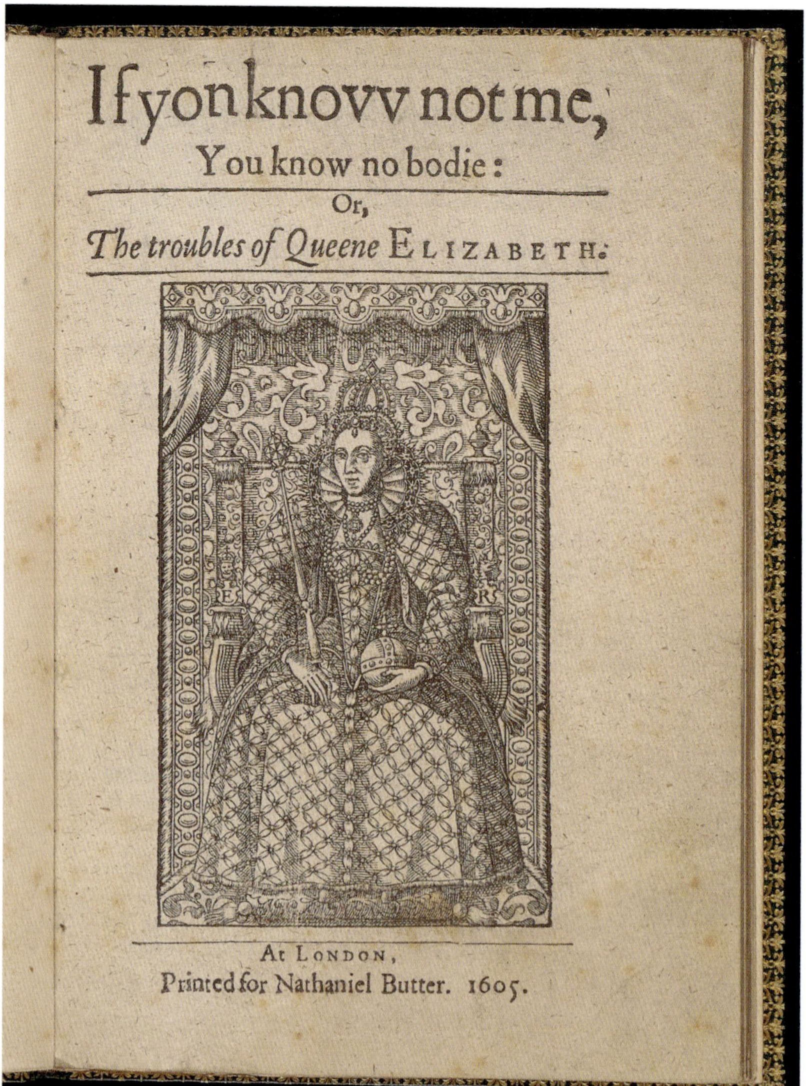

Figure 3.11 Title page of an inaccurately repaired copy of *1 If You Know Not Me, You Know Nobody* at the Elizabethan Club, Yale University (Eliz 96), under normal lighting and backlit.

If you knovv not me,
You know no bodie:
Or,
The troubles of Queene ELIZABETH.

At LONDON,
Printed for Nathaniel Butter. 1605.

Figure 3.11 (*Continued*)

Bartlett lists only the Folger *1 Henry IV* and six other copies as having any part of their imprint repaired in facsimile, out of the 1,222 copies of Shakespeare's plays in her 1939 *Census*. All of these six copies are similar to the Folger *1 Henry IV* in repairing the entire bottom margin or the title page more generally.[40] This comparison thus provides a check against the possibility that the prevalence of tear-and-repair copies of Jaggard Quartos is simply an artifact of my having looked more closely at more copies of those editions than of others. By contrast to all these other copies, the precision of the repairs around the dates on the Jaggard Quartos shows that they were addressing something out of the ordinary—something that has now been lost to us.

For the rest of this chapter we are faced with a series of branching paths, and depending on which ones we take, our conclusions will differ. To begin with, there are two possibilities for the appearance of these title pages immediately before their repair, for this "something out of the ordinary" that was being remedied. Either there was nothing at all where the new paper was blended onto the existing title page, just a torn corner or a hole where the date had been; or there was something there that it was thought desirable to remove before beginning the repair work. Either the new paper with pen facsimile was added to fill a gap in the original title page; or the original paper was torn, cut, or punched out in order to create the optimal conditions for grafting the new paper with its pen facsimile onto the title page. Either a prior "tear" necessitated the early nineteenth-century "repair"; or the tear and repair was a single nineteenth-century process of restoration caused by some unknown previous process.

In his 1924 catalogue of the library of John Clawson, who owned the Akron *Henry V*, Seymour de Ricci wrote that the "lower corner of the title, with the date, has been torn off at the time, probably by the publisher as it also occurs in other copies (now completed in fac-simile . . .)."[41] De Ricci does not say which other copies he has seen, and while he seems to be referring to other copies of *Henry V*, he might simply be referring to tear-and-repair copies of other Jaggard Quartos. I have not located another copy of *Henry V* with anything unusual about the imprint. But the Quaritch manager E. H. Dring certainly reported having seen multiple tear-and-repair copies of the same play, although not *Henry V*. And Dring too thought that the tears were done early in the life of these books, with only the repairs done in the nineteenth century. Dring wrote to Pollard in 1910 that he had seen "at least 3 copies of the

M. N. D. J[ames] R[oberts] 1600, with the date torn out & added; & also the 1608 King Lear & the T. P. 1600 Oldcastle." Perhaps Dring was simply misremembering: I have found no extant manipulated copies of *Dream*, only the mention of one such copy in the 1894 Quaritch catalogue. But then again maybe Dring and de Ricci had indeed seen these additional copies, which will turn up someday. Dring added that Quaritch's chief cataloguer, Michael Kerney, "had noticed [the torn and repaired title pages] himself but had never been able to assign any reason for it having been done, although he was sure it had been done intentionally and most probably when issued."[42]

Both Dring and de Ricci were writing after Greg's "On Certain False Dates," and their speculation that the dates were originally torn off these copies "by the publisher" "when issued" clearly results from their familiarity with the New Bibliographic narrative of the 1619 quartos. But their comments never entered the scholarly discourse around the Jaggard Quartos. Pollard did not pick up on Dring's recollections, perhaps thinking the case had already been definitively solved by Greg. Or perhaps Pollard neglected those recollections because, even though Dring told him that "this had some little bearing on your ingenious discoveries," Dring's and de Ricci's theory actually sits somewhat uneasily with the New Bibliographic explanation of the Jaggard Quartos.[43]

After all, if the tear-and-repair copies were localized only to those with the date 1619—the BPL copies of *Pericles, Yorkshire Tragedy*, and *Merry Wives*—it would be easy enough to assimilate this evidence into the traditional theory. After falsifying the dates on the title pages of the plays printed later in the series, one might speculate, Jaggard went back and defaced the title pages of some copies of the plays printed earlier to erase evidence of the actual date of printing. By removing 1619 from their title pages, these plays were made to appear just like the other plays in the set: old copies, not newly printed ones. But it is much harder to understand the tear-and-repair copies of *Merchant*, *Oldcastle*, *Lear*, *Dream*, and *Henry V*—and perhaps multiple copies of the last two if Dring and de Ricci were remembering correctly. These plays were already falsely dated to 1600 or 1608. Why would Jaggard or Pavier have torn off these fraudulent dates from the title pages "when issued"? This evidence is hard to square with the dominant understanding of the Jaggard Quartos since the New Bibliography.

At the same time, the oddity of manipulating the already false imprints provides important evidence that, whatever these repairs were addressing, it was likely *not* a change made by a later collector or dealer to enhance the value of the copy. The tear-and-repair title pages include four copies that would have already appeared to everyone in the eighteenth and nineteenth centuries to be first editions, or at least the second of two editions printed in the same year.[44] The tear-and-repair copies are not, in other words, restorations of the "correct" date made by a nineteenth-century owner in order to fix a fraudulent transformation of that date by an eighteenth-century bookseller. The same evidence that makes it hard to understand Jaggard's motivation for tearing the date off these title pages in 1619 also makes it highly unlikely that they were altered later.

We should therefore consider the second of our branching paths: the tear was part of the nineteenth-century repair, addressing some change made to these imprints in the early seventeenth century. If so, evidence from other copies may offer a clue to the appearance of these title pages before a portion was removed from them to enable the repair. Several Jaggard Quartos have been manipulated, post-printing, precisely around their dates, but without any Victorian repairs. So far as I am aware, only one of these copies has been much noticed before: a *Yorkshire Tragedy* in the George III collection at the British Library (SC 1725).[45] Here the paper was scraped like parchment to erase the "19" in the imprint date. With transmitted light, one can even see pinprick holes where the scraping went too far (Figure 3.12). Then "08" was added to create the date of the true first edition of the play, 1608, but the remnants of the original "19" can still be seen when viewed from the verso (Figure 3.13). Greg saw this copy while preparing his *Bibliography of English Printed Drama* and suggested the manipulation was done "possibly at the time of issue" by "erasure and stamping," that is, by inking two pieces of movable type and stamping them onto this copy by hand.[46] If we knew that were the case, we could be sure the alteration was made by Jaggard, since it is hard to imagine that the copy would have found its way back to a printing house in the centuries that followed.

But in fact the numerals seem more likely to have been handwritten, as a magnified image suggests (Figure 3.14). The margins of the numerals are blurrier than the crisp edges of the movable-type "16" immediately adjacent, and the ink in the 8 appears to overlap at the intersection of the two loops, which occurs when the numeral is drawn by hand but not when impressed by a typeface. The 0 and the 8 have discolored the page over time very differently from the printed numerals, as can be seen under ultraviolet light, a yellowing typical

Figure 3.12 The scrape-and-ink copy of *Yorkshire Tragedy* at the British Library. © The British Library Board, C.12.g.26.

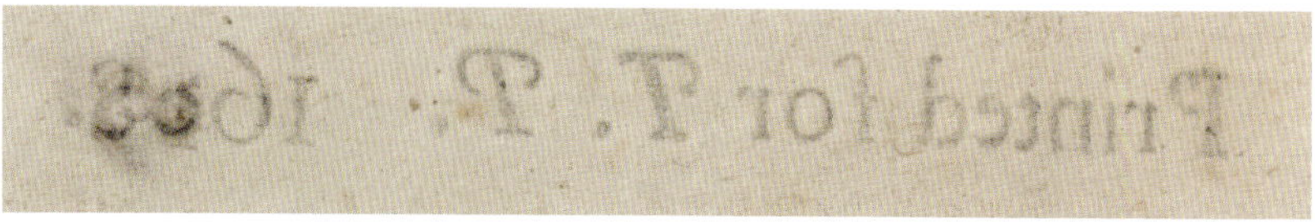

Figure 3.13 The verso of the BL *Yorkshire Tragedy* shows that the original "19" has not been completely erased. Photograph by Christina Duffy, imaging scientist, British Library. © The British Library Board, C.12.g.26.

Figure 3.14 Magnified image of the imprint date on the BL *Yorkshire Tragedy*, under a combination of ultraviolet light with a red, green, and blue filter. Photograph by Christina Duffy, imaging scientist, British Library. © The British Library Board, C.12.g.26.

of iron-gall writing inks. The ink on each numeral pools at the bottom, which implies an ink liquid enough to settle downward when written on a slightly inclined surface, and printer's ink was far more viscous than writing ink.[47] Of course, printing houses would have had plenty of writing ink around, as any business would, and so the fact that the numerals were handwritten in no way rules out the change having been done in Jaggard's shop.

Even if the new numerals were written, rather than stamped, the existence of several similarly treated copies strongly suggests that all these title pages were manipulated at the same time, by the same person. For instance, a copy of *Pericles* in the Auckland Free Library (SC 1007) was transformed in exactly the same way as the BL *Yorkshire Tragedy*. The original date 1619 has been altered: with transmitted light, you can see that the numeral 1 has been erased, leaving only its outline where the paper was scraped thin (Figure 3.15 and Figure 3.16). While the library catalogue (probably following Greg's note

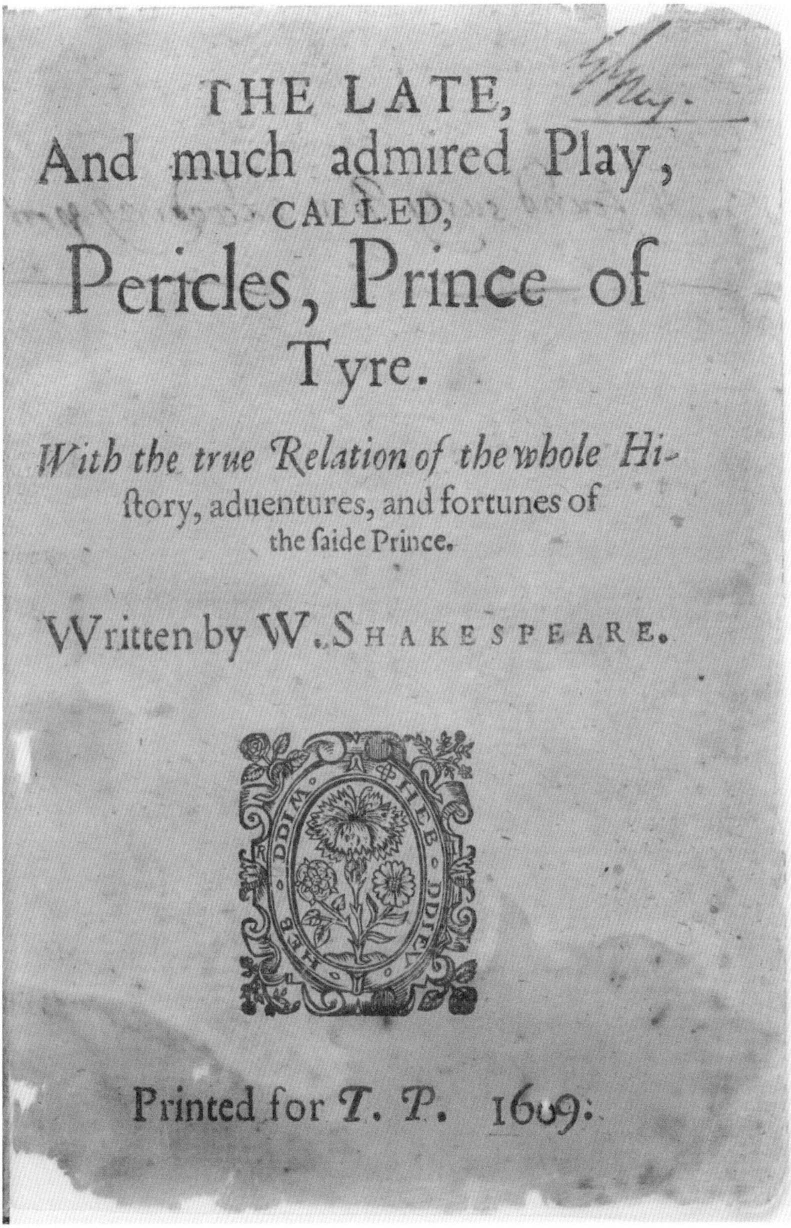

THE LATE,

And much admired Play,

CALLED,

Pericles, Prince of

Tyre.

With the true Relation of the whole Hi-

ſtory, aduentures, and fortunes of

the ſaide Prince.

Written by W. SHAKESPEARE.

Printed for *T. P.* 1609.

Figure 3.15 Title page of the scrape-and-ink copy of *Pericles* in Auckland. From the Sir George Grey Special Collections, Auckland Libraries, RBR.1619.SHAK.Safe.

Figure 3.16 A backlit image of the verso of the Auckland *Pericles* reveals the outline of the erased "1." From the Sir George Grey Special Collections, Auckland Libraries.

on *Yorkshire Tragedy*) suggests that the date was "altered by erasure and stamping, possibly at the time of issue," when viewed closely the numeral 0 appears more likely to have been handwritten, since it too lacks the clear borders of the numerals printed from type.[48] Furthermore, the numeral 0 that Jaggard used for the imprints on other Jaggard Quartos is wider than the loop of his numeral 6, but in the case of both the Auckland *Pericles* and the BL *Yorkshire Tragedy* the 0 is narrower.[49] Like the BL copy, therefore, this imprint seems to have been altered by scraping the undesired numeral and then inking over it by hand.

While it is conceivable that these two copies were once owned by the same later collector who forged the dates, there is no known overlap in their provenance. The BL copy of *Yorkshire Tragedy* was already in the George III collection by about 1812, when it appears with the date 1608 in the catalogue prepared by the king's librarian Frederick Barnard, indicating that the alteration was already made.[50] Meanwhile, Sir George Grey purchased the Auckland *Pericles* in 1862, but its current binding dates from around 1820: in the lower compartment of the spine is "1609," making the date of rebinding the terminus ad quem for the alteration of the imprint.[51] Either the early nineteenth-century binder of the Auckland *Pericles* and (presumably) its owner at the time were taken in by the alteration or they were themselves engaged in deliberate fraud. The more examples we find of this kind of alteration, though, the less likely this latter explanation becomes. If we find several such title pages, with no obvious later overlap in provenance, the simplest explanation becomes that they were all changed when they were in the printing house or bookshop, by the same person, at the same time, in 1619 itself.

A copy of *Henry V* at the National Library of Scotland (SC 336) has also been altered by scraping, although without the inking afterward.[52] The imprint appears to read 1608 as it should, but this is a later (fairly crude) handwritten restoration (Figure 3.17).[53] A closer look with transmitted light reveals the sequence of events that must have resulted in the imprint's current appearance. The light shining through the top of the original 8 shows that the paper has been scraped and the top loop of the 8 removed to create the illusion of a publication date of 1600 (Figure 3.18). Here again we are faced with the oddity of altering an already false date. The other examples we have seen of this kind of manipulation are on copies of plays dated 1619, *Yorkshire Tragedy* and *Pericles*. But *Henry V* is the only misdated Pavier edition that is *mis*-dated in another sense. It refers to an earlier edition that, so far as we know, never existed. There was no 1608 edition of *Henry V*, whereas all of the other plays are, we might say, *accurately* misdated to the year of a real earlier edition. Perhaps someone realized the problem: the faulty fraud has been detected and remedied, with the date altered to 1600, the date of the actual first edition of *Henry V*. In other words, this title page was made by someone to mimic the true first edition exactly as on the original imprints of other Jaggard Quartos. And the similarity of the erasure process here and in the British Library *Yorkshire Tragedy* and Auckland *Pericles*—scraping the paper as if it were a parchment manuscript—strongly suggests the same hand was behind them.

On the title page of this copy of *Henry V* is the number 15299, which links it with the BL *Yorkshire Tragedy*, which has 15383 written on its title page (see Figure 3.12). Both numbers refer to items in the *Catalogue of Books* printed by Thomas and John Egerton in 1791 and 1792, featuring "a singular Assemblage of Old English Poetry and Plays."[54] Furthermore, 15299 on the *Henry V* title page is overwritten on an earlier number, 500; and on the *Yorkshire Tragedy* title page, the number 501 has been crossed out. These earlier numbers refer to the Egertons' *Catalogue of Old Quarto Plays* (1790), and they were clearly updated when that catalogue was incorporated into the much larger, general catalogues for 1791 and 1792. Two of the manipulated copies can thus be traced to the same owners in the 1790s, a brief overlap in their provenance.

Might this shared provenance suggest that the date manipulations were done by someone in the eighteenth or early nineteenth century, to increase

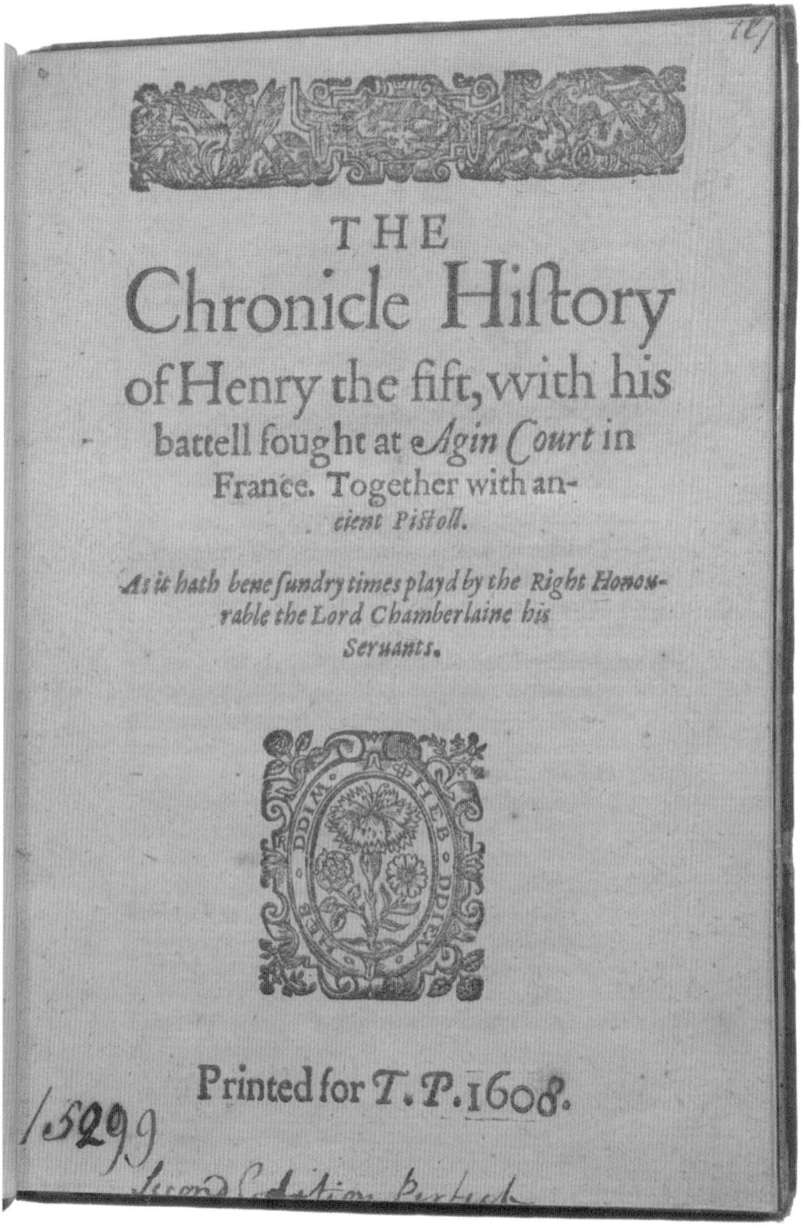

Figure 3.17 Title page of the scraped copy of *Henry V* at the National Library of Scotland (Bute.485).

Figure 3.18 Detail of the imprint date on the NLS *Henry V* with backlighting.

their value? The Egertons themselves made no effort to pass them off as earlier, more valuable editions: in all three of their catalogues, both plays are listed by their original printed imprint dates. After the Egerton sale, the two copies seem to have gone their separate ways, since one soon passed into the royal collection—taking it off the rare book market and thus eliminating the main incentive for someone to alter the date—and the other passed through different hands on its way to Scotland. It seems unlikely, therefore, that the title pages were manipulated following their sale by the Egertons. The most likely explanation is that they were already altered by the time the Egertons acquired them, but that the booksellers simply listed the plays by their correct dates, which they knew from other evidence. Their catalogues offer almost no details about the specific condition of any of the books, only occasionally pausing to mention a particularly nice binding, so this would not be unusual. Furthermore, the Auckland *Pericles* is altered so similarly that it seems certain to have been done by the same hand, but it was never part of the Egertons' catalogues, and indeed we know of no overlap at all of its provenance with the *Henry V* and *Yorkshire Tragedy*. Since we know that the date on the Auckland *Pericles* was altered by the time of its binding in the early 1800s, there appears again to have been too little time between the Egerton catalogues and this binding for all three copies to have passed into the same hands and been altered by that owner. We are pushed back to the conclusion that they were altered when they last seem to have been together, in 1619.

Not all of the Jaggard Quartos whose dates have been manipulated were scraped in this way before being inked with a false date. Since *Whole Conten-*

tion had no date to begin with, erasure was unnecessary, as can be seen on a copy (SC 1703) at the New York Public Library that has been altered so that it appears to have been printed in 1600, the date of earlier editions of both *2* and *3 Henry VI* (Figure 3.19). Some effort has been made to copy the form of the numerals in Jaggard's shop, although this pen facsimile is nowhere near as sophisticated as the work of John Harris and his nineteenth-century colleagues. The 1852 sales catalogue of Edward Utterson (whose bookplate appears in the copy) shows that the false date was already there, and this is the earliest record of the copy that I can find. Interestingly, Utterson's catalogue notes "date on title *mended*," as if the inked date were simply restoring a damaged printed date. And a note on the flyleaf highlights the distinctiveness of "a copy like this with the *printed date* 1600." This former owner thus seems to have been convinced that the pen facsimile was in fact printed ink. By 1874, the facsimile was apparently easier to detect: the catalogue for the auction of William Tite's collection noted of this same copy that the "date is undoubtedly a forgery to palm off this copy as an unknown edition," since the "typographical errors and the slipped letters . . . prove that it is identical with the impression issued with Pericles" in 1619.[55] It is not that the author of the Tite catalogue was simply a better bibliographer than whoever wrote the note on the flyleaf. Rather, our perception is culturally situated, and some things become easier or harder to see depending on the observer's historical context.

All of which goes to show that untangling the bibliographic evidence of the highly variable copies of these editions was difficult enough in the nineteenth century—after more than a hundred years of serious collecting and comparing of copies. It must have been much more so in the early seventeenth century when the Jaggard Quartos appeared in bookstalls. Could this handwritten "1600," which may seem fairly crude to us today, have fooled the first readers of *Whole Contention*, much as it did some readers in the nineteenth century?

Two other copies of Jaggard Quartos present more doubtful cases of alteration, and I would likely not have considered them to have been deliberately manipulated were it not for the evidence of the imprints that have clearly been intentionally altered. Both involve a second copy of a play we have already seen scraped and inked. On a copy of *Pericles* at the Huntington Library (SC 1022), a numeral was scraped just as on the Auckland copy, but in this case the 9 rather than the 1 (Figure 3.20). The intention may have been to make the imprint date read 1610, since only the descender was scraped

THE
Whole Contention
betweene the two Famous
Houses, LANCASTER and
YORKE.

With the Tragicall ends of the good Duke
Humfrey, Richard Duke of Yorke,
and King Henrie the
sixt.

Diuided into two Parts: And newly corrected and
enlarged. Written by *William Shake-*
speare, Gent.

Printed at LONDON, for T. P.
1600

Figure 3.19 Title page of a copy of *Whole Contention* at the NYPL, with added manuscript date. *KC 1619 (Shakespeare, W. *Whole Contention betweene the two Famous Houses, Lancaster and Yorke*) copy 1. Rare Book Collection. The New York Public Library. Astor, Lenox and Tilden Foundations.

Figure 3.20 Microscopic photograph of the imprint date on a copy of *Pericles* at the Huntington Library, showing scraping and over-inking. Courtesy of the Huntington Library, San Marino, California, 69347.

while the loop was left intact, although it doesn't appear to have been done as carefully or thoroughly as in the other copies. And while the entire 9 was restored in ink at a later stage, the staining around the loop suggests that it had previously been overwritten to emphasize its new status as a zero, since the stain does not appear on the descender. The BL *Yorkshire Tragedy* shows a similar staining around the 08 due to the composition and age of the ink. This case is questionable, however, not only because the physical evidence is not as clear—perhaps it was accidental—but also because the other cases all redate the play to the date of an actual, earlier edition, whereas there was no *Pericles* printed in 1610.[56]

Another possible case is at the Folger: a copy of *Henry V* (SC 327) with the lower loop of the 8 in the imprint scraped, although not completely (Figure 3.21). The copy at the National Library of Scotland shows that the better choice for scraping was clearly the top loop. The resulting date on the Folger copy—even if the scraping had been carried out completely—would

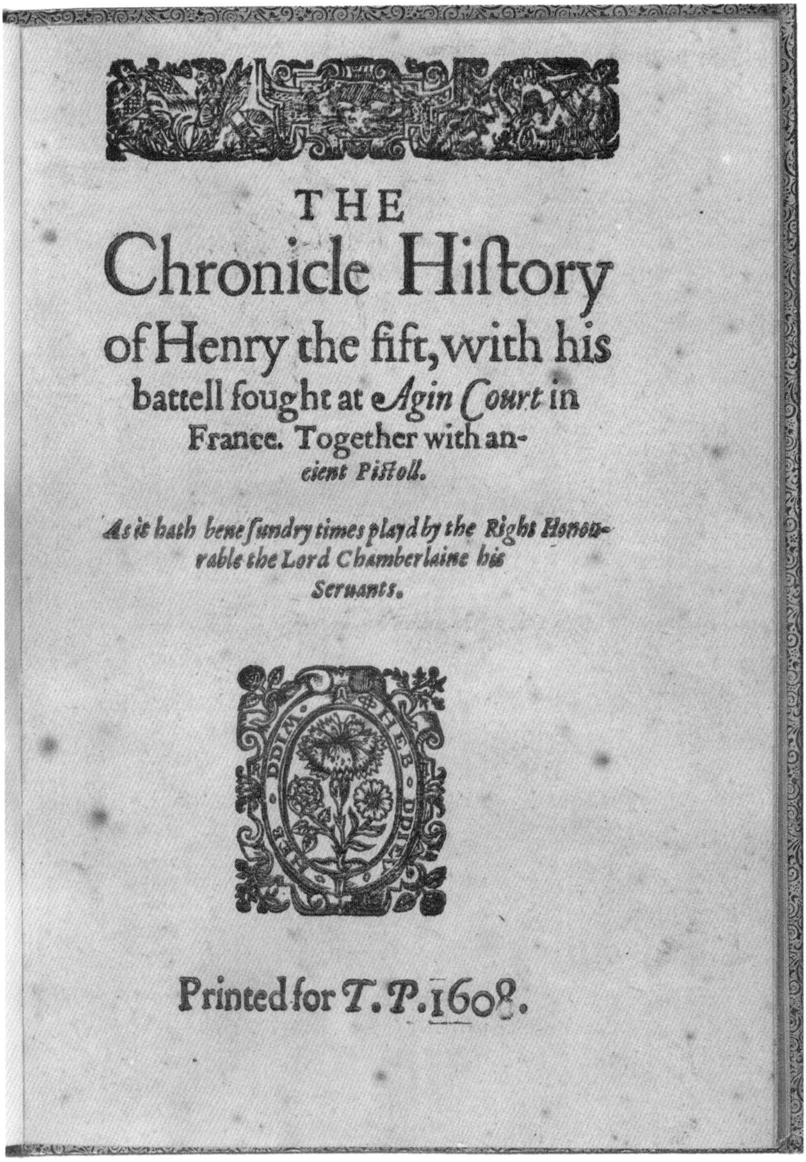

THE

Chronicle Hiſtory

of Henry the fift, with his battell fought at *Agin Court* in France. Together with ancient *Piſtoll*.

As it hath bene ſundry times playd by the Right Honourable the Lord Chamberlaine his Seruants.

Printed for *T. P.* 1608.

Figure 3.21 Scraping of the lower loop of the "8" in the imprint date on a copy of *Henry V* at the Folger. Used by permission of the Folger Shakespeare Library, STC 22291 copy 3.

look far too awkward, to my eyes anyway. Perhaps this was simply accidental damage, or perhaps it was a trial run, abandoned midway, and the decision was made to scrape the top loop instead as the way to hide the "false" false date.

Two different methods of changing a title-page date, tear-and-repair and scrape-and-ink, each with multiple examples: eight title pages that we know of with the tear-and-repair method; three (or five if we include the doubtful cases) with the scrape-and-ink technique, plus *Whole Contention*, which could be inked without first scraping away part of an existing date. As discussed above, we cannot know what the tear-and-repair title pages looked like before they took their current form. Any theory of their meaning, and consequently of the meaning of the scrape-and-ink title pages as well, will depend on how we imagine their appearance before they were repaired.

If they in fact looked something like the scrape-and-ink title pages, then we are dealing with a single method of alteration that has been made, over the centuries intervening between 1619 and today, to appear as two methods. If these title pages had been damaged by scraping—and the BL *Yorkshire* and Auckland *Pericles* are fairly damaged, with the paper completely worn away at points—then perhaps when repairing them in the nineteenth century it was thought best simply to remove part of the page before attaching new paper and writing the original date in pen facsimile. The BPL *Yorkshire Tragedy*, with only the date punched out and patched, offers the best evidence that previous damage caused by scraping required the tear-and-repair procedure.[57] But possibly the copies with the entire corner torn off had also suffered enough paper damage from the original process of changing their dates that it seemed easier to the later restorer to remove the corner entirely before beginning the repair.

If all of the manipulated copies of Jaggard Quartos once formed a single group with transformed imprint dates, the case for their having all been done at the same time, by the same person, becomes even stronger, since we know of twelve such playbooks (or fourteen, including the doubtful cases), with a diverse range of provenance histories that include no known overlap. The last common source for all of these copies was therefore most likely the printing house or bookshop in 1619. But we still need to explain the appearance of the imprints of *Dream, Oldcastle, Lear, Merchant of Venice,* and *Henry V*—the Jaggard Quartos that already had false dates—before they were repaired. The copies of *Henry V* at the National Library of Scotland and the Folger might suggest that the tear-and-repair copy of that play, now at Akron, had likewise been altered to 1600, the date of the true first edition. But the other four plays with tear-and-repair copies were already dated to their first edition, and so they must have been handled differently.

Could those copies have been scraped and altered to display the date of a nonexistent edition? Such a strategy would fly in the face of everything we have thought about the Jaggard Quartos, since from the beginning we have assumed they were designed to resemble the first editions. Despite what many revisionist critics have supposed, the theory advanced by Greg did not quite require that they be mistaken for actual copies of the first editions, as he made clear in an imagined conversation between Pavier and "some impertinent bibliographer" who pointed out the differences between his edition of *Lear* and the one "issued from the Pied bull in that year": "Have you any reason to believe," Pavier responds, "that there were not two editions printed that year?"[58] Nonetheless, ever since Greg's discovery, it has been fundamental to the story that these editions were made to appear as if they had been printed in the same year as their first editions (with the date on *Henry V* likely a mistake resulting from keeping type standing after printing the title page for *Lear*). The tear-and-repair copies of plays that were already falsely dated to the year of the first edition at least raises the possibility that we have been wrong about this, that Jaggard changed his mind, or was made to change his mind, about how to falsify these title pages. The true date 1619 needed to be hidden, of course, and copies of those title pages were scraped and inked to make that date disappear, but possibly Jaggard realized that the fraudulent printed dates had to be hidden as well. After all, altering the date on some copies of these editions to that of a nonexistent edition would make the playbooks, and bound sets of them, appear even more variable.

On this theory, we would need to imagine a three-step process for the Jaggard Quartos, one that shows how the scheme continued to develop after printing had been completed—or, we might say, how the stationers continued to scramble to hide what they had done. First, the Lord Chamberlain's order causes Jaggard to issue some of the plays with false printed dates in the imprints. Second, after printing is completed, Jaggard realizes that he needs to go back to some of the copies dated 1619 and alter them so they appear to have been printed in the same year as their first editions, and he realizes that he needs to alter some copies of *Henry V* so that they too have the "correct" false date. Finally, Jaggard realizes (or is forced to realize?) that making his editions appear to have been printed in the same year as the first editions will not suffice, and he alters some other copies of them so that they appear to have been printed in completely different years.

This hypothetical narrative may seem far too complex, and it is hard to understand exactly why Jaggard might have felt the need to take this third step. Would Lawrence Hayes have complained about the date on *Merchant of Venice*, which had been published by his father in 1600? Was Thomas Fisher, who had published *Dream* in 1600, even still alive in 1619? We have no records of him at all after 1602. Would the King's Men or Edward Blount have insisted for some reason that the imprints be altered yet again, after discovering the initial fraud, as part of their attempt to eliminate a competing Shakespeare collection? Readers may well be feeling the time has come to deploy Occam's razor.

It may seem simpler, therefore, to return to the first of our branching paths and conclude that these two different groups of title pages as they appear today, tear-and-repair and scrape-and-ink, do indeed testify to two different ways of altering the Jaggard Quarto title pages. One group of copies—at least one of each play except *Whole Contention*—had their dates removed entirely simply by tearing a corner of the title page or punching a hole in it. Another, smaller group had their dates altered to make them appear to have been printed earlier.

On this theory, we might be less confident that the two kinds of alteration were done by the same person at the same time. It may be only coincidence, but all of the scrape-and-ink title pages that I have seen have the imprint "Printed for T.P.": *Pericles*, *Yorkshire Tragedy*, *Henry V*, and if we include the New York Public Library copy in this group, *Whole Contention*. And all of them have imprints that, for reasons that are relatively easy to understand, might need to be disguised: the 1619 on *Pericles* and *Yorkshire Tragedy*, of course, but also the "false" false date on *Henry V* and the dateless *Whole Contention* that could easily be assumed to have been contemporary with the 1619 *Pericles* that follows with continuous signatures. We might wonder, therefore, whether Pavier employed one method to alter copies of the books he was selling from his shop, while Jaggard used another. Was Pavier attempting to hide his own involvement in the 1619 scheme—after it was discovered by the King's Men, say, or by his fellow stationers—by altering the copies that bore his initials so as to suggest they too had been printed years earlier?

The tear-and-repair copies might thus belong to Jaggard, who altered a full set of the plays in this manner in response to some objection from the King's Men or their main collaborator, Blount. But we are again faced with the question of why the plays with already fraudulent dates would have had their dates torn off, and how a ripped title page could have sufficed to deceive anyone. Perhaps removing the dates was considered sufficient to make clear that the Jaggard Quartos were not a proper Shakespeare collection that could compete with the forthcoming First Folio. Or perhaps—and this seems more likely to me, if we assume that Dring and de Ricci had in fact seen multiple copies of the same play manipulated in this way—these copies had already found their way to the bookshops of stationers with no earlier involvement in the project, who learned of official objections and tore off the dates on their copies so as not to lose the chance to sell them.

Whatever the causality behind the variously manipulated copies, the vast majority of extant copies show no damage or alterations to their imprints at all. For the publishers' purposes, maybe it was sufficient to keep merely one or two altered copies on hand to show to authorities when necessary. But we also need to consider how the Shakespearean archive as it comes down to us may have been transformed by the very processes we are studying: it seems entirely possible that a much larger number of copies was altered, but that for some reason those copies have been disproportionately lost in the intervening years.

If all of these imagined scenarios risk toppling under the weight of their own assumptions, it nonetheless remains hard to believe that the tear-and-repair copies represent either merely accidental damage over the years or deliberate falsification by later collectors. The tears are far too localized to be accidental; the repairs make no effort to falsify the dates of the plays to increase their value; plays already bearing the year of the first edition are included in the group. The scrape-and-ink copies confirm that someone was manipulating the dates of Jaggard Quartos after their initial printing, and probably not long after. Repeatedly we are pushed back to the conclusion that all of these title pages were altered early in the life of these copies. And yet every coherent explanation for those alterations seems unduly complex and hypothetical.

"How often have I said to you," Holmes famously reminds Watson in *The Sign of Four*, "that when you have eliminated the impossible, whatever remains, *however improbable*, must be the truth?"[59] But the problem lies precisely in determining where the boundaries lie between the impossible, the improbable, the possible, the probable, the demonstrable.[60] When bibliography can establish historical facts with some certainty or at least probability, we need not shy away from them. But even when bibliographic facts seem fairly certain, the question is always how far we can push them toward historical explanation. We must remain wary of the detective genre's march toward a triumphant unmasking, or we risk succumbing to "the hypnotic influence that traditionally accepted facts exercise even over the most critical mind."[61]

I have stressed the need to take another close look at all these books, which we have not done since the New Bibliography. Nor do I imagine my own reexamination as in any way the final one. Bibliography is fundamentally a humanistic discipline, however much it has sometimes been presented as a science, and however technical its methods and subjects may be. *Hamlet* is no more "solvable" as an object of bibliography than it is as an object of literary criticism. I therefore conclude by laying out a new narrative we might tell about the Jaggard Quartos based on the evidence detailed here, but also a number of significant questions that evidence raises. My findings are based on a study of 342 copies (see Appendix C), but there are at least thirty remaining that I have not been able to examine at all, and there are another five copies that Henrietta Bartlett listed in the two editions of her *Census* that are currently untraceable, perhaps in private hands.[62] More important, I have surely not seen all there is to see in the copies I have studied. Some of the questions I pose in my conclusion may prove finally unanswerable, but then again, every time we look bibliographically at these books, we see something new. There is much more evidence out there, and each piece that we discover should force another revision of our narratives.

First, however, one last ghost, the most mysterious one I have seen.

CONCLUSION

Questions

> Those, my friend, are the questions with which I am tormenting myself. If I could answer those, I should feel happier in my mind.
>
> —Agatha Christie, *Thirteen at Dinner*

Part of what sparked my interest in the 1619 quartos was the ghost of *A Woman Killed with Kindness* discovered by Jeffrey Todd Knight on the last verso of the Huntington *Henry V* (SC 334). Knight's crucial 2010 discussion of that ghost was the first I had heard of this bibliographical phenomenon, and it led me to hunt for others. I saw this particular ghost firsthand in 2017 while examining all of the Jaggard Quartos at the Huntington. Having confirmed with my own eyes Knight's reading of the key words in the title of the ghost, and thinking that I had thereby done my due diligence, I moved on to other copies in the collection. Fortunately, I decided to have another look.

My second session of staring at the last verso of *Henry V* revealed to me, in miniature, the need for bibliographic reexamination. I had been under the "hypnotic influence" of "traditionally accepted facts." The discovery by Knight was absolutely fundamental for my own research: I would never have looked for other ghosts, and *Ghosts, Holes, Rips and Scrapes* would not have been written, had I not read his article. Yet its very centrality to my work also made it harder for me to see this ghost with fresh eyes. I had seen what Knight saw, because he saw it. But there was more on the page to be seen. This pattern repeated itself again more than a year later as I was completing the manuscript of this book and looking again at a high-resolution image of the page. Suddenly I could see something else that I had never seen previously. How is it possible to stare at a ghost like this for hours, repeatedly over time, under every variety of light, and still miss something? How is it possible for something to appear, seemingly out of nowhere, when you look at the page with fresh eyes? Because this case demonstrates so emphatically the importance of returning to the same copies we have studied before, I will describe the development of my thinking about this copy of *Henry V* over time, rather than (as more typically) simply summarizing the end result of that process.

When I looked again at the last blank page, signature G4v, of the Huntington *Henry V* in 2017, I covered the top part of the page, where the ghost title appeared, with a sheet of paper. And suddenly I could see something toward the bottom of the page, where the imprint of *Woman Killed* would have pressed against this blank verso: "1608" in mirror image (Figure 4.1). A ghost in every sense: no extant copy of *Woman Killed* bears this date. Again I was confronted with two branching paths. When this ghost date is viewed in isolation, without considering everything I discussed in the previous chapter, the obvious explanation would be that the date offers the only evidence we have of a lost edition of Heywood's play. The 1617 edition claims on its title page to be "The third Edition," and scholars have long suspected that an edition of the play has been entirely lost, while debating whether the 1607 edition represents the true first or second edition.[1] Did this ghost date reveal that the lost edition was the second quarto, printed only one year after the first edition and indicating that the play had been popular enough to sell out rapidly?

Given the number of copies of Jaggard Quartos that show some kind of manipulation of the imprint and specifically the date, however, I began to investigate a second possibility: a copy of the 1617 *Woman Killed* had been altered so that it appeared to have been printed in 1608. Comparing the title pages of the two extant editions of *Woman Killed* to this ghost image showed clearly that the ghost has far more in common with the 1617 title page than it does with the one printed in 1607. On the 1607 title page, the word "WOMAN" is 6.8 cm wide, while on the 1617 title page it measures 8.2 cm. The ghost "WOMAN" is 8.3 cm wide, essentially identical to the 1617 title page, given the difficulty of accurately measuring a ghost image.[2] This demonstrates that the ghost title page could not simply have been a variant of the 1607 title page with the date altered while the type was still standing, as in the two issues of Q2 *Hamlet* (1604/1605); it must be a different setting of type. Furthermore, while it is theoretically possible that a word on a title page printed in 1608 could have been set to almost precisely the same measurement as the same word on a title page printed in 1617, it is not easy to do so, nor would there have been any reason for Jaggard's compositors to try. And in fact, when I superimposed images of the ghost title and the 1617 title page, not only the word "WOMAN" but also the very faintly visible "A" before "WOMAN," the word "with," and the "K" of "Kindnesse" lined up precisely. Neidig's composite photography, used in 1910 to reveal the standing type for the title pages of the Jaggard Quartos, likewise revealed to me that the ghost title and the 1617 title were almost certainly printed from the same setting of type. This ghost, I decided, must not derive from a lost edition of *Woman Killed with Kindness*.

The only area visible to me at the time that diverged from the 1617 title page was the date 1608, which is located more centrally than the date 1617. If this was indeed an altered 1617 title page, I reasoned, it must have been manipulated somewhat differently from the scrape-and-ink copies that we have seen, since on those copies the falsified handwritten date necessarily appears precisely where the scraped printed date had been. The location of "1608" suggests a shorter line than "Printed by Isaac Iaggard, 1617." As this is the only title page in the collection that includes his name, could Jaggard have somehow removed this telltale sign of his involvement while altering the date? Doing so would help to cover his tracks by removing the clearest link in the entire set of quartos between his name and the "HEB DDIEV" device.

But he could hardly scrape away "Isaac Iaggard" along with the date with any hope of subtlety. When faced with typos, printers sometimes resorted to printing the correct reading on small slips of paper that they then pasted over the misprinted word, especially when the misprint was significant enough to warrant the intervention and when the type for that forme had already been distributed.[3] Likewise, when stationers wanted to reissue an old book that had failed to sell, they generally printed a new title page with the current date, but they sometimes used a cancel slip, as Richard Davis did when he inserted copies of Jasper Mayne's 1648 play *The Amorous War* into his 1658 collection of Mayne's *Two Plays* with a slip pasted over original imprint, reading: "OXFORD, Printed for *Ric. Davis*. 1658" (Figure 4.2).

Like all early modern printers, Jaggard was familiar with this mode of correction. In fact, in the same year as the Jaggard Quartos, he used cancel slips to correct errors in Ralph Brooke's *Catalogue and Succession of the Kings, Princes, Dukes, Marquesses, Earles, and Viscounts of This Realme*. This was the book that Augustine Vincent attacked in his *Discoverie of Errours*, which Jaggard printed in 1622 and which caused delays in the production of the First Folio. There too Jaggard used cancel slips on several occasions, "the work being done so skilfully that the correction is easy to overlook."[4]

Could Jaggard have printed one of these cancel slips to cover the entire imprint on at least one copy of the 1617 title page? I found it suggestive that

Figure 4.1 Color-altered image of the last blank verso (sig. G4v) of the Huntington copy of *Henry V*, with a color-altered and mirrored close-up of the imprint area. Courtesy of the Huntington Library, San Marino, California, 69323.

Figure 4.1 (*Continued*)

the date was one of the two chosen for the fraudulent imprints of the Jaggard Quartos. And Jaggard does not seem to have used the distinctive set of numerals that appear in the imprints of the Jaggard Quartos, and in the ghost "1608," before around 1619.[5] Might he have used some type already set for one of the other 1619 title pages, or even cannibalized an actual title page to provide the slip? The short imprint for *Henry V* ("Printed for *T. P.*1608.") fits the location of the date on this ghost perfectly. A 1617 title page, with a slip cut from the title page of another copy of *Henry V*, would account nicely for all the aspects of the ghost image that I could see. So too would a newly composed and printed imprint such as "Printed in the Year 1608"—the kind of imprint sometimes found on surreptitious or risky publications like Thomas Middleton's *Game at Chess*.

Analysis of the page at the Huntington with some sophisticated multispectral imaging techniques failed to reveal anything else, and at that point I decided that it was impossible to push the argument any further given the information I had. As I was going through the illustrations while revising the manuscript of this book, however, I suddenly thought I could see part of the word "London" next to the date 1608 (see Figure 4.1). This guess turned out to be wrong, but it led to an extended discussion with Aaron Pratt and Alan Farmer, in which Pratt was able to determine that what I had read as fragments of "London" was in fact part of the word "Isaac" in the original imprint of the 1617 edition. By superimposing the 1617 title page on the ghost image, Pratt also enabled us to see, for the first time, a very faint ghost of "1617." The ghost date 1608, it became clear, was superimposed on the ghost name "Iaggard,"

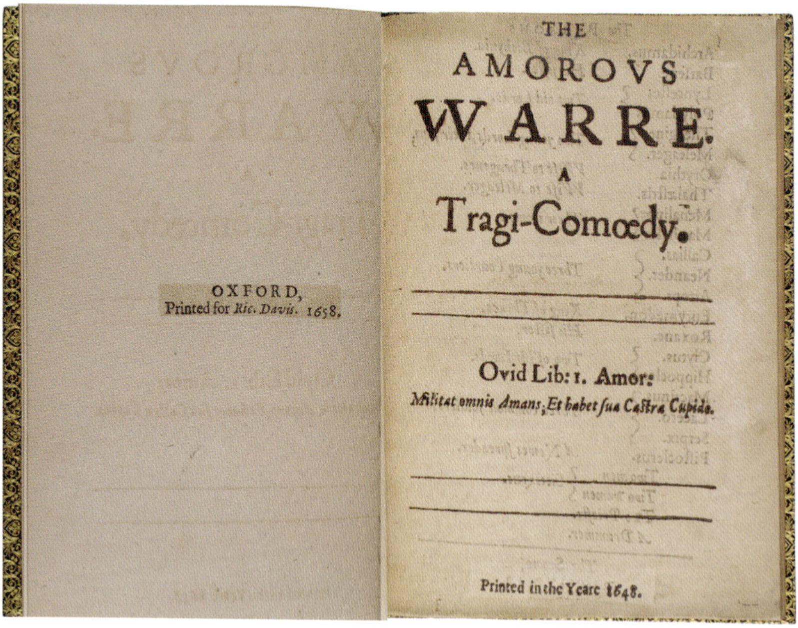

Figure 4.2 A copy of *The Amorous War* that shows both the original imprint and the slip cancel, which a later owner has removed and pasted onto the flyleaf. Used by permission of the Harry Ransom Center, University of Texas at Austin, Wh M454 658c WRE.

with the lower loop of the 8 practically enclosing the comma after the printer's name. Instead of a single ghost date, we were dealing with a ghostly palimpsest.

This new information confirmed my earlier suspicion that the title page did not represent a lost edition of *Woman Killed*. But it left me with another set of alternatives to explain the ghostly palimpsest, again one more ordinary and one stranger. Were it not for all the other evidence of manipulated imprints, the first possibility would surely seem the likeliest: this last blank leaf of *Henry V* had been bound at one point in its history before the title page of a copy of *Woman Killed with Kindness*, and at another point before the title page of a different copy of *Henry V*. The two layers of this ghost, on this theory, would attest to two discrete moments in time collapsed into two dimensions on the page.

But how exactly would a second copy of *Henry V* come to be bound after this one? The binding on the Huntington copy dates from the early nineteenth century, and so if two copies of the play really were bound back-to-back, it must have been before then. Because the Huntington copy lacks stab-stitch holes, indicating it was initially sold as part of a larger volume, and because we know that copies of the Jaggard Quartos were often sold with *Woman Killed* included, most likely the *Woman Killed* layer of the palimpsest dates from its initial binding. But at some point after this set of Jaggard Quartos was disbound—between, say, the 1650s and the 1820s—was the Huntington *Henry V* rebound in a sammelband containing a second copy of *Henry V*? Certainly it is possible, but it does not seem particularly likely that two copies of the same edition would have been bound next to each other. The duplicates in David Garrick's collection, for instance, are scattered around the various volumes as they were arranged by Edward Capell. When presented to Trinity College, Capell's own collection of Shakespeariana contained virtually no duplicates at all, and none bound consecutively, in part because Capell was seeking to acquire simultaneously one copy of each play for himself and one copy for Garrick's collection. Edmond Malone's collection, now at the Bodleian Library, never binds duplicates in the same volume, much less consecutively.[6] And before these great eighteenth-century collectors, early readers tended to bind up their sammelbands as they acquired enough plays, not to organize them afterward according to a more modern bibliographic logic that might group copies of the same edition together.

If the odds of two copies of *Henry V* being bound consecutively seem small, perhaps this layer of the palimpsest occurred outside a binding. Occasionally one finds a ghost that seems to derive from the way that printed sheets were stored in the warehouse: typically all the sheets needed to make up one copy of the book were gathered in order, with sheet A on top; they were then folded once and stacked with the other copies.[7] Since sheets were not folded into the format of the book before warehousing, therefore, the blank G4v of the Huntington *Henry V* would not have come into contact with the title page of the copy stacked either above or below it. Instead, sheet G of each copy would be folded in the center of the stack, while sheet A would form the outside wrapper, contacting sheet A of the copies above and below it.

Another hypothesis that does not involve binding two copies together: what if the final blank leaf of the Huntington *Henry V* had at one point been wrapped around to the front of the book to serve as a makeshift cover? We have evidence of this practice in the early modern period, and if the blank leaf G4 had been pulled around the spine to the front, its verso would have been in the correct position to receive a ghost image of the title page of this same copy.[8] On this theory, in other words, we need not postulate any second copy of this edition to produce this ghost. But this copy of *Henry V* appears to have been sold initially as part of a set of Jaggard Quartos, not as a single pamphlet, and this kind of sale would obviate any need to wrap around the final blank. After all, the purpose of the wraparound blank was to protect the title page of a stab-stitched pamphlet, which would otherwise be more exposed to damage, but this copy lacks stab-stitch holes and was apparently sold bound before *Woman Killed*.[9] The wraparound blank therefore seems even more unlikely than the warehousing explanation.[10]

Another aspect of this ghostly palimpsest challenges not only these explanations but in fact any explanation of how a title page of *Henry V* came into contact with this blank verso: while the ghost of "1608" is fairly strong (although not as strong as the title of *Woman Killed*), no other part of the title page of *Henry V* can be perceived (at least at the moment). In my experience, the larger type and particularly the uppercase letters in titles like "THE Chronicle History" tend to create ghosts more forcefully and frequently than the imprint. If this blank verso came into contact with a title page of *Henry V*, either from another copy or from the same one, we might expect to see at least a few letters of the title in the upper portion of the page.

The stranger alternative returns us to the idea of a cancel slip pasted over the imprint of *Woman Killed with Kindness*. I have seen numerous examples where the oil from type has traveled through the page to create a ghost. The title page of a copy of the 1684 *Julius Caesar* at the Harry Ransom Center (SC 398), for instance, has ghosted onto the verso of the flyleaf adjacent to it, but so too has the "Dramatis Personae" from the verso of the title page, which appears on the flyleaf as a positive (not mirror-image) ghost because it has passed through the leaf (Figure 4.3).[11] If Jaggard used a cancel slip to cover the imprint of the 1617 *Woman Killed*—so as to hide his name and the more recent date—then both the underlying original imprint and the cancel might have ghosted onto the last blank verso of the Huntington *Henry V*. The ghostly palimpsest might testify not to different moments in the history of this copy of *Henry V* but rather to the palimpsestic imprint on this one copy of *Woman Killed* itself.[12] Perhaps the ghost of the original 1617 imprint is so much weaker than the ghost of the title and "1608" because it was transmitted through the intervening cancel slip—although this still leaves the question of why the rest of the cancel-slip imprint has left no trace other than "1608."

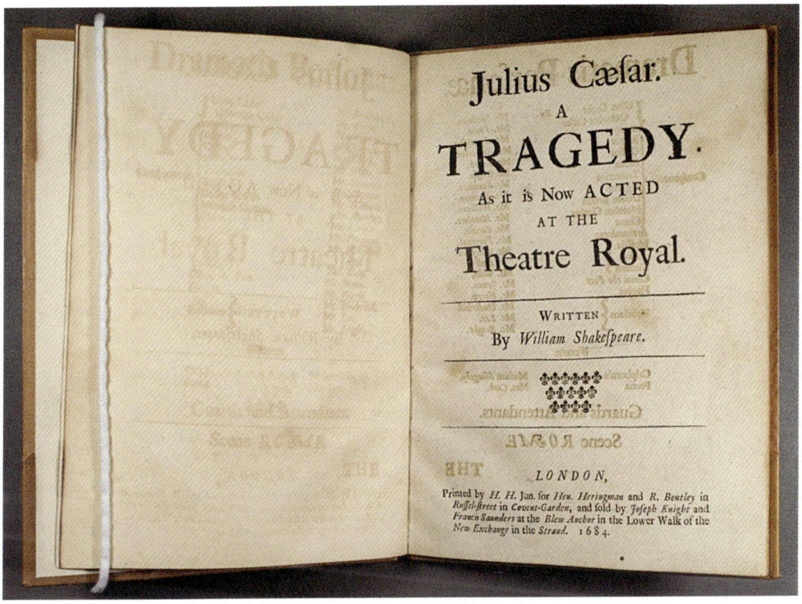

Figure 4.3 A ghost image passes through the title page of *Julius Caesar* (1684) from verso to recto and onto the adjacent flyleaf. Used by permission of the Harry Ransom Center, University of Texas at Austin, Ag Sh15 623jb.

At the moment, it is impossible to explain this palimpsest satisfactorily; we are left at an impasse. This ghost image presents us with a particularly vivid example of a more general tension in bibliographic analysis. Put simply, we can only see what we can see, and we can't see what we can't. Over time, we may be able to see more, just as I was suddenly able to see some lettering I had not seen in all of my previous examinations of the ghost, and just as Aaron Pratt was able to see something I had not. Likewise, even if multispectral imaging did not reveal more of this ghostly title page, some future technology might well do so, and thereby provide some answers to the questions it poses. But there will always be much that remains invisible to us. This is not to suggest that bibliography is different from any other historical study in this regard—quite the opposite in fact: it is to say that bibliography, despite its empiricism and its often technical or even scientistic discourse, is a humanism. While it can reveal historical facts, those facts are embedded in historical narrative, and those narratives have constitutive blind spots. Again and again, in researching the Jaggard Quartos, I have been confronted with irresolvable alternatives like the ones presented by this ghost. Each possibility in these alternatives presents a different, often mutually exclusive, narrative. It is easy for conjecture to fossilize into fact, easy to believe that "you have eliminated the impossible," and that therefore "whatever remains, *however improbable*, must be the truth," as Holmes would maintain. The problem is that every time we return to a case, we seem to find something more. How can we be confident we really know what "remains"?

I conclude, therefore, by moving in the opposite direction to Holmes. Whereas the typical detective story moves from bafflement to revelation, from scattered and seemingly unconnected clues to a unified solution, I begin my summation of the case with what I think we can be most sure of, the new facts revealed by a return to primary bibliographical analysis of the Jaggard Quartos. I then lay out a possible narrative we might now tell, rooted in those facts but nonetheless hypothetical and highly open to change as more evidence becomes available. Finally, I turn to what we do not know, the ongoing mysteries that have continued to trouble my narrative explanations and that I hope future bibliographers will explore.

What the new bibliographic facts I have discussed can tell us most assuredly is that the Jaggard Quartos are not quite the Shakespearean collection we have always thought they were. The scholarly attention they have drawn over the past century, of course, derives entirely from their connection to Shakespeare. But while Jaggard apparently set out with a purely Shakespearean collection in mind, he must have thought that customers would be happy to buy the volume with *Woman Killed* included, and indeed many customers do seem to have bought it. The evidence makes clear that the insertion of Heywood's play into the collection was not a one-off; the work found its way into a good proportion of the bound sets. Among publisher-issued collections of professional plays, the bound volumes of Jaggard Quartos that included *Woman Killed* are thus the single exception to the rule: the principle of collection for volumes of professional plays was otherwise always authorial. Readers often bound up items without regard for their authors, in part because they were collecting and binding together plays (and other pamphlets) as they happened to acquire them. But when issued by the book trade, dramatic collections bound plays by author. In this way, they served a canonizing function, since, as Roger Chartier and Peter Stallybrass write, "one way of defining an author is as someone who is bound with him or her self."[13] Of course many bound sets of Jaggard

Quartos did include only the "Shakespearean" plays, without *Woman Killed*: Shakespeare remains at the heart of Jaggard's project, at least as authorial name if not always as actual playwright, given the presence of *Yorkshire Tragedy* and *Oldcastle*. But what is striking is the ease with which Heywood's play could find its way into this collection. Only later in the lifetime of these books did *Woman Killed* come to seem an oddball in the group, causing it to be removed, for instance by Capell in the eighteenth century. The Jaggard Quartos do have a central place in the history of Shakespearean authorship, but they fit less easily than we have assumed.

We know now, too, that a sizable number of bound volumes of Jaggard Quartos were sold from London bookshops, far more than most scholars assumed in the past. The collection was not "stopped" in quite the way we have thought. It seems to have taken a new form following the Lord Chamberlain's order, but Jaggard's continued printing of plays, even after that order, was designed not simply to sell them individually but precisely so that they could make up a bound collection. Given the number of such volumes we now can trace in the surviving archive—as many as nineteen, and the actual total circulating in the years after 1619 must have been significantly higher—Jaggard and his collaborators must have succeeded in marketing these collections *as collections* to their customers.

I think we can be reasonably sure as well that Jaggard intended to deceive someone, almost certainly the King's Men and the Lord Chamberlain, and possibly also Edward Blount, who may have already been working with the King's Men. This deception went beyond even the false imprints, which recent scholars have suggested were not necessarily meant to deceive either the Stationers' Company or the King's Men. The fact that *Whole Contention* and *Pericles* never appear consecutively in the binding order of volumes we know about, the highly variable order of those bindings in general, and, most important, the evidence of post-printing manipulations of the title pages make clear that the deception was far more thoroughgoing than we have imagined.

Finally, the presence of *Woman Killed* strongly suggests that Jaggard was at the center of the project, not Pavier. Unlike Pavier's involvement, which is made evident by the initials on the 1619 title pages, Jaggard's was more hidden, indicating that the attempts at deception were more likely Jaggard's than Pavier's. No doubt the "HEB DDIEV" device could have told any interested stationer who printed the 1619 volumes, but its use on the title pages with older dates would not necessarily have pointed to Jaggard, as it had changed hands several times in the previous decades.[14] And the later alterations of the dates in these imprints—particularly the date 1619—would have made it harder to uncover his role in the collection, effacing the link between him and the "HEB DDIEV" printer's device just as Jaggard may have worked to efface that link in the imprint of at least one copy of the 1617 *Woman Killed.*

Now I have already begun to create more speculative narratives from the bibliographic facts. It is easier to maintain the distinction in theory than in practice. How should the new bibliographic evidence I have presented change our interpretation of the Jaggard Quartos? Here is one narrative we might now tell, which features Jaggard at the center rather than Pavier. The shift is important: for the New Bibliographers, it was something of a scandal that Jaggard was involved in both the 1619 quartos and the First Folio; this continuity undermined their desire for a clean division between the "bad" and "good" texts of Shakespeare, and consequently undermined the authority of Shakespeare's texts. For this reason, the blame was most often placed on Pavier, with Jaggard's "embarrassing" role greatly diminished or otherwise "explained away."[15] The new evidence suggests that the idea for the collection came from Jaggard and that he gathered a group of copy-owning stationers, including Pavier, Butter, and Johnson, to bring it to press.

Furthermore, Jaggard deliberately foregrounded his favorite printer's device—as shown by the fact that the title pages of *Pericles* and *Yorkshire Tragedy* were each printed on the final leaf, to be later pasted in at the front, apparently to ensure the availability of the device when the other title pages were printed.[16] Even once any possible plan for a general title page would have been abandoned, the device was left standing in the forme, and the presence of a different device only on *Dream* suggests that concurrent printing was ongoing but had, uniquely, made the device unavailable for this title page.

In other words, strange as it may seem given all the new evidence of deception I have presented, Jaggard appears to have wanted this device on all these books and gone to some lengths to ensure it. Perhaps he hoped it would provide some uniformity in an otherwise disparate collection with plays gathered from three different stationers—Pavier, Butter, and Johnson—who all wanted their names or initials in the imprints. The name of the other publisher who appears in the imprints, the dead one, is also important and helps to explain this apparent contradiction: Jaggard had succeeded to the printing house of James Roberts, and he inherited his printer's devices along with his type. The false imprint substitutes the very printer from whom Jaggard could quite plausibly claim he had inherited these old playbook copies printed in 1600. This way no one could challenge him—not living publishers like Lawrence Hayes with a copyright claim, not the King's Men or his future partner Blount asking where he got hold of these quartos. The printer's device could serve to unify the collection while still providing plausible deniability in the event of any official investigation.

This plausible deniability may have been enhanced by the fact that Jaggard seems generally to have reserved the "HEB DDIEV" device for his trade printing, not his own publishing. In a new analysis of the Jaggard printing and publishing business, Ben Higgins notes that of sixteen other books featuring this device that emerged from the Jaggards' shop, only two were the Jaggards' own publications, the 1617 *Woman Killed* and the 1618 *Catalogue of such English Bookes, as lately haue bene, and now are in Printing for Publication*. Furthermore, the device used on *Dream* "never appeared on a book within Jaggard's publishing imprint." Higgins concludes not only that Jaggard typically "diminished his visible presence in [his trade printing] just as he foregrounded his agency in the books he financed" but, more specifically, that these two printer's devices were ones that "Jaggard turned to in order to distance himself from a project, rather than to advertise his identity."[17] Given the way that Jaggard had previously used the "HEB DDIEV" device, it could effectively perform double duty as a disguise and a unifying aesthetic.

Jaggard was able to sell a number of copies of these plays individually—both those dated 1619 and those dated earlier—as evidenced by the stab-stitch holes we can still find in many of them. But in the sets that were sold in bindings (whether directly from his own shop or via other booksellers to whom he sold gathered sheets wholesale), Jaggard varied the order of plays; he separated the two with continuous signatures, which must have required either explicit instructions or implicit signals to the binder; and he inserted *Woman Killed* into a good number of copies. These manipulations made the collection appear more like a reader's sammelband, or a nonce collection of a few new plays with a bunch of old ones, than like a newly planned, publisher-issued *Works*. Because he was selling quite a few of these bound volumes, however, Jaggard still feared being discovered, so he excised or altered the dates on some copies to make them seem even more variable. These copies included not only those dated 1619, which would eliminate the link between the printer's device and his shop, but also those already falsely dated, thereby muddying the waters more generally. On at least one copy of *Woman Killed*, Jaggard altered the date of publication. But since the presence of both his name and the "HEB DDIEV" device on its title page would risk giving away the origins of the other falsely dated plays in the collection, he used a cancel slip to replace the imprint on this copy altogether, rather than merely scraping away the "17" and overwriting the "08" in its place.

This kind of post-publication transformation of the title page was a strategy Jaggard had employed before with his Shakespeare publications, albeit in a slightly different way. His 1612 expanded edition of *The Passionate Pilgrim* exists in two issues, one with Shakespeare's name on the title page, and the other without. This latter version was apparently printed after complaints from none other than Thomas Heywood, who feared that Jaggard's insertion of some of his poems into this putatively Shakespearean collection "may put the world in opinion I might steale them from [Shakespeare]." Heywood added that Shakespeare himself was "much offended with M. *Iaggard* that (altogether vnknowne to him) presumed to make so bold with his name."[18] In 1612, Jaggard seems to have accommodated Heywood and Shakespeare with a cancel title page, but seven years later, after Shakespeare's death, he did not hesitate once again to insert Heywood into a supposed Shakespeare volume. For Jaggard, the author was a figure who could help sell books, sometimes an annoyance to be managed or worked around, but in no way important enough to derail his publishing plans.

Did the variously altered title pages succeed at deceiving anyone? Only a few copies survive with this treatment, while many other copies—far more than typical for a Shakespeare quarto—remain extant with no alterations at all. How could the comparatively few copies manipulated post-printing have been used as a ruse? Possibly Jaggard simply presented a complete set of defaced title pages to the King's Men or the court of the Stationers' Company as evidence that he had not violated the Lord Chamberlain's order. The company might well have gone along with even a seemingly feeble ruse so that two of its more prominent members, one of whom (Pavier) was a member of the Court of Assistants responsible for such orders in the first place, would not be financially harmed. Since the Lord Chamberlain and the King's Men had no legal authority over printing, it was up to the Stationers' Company to enforce this order, and given Pavier and Jaggard's positions, the company likely had little interest in doing so proactively. The fig leaf of a few copies with altered dates—or with defaced title pages with the date torn off or punched out—may have sufficed.[19] We will likely never be able to reconstruct precisely what happened, but for some reason Jaggard decided to go beyond the original fraudulent imprints to hide his involvement in the collection—and beyond that, to hide that it truly *was* a publisher-issued collection at all.

All of this new evidence suggests, paradoxically, that we have been both too skeptical and too credulous about the deception involved in the Jaggard Quartos. Too skeptical in accepting the revisionist argument that the title pages are not sufficiently sophisticated frauds to have deceived contemporaries. For one thing, we have not previously seen all the evidence of deception. More important, we have assumed that contemporaries had access to all the information we currently have, and to all that information at once, and to the same information as each other. We need always to bear in mind that until Greg's article in 1908, these false imprints were universally accepted as authentic. While Jaggard's editions do not precisely match the genuine earlier one, that kind of forgery was not necessary. They merely had to pass as what Pollard himself had believed they were: copies of a second edition printed in that same year. Individual copies of these plays, and bound volumes of them, would have looked very different from each other, with varying plays, varying dates, or even no date at all, just a hole where the date had been. And the very idea of a printed collection of professional drama was still nascent, its form far from settled. Given this unprecedented variability, sorting out the evidence would have been all the more difficult for stationers, customers, and the King's Men.

At other times, however, we have been too credulous about the deception, downplaying the ability of contemporaries to discover the fraud. Greg's hypothetical drama in which "some impertinent bibliographer" questions Pavier about the falsely dated *King Lear* imagines that such a question would be easily enough turned away: "Have you any reason to believe that there were not two editions printed that year?"[20] And it has been "generally accepted," as Gerald Johnson writes, that, once the Lord Chamberlain's order put a stop to the project of issuing the plays as a true collection, the fraudulent imprints allowed Jaggard and Pavier "to pass off these texts as remainders or twin editions."[21] But the rips, scrapes, and inked dates reveal, importantly, that the deception was a staggered process, not a single event. The decision to alter even the fraudulent imprints after printing implies that Jaggard had at least become worried that someone might see through them, or that someone already had. And if even the date on a copy of *Woman Killed* was altered, it makes all the more clear this concern about being found out: that play could hardly be seen to violate the Lord Chamberlain's order, because it bears Heywood's name (not that of the King's Men's most important playwright) and states clearly on its title page that it was acted by the Queen's Men (not

Shakespeare's troupe). Perhaps Jaggard simply wanted to hide his involvement from the King's Men, and from Blount, but we may have also concluded too quickly that other members of the Stationers' Company could not have been a target of deception. The title pages of at least one and perhaps several copies of the already falsely dated *Dream*, last published by Thomas Fisher, were also altered after printing, as was the title page of a copy of the already falsely dated *Merchant of Venice*, which Lawrence Hayes entered in the Stationers' Register only two months after the Lord Chamberlain's order, as if to secure his rights. The post-publication alterations of the imprints suggests that Jaggard thought additional steps had to be taken to protect his investment in these quartos, and given this new evidence, we should probably not foreclose any possibilities about whom exactly he feared or to whom exactly he was responding with these rips and scrapes.

Perhaps this multistage process of deception did work, since Jaggard was later chosen to print and help publish the First Folio. Or perhaps it has been more important to us, after the New Bibliography, than it was to Shakespeare's friends Heminges and Condell that there be no overlap between the publishers of the 1619 collection and the First Folio. The King's Men may not have been concerned with punishing Jaggard, and Edward Blount may not have resented Jaggard's attempt to sell another Shakespeare collection in quarto while collaborating with him on the one planned in folio, even if they did see through his false imprints. Jaggard was a good and experienced printer of plays, and the Folio project was by no means a guaranteed success that any stationer would have jumped at.[22] The King's Men's main goal was to quash this rival collection. In that they were largely successful, even though many bound sets were in fact sold, because what emerged from Jaggard's shop in 1619 did not resemble anything like a typical publisher's collection: no general title page, no continuous signatures, no list of the plays included, no consistent order of binding, a wide range of dates in the imprints (both printed and overwritten), and the miscellaneous inclusion of a play by another dramatist. This was a collection of sorts, certainly, but it was far from the kind of book that the King's Men were contemplating. By forcing this material transformation of the project, the King's Men protected their investment in Shakespeare and their power to establish exactly what his works were. The Folio, of course, creates the Shakespearean canon that we still largely follow today. Had this earlier collection succeeded in doing what the King's Men apparently feared, scooping their own 1623 folio, the "Complete Works of William Shakespeare" might have meant something quite different. The evidence of ghosts, holes, rips and scrapes is a quiet bibliographic reminder of that power struggle.

The need for bibliographic reexamination is ongoing. My own fresh look at copies of the Jaggard Quartos has generated new evidence and, I hope, some productive (if always hypothetical) narratives constructed from that evidence. Many questions remain, and some of them may be answered by future bibliographic reexamination. When I looked at all of these copies, I could see things that the New Bibliographers could not, simply because their scholarly context is not my own. This is not to say that scholarship inevitably progresses and our understanding increases: we have seen that the blind spots of one generation can actively reshape the archive and make things far more difficult for the next. Capell removed *Woman Killed* from his volume of Jaggard Quartos because, according to everything he knew, it did not belong. In the mid-twentieth century the Folger curator Giles Dawson disbound the Goodman-Orlebar volume and rebound *Whole Contention* and *Pericles* together, in part because he thought that "the presence of the non-Pavier *Woman Killed* pretty well guarantees that the original collector had no special plan in view and therefore that the arrangement in Miss Orlebars's volume was hit or miss."[23] Both Capell and Dawson were preeminent scholars, and these decisions are not simply "mistakes"; they are justifiable given the frameworks of collection and conservation within which the two men were working. But their decisions had the effect of obscuring important evidence for decades or centuries.

No doubt we are making decisions like these today. We do not simply learn more over time. But just as I could see evidence in these copies that W. W. Greg could not, although he was a far greater bibliographer than I am, future bibliographers will inevitably see things that I could not.[24] These future bibliographers too will have their blind spots, but the evidence they will be able to see just might answer some of the questions that remained unanswerable for me. Here are a few of the most important, beginning with the more technical ones and moving to the larger theoretical ones upon which they bear.

Does the current appearance of the manipulated title pages, the tear-and-repair and scrape-and-ink imprints, represent one method of post-printing alteration, or two, or more? Knowing the answer to this question would illuminate exactly who altered the title pages (Jaggard? Pavier? someone else?), when, and why. There may be relevant evidence on some of the copies that I have not been able to examine, and further ghost images, along the lines of the "1608" *Woman Killed*, may also help. The altered copies of *Dream* and *Oldcastle* may yet turn up, and if we could confirm or refute Dring's and de Ricci's claims that multiple copies of some of these plays were manipulated in the same way, we could better understand the kinds of deception that occurred even after the Jaggard Quartos were printed.

Are the altered dates written or stamped? The current evidence points to the alterations having been written, but we need more analysis of these marks, especially those on the BL *Yorkshire Tragedy* and the Auckland *Pericles*. Chemical testing of the ink could reveal its components and tell us more certainly whether it is printer's ink or writing ink. And more detailed imaging could perhaps reveal whether the numerals bite into the page from having been stamped (which I could not perceive myself). If the numerals were stamped, we would have the clearest proof possible of my hypothesis that these alterations were made in the print shop in 1619.

What does the "1608" *Woman Killed* palimpsest represent? Seeing almost any other part of the title page of *Henry V* in this ghost would allow us to rule out a cancel slip and would suggest that, "however improbable," one of the more ordinary explanations for this ghost "must be the truth." But it is much harder to establish positively that Jaggard did paste a new imprint onto this copy. If we discovered evidence of post-printing manipulation on any surviving copies of the 1617 *Woman Killed* (at least one of which I have not been able to examine), or if we found further strange ghosts like this one, we would have strong corroboration. It is entirely possible that this evidence is waiting for us in the archive. Or not.

Are there more ghosts out there? Knowing more about the process that produces these ghosts would tell us which scientific tools would be most likely to make them visible. Given the frequency with which I have found ghosts on copies of the Jaggard Quartos, examination of the remaining copies that I have still not been able to see may well reveal one or two more. These would probably be ghosts of the plays traditionally included in the set, but possibly another ghost of *Woman Killed* will appear, and there is always the outside chance that a different play altogether will turn up, which would raise the crucial question of whether it was bound with the set in 1619 or in the ensuing centuries.

Why didn't Jaggard print cancel title pages for the plays dated 1619 once the decision was made to put fraudulent dates on the other ones? It would have been easy enough to produce a new title page for *Pericles* that was dated 1609, a *Yorkshire Tragedy* dated 1608, and a *Merry Wives* dated 1602, to make them seem (like the others) to have been printed in the same year as the first edition. Why was the deception not carried through to this degree?

This last question becomes even more puzzling if we consider the post-printing manipulation of the imprints of some copies (both tear-and-repair and scrape-and-ink). If this was indeed done by Jaggard or Pavier, as I have argued, why not simply produce cancel title pages instead? Again, it would help to know more about the alteration of the imprints to answer this question, but cancel title pages were not time-consuming to compose and print, and they would surely have looked more convincing than do the altered scrape-and-ink imprints, good as they are. Perhaps this points toward Pavier or even some other booksellers who had copies in their shops as the ones responsible for the alterations, not Jaggard, but perhaps there is another explanation. Is it possible that the altered appearance of the title pages was in fact meant to be noticed, for example to show the King's Men or the Stationers' Company that they had been defaced, or the date entirely torn off—in other words, to demonstrate that Jaggard (and Pavier) had acquiesced, even if only pro forma, to the demands of the authorities? This kind of obvious alteration or excision of the date looks like the censorship that is sometimes evident in early printed books. On multiple copies of *The Malcontent* (1604; STC 17481), for instance, the words "the Church" have been cleanly cut out of the page on signature B1v in a way that both hides the word and draws attention to its censorship.[25] Perhaps Jaggard or Pavier did something similar to these title pages?

Who exactly was being deceived? All of the above questions impinge on this one, which has long been at the heart of scholarly studies of the Jaggard Quartos. The evidence of ghosts and holes has suggested that the collection was important to Jaggard precisely *as a collection*, which points toward the King's Men, and perhaps Blount, as the key people he needed to deceive. But we should remain open-minded on this question as we gather more evidence.

What determined the precise makeup of this collection? If Jaggard was initially attempting to create a volume of "rediscovered masterpieces," how did his decision to insert *Woman Killed* alter that design? Why not include Nathaniel Butter's *London Prodigal*, another play that had only been published once, more than a decade prior? Why were *Dream* and *Merchant* in particular included, when none of the stationers involved seems to have had any rights over these plays, as opposed to various other old, "forgotten" Shakespeare plays that they likewise had no clear right to publish, such as *Love's Labors Lost* (1598), *Much Ado About Nothing* (1600), or *2 Henry IV* (1600)? John Smethwick had entered his right to *Love's Labors Lost* in 1607, and William Aspley had published *Much Ado* and *2 Henry IV*. Both men would soon be listed in the colophon to the First Folio, alongside William Jaggard and Edward Blount, and so the choice of *Dream* and *Merchant* rather than these plays may indicate that they refused to participate in Jaggard's syndicate for the earlier collection because plans for the Folio were already under way. Or perhaps Jaggard did not approach them at all, already anticipating objections from the King's Men and not wanting to risk alerting them to his plans. We need to learn more about how Jaggard came to collaborate with the particular three booksellers who worked on the project (Pavier, Butter, and Johnson), and whether he attempted to negotiate with anyone else over the rights to plays they owned.

How was this collection understood by readers in the early seventeenth century? From a post-Folio perspective, the Jaggard Quartos include a number of plays excluded from or marginal to the Shakespearean canon: *Pericles*, *Oldcastle*, and *Yorkshire Tragedy*, as well as *Whole Contention*, which does not appear by that name in the Folio. But how did this collection appear to readers in 1619, rather than in 1623 and after? In the Jaggard Quartos, readers could find bound together two domestic tragedies taken from recent news stories (*Yorkshire Tragedy* and *Woman Killed*), a genre in which it is often said Shakespeare never truly wrote, making his "nearest approach" in *Othello*.[26] We find *Henry V* alongside its rival play *Oldcastle*, *Whole Contention* alongside another play about British civil war, *King Lear*. Does any evidence survive of readers' engagement with these plays specifically in this collection? And does anyone comment on the presence of *Woman Killed with Kindness* in particular? I have not found any such evidence on the playbooks themselves, but commonplace books and other kinds of readerly documents may offer clues. Part of what I have been arguing is that our ideas about a "collection" of works has obscured some of the evidence in this case. Did early modern readers leave us any sense of their possibly quite different understanding of a dramatic collection?

Ending on a series of unanswered questions is no doubt anticlimactic. I do so not only to suggest the areas in which future researchers should take up this work but also because I think such open-endedness offers a way to combat "the hypnotic influence that traditionally accepted facts exercise even over the most critical mind," as W. W. Greg wrote more than a century ago. Our own investments in Shakespeare in 1619 have transformed these quartos into Quartos (Pavier or Jaggard). Our scholarship has quite literally changed the object of our investigation. A bibliography that dwells in the longue durée must account for these effects as it seeks to understand how these books came to be the way they are, a process that stretches from 1619 (or from 1617) to the present, and the future. The Jaggard Quartos as they appear to us today in fact result from two historical processes across this long history: first, the successful effort by the King's Men in 1619 to construct them as fraudulent, which resulted in their material transformation in the printing house; and, second, the New Bibliographic effort in the early twentieth century to reconstruct them as the fraudulent forerunner of the First Folio. That latter effort has reshaped their material existence in the Shakespeare archive and obscured the evidence of their earlier form, both from the New Bibliographers themselves and from us, their inheritors. Fortunately, that evidence can still be perceived, embedded within centuries of accreted history, if we look closely enough—and again and again.

APPENDIX A

CENSUS OF KNOWN SETS OF THE 1619 QUARTOS

#	Abbreviation	Early Provenance	Current Location	# of Playbooks Included
Still in seventeenth- or eighteenth-century binding				
(1)	EG	Edward Gwynn	Folger Shakespeare Library	9
(2)	HP	Hannah Plat	Texas Christian University	9
(3)	EC	Edward Capell	Trinity College, Cambridge	10
(4)	N	William Henderson	Newberry Library	3
Known from a former binding				
(5)	EH	William Neile? / Edward Hussey	Shakespeare Birthplace Trust / Meisei / Harvard / Folger / unknown	9
(6)	TG-MO	Thomas Goodman / Mary Orlebar	Folger / unknown	10
Known from booksellers' and library catalogues				
(7)	JH	John Henderson	unknown	9
(8)	BW	Benjamin White	unknown	10
(9)	TR	Thomas Randolph	unknown	9
Known from ghost images				
(10)	DG	David Garrick	British Library	4
(11)	BPL	unknown	Boston Public Library	2

#	Abbreviation	Early Provenance	Current Location	# of Playboo[ks] Included
(12)	Y-E	unknown	Elizabethan Club, Yale University	2
(13)	Pr	unknown	Princeton University	2
(14)	HRC	unknown	Harry Ransom Center, University of Texas	2
(15)	F 1	unknown	Folger Shakespeare Library	2
(16)	F 2	unknown	Folger Shakespeare Library	2
(17)	Hunt	unknown	Huntington Library	2
(18)	V&A	Alexander Dyce / Thomas Richardson	Victoria and Albert National Art Library	2
Known from early marginalia				
(19)	Eton	Anthony Morris Storer	Eton College	2

APPENDIX B

ORDER OF PLAYS IN KNOWN BINDINGS OF THE 1619 QUARTOS

(1) EG: *WC, MND, Old, MV, H5, Lr, Per, MWW, YT*
(2) HP: *WC, YT, Per, H5, Old, Lr, MND, MWW, MV*
(3) EC: *YT, MWW, MND, Lr, MV, Old, H5, WKK, Per, WC*
(4) N: *MWW, Old, WC*
(5) EH: *WC, YT, H5, Per, Lr, MND, MV, MWW, Old*
(6) TG-MO: *WKK, H5, WC, MV, Lr, MND, MWW, Old, YT, Per*
(7) JH: *YT, Per, H5 . . . Lr, WC, MV . . . MWW, MND, Old*
(8) BW: *MND, H5, MWW, Old, MV, YT, Per, Lr, WC, WKK*
(9) TR: *WC, YT, MV, Per, H5, Old, Lr, MWW, MND*
(10) DG: *WC, Per* [?] . . . *MV, Old . . . Lr, H5*
(11) BPL: *Per, Lr*
(12) Y-E: *Old, H5*
(13) Pr: *Old, H5*
(14) HRC: *MND, MV*
(15) F 1: *Lr, Old*
(16) F 2: *H5, YT*
(17) Hunt: *H5, WKK*
(18) V&A: *Old, WC*
(19) Eton: *Per, MND*

ABBREVIATIONS

H5: *Henry V*; *Lr*: *King Lear*; *MND*: *Midsummer Night's Dream*; *MV*: *Merchant of Venice*; *MWW*: *Merry Wives of Windsor*; *Old*: *1 Sir John Oldcastle*; *Per*: *Pericles*; *WC*: *Whole Contention*; *WKK*: *Woman Killed with Kindness*; *YT*: *Yorkshire Tragedy*

NOTES

1. JH is listed in three separate volumes, and the original sequence of these volumes is unknown.

2. DG currently binds *WC* and *Per* together, but date of this binding is unknown.

3. DG includes two distinct ghosts, which are combined into a single copy here, but it is not certain they once belonged to the same binding.

APPENDIX C

COPIES CONSULTED

Listed by the SC reference number from the Shakespeare Census, shakespearecensus.org, and current location, except for the 1617 *Woman Killed with Kindness* (current location only); * indicates a copy examined by someone else on my behalf. Abbreviations for libraries are given below.

***Henry V* (35 copies seen personally, 6 by others)**: SC 312* (BNF), 313 (Birm), 314 (BPL), 315 (BL), 316 (BL), 317 (JCB), 318 (C-K), 319 (C-T), 320 (CU), 321* (Dar), 323 (E), 324 (Eton), 325 (F), 326 (F), 327 (F), 328 (F), 329 (F), 330 (F), 331 (F), 332 (Hvd), 333 (Hav), 334 (Hunt), 334.5 (JHU), 335 (Bmer), 336 (NLS), 337* (Pet), 338 (NYPL), 339 (Newb), 340* (OSU), 341 (O), 342 (PML), 343 (Pr), 344 (Pr), 345 (TCU), 346* (Akr), 347 (Clk), 349 (Penn), 350 (Penn), 351* (HRC), 352 (V&A), 353 (Y-E)

***King Lear* (29, 5)**: SC 484* (BNF), 485 (BPL), 486 (BL), 487 (BL), 488 (BL), 489 (C-T), 490* (Dar), 491 (E), 492 (Eton), 493 (F), 494 (F), 495 (F), 496 (F), 497 (F), 498 (F), 499 (Hvd), 500 (Hav), 501 (Hunt), 502 (Bmer), 503 (NLS), 504* (Pet), 505 (NYPL), 506 (Newb), 507 (O), 509 (PML), 510 (Pr), 511 (Pr), 512 (SHL), 513 (SBT), 514 (TCU), 516 (Penn), 517* (HRC), 518* (UVa), 519 (Y-E)

***Merchant of Venice* (28, 3)**: SC 640* (BNF), 641 (Birm), 642 (BPL), 643 (BL), 644 (BL), 645 (C-T), 646* (Dar), 647 (E), 648 (Eton), 649 (F), 650 (F), 651 (F), 652 (F), 653 (Hvd), 654 (Hav), 655 (Hunt), 655.3* (IU), 655.5 (JHU), 656 (Bmer), 657 (NYPL), 658 (Newb), 659 (O), 660 (PML), 661 (Pr), 662.5 (Rut), 663 (SBT), 664 (SBT), 665 (TCU), 666 (Clk), 668 (Penn), 669 (Y-E)

***Merry Wives of Windsor* (30, 7)**: SC 714* (BNF), 715* (BNF), 716 (BPL), 717 (BL), 718 (BL), 719 (C-T), 720* (Dar), 721 (F), 722 (F), 723 (F), 724 (F), 725 (F), 726 (F), 727 (F), 728 (F), 729 (Hvd), 730 (Hunt), 731 (Bmer), 732 (NLS), 733* (Cha), 734 (NYPL), 735 (NYPL), 736 (Newb), 737* (OSU), 738 (O-B), 739 (O), 740 (PML), 741 (Pr), 742 (SBT), 743 (SBT), 744 (TCU), 745* (Akr), 746 (Clk), 748* (HRC), 749 (V&A), 751 (Y), 752 (Y-E)

***Midsummer Night's Dream* (26, 5)**: SC 772* (BNF), 773 (BPL), 774 (BL), 775 (BL), 776 (C-T), 777* (Dar), 778 (E), 779 (Eton), 780 (F), 781 (F), 782 (F), 783 (F), 784 (F), 785 (F), 786 (F), 787 (Hvd), 788 (Hunt), 790 (NLS), 791 (NYPL), 792 (Newb), 793* (OSU), 794 (O), 795 (PML), 796 (Pr), 797 (Pr), 798 (SBT), 799 (TCU), 800* (LC), 801 (Clk), 803* (HRC), 804 (Y-E)

***Pericles* (30, 3)**: SC 1007* (Auck), 1008 (BPL), 1009 (BL), 1010 (BL), 1011 (C-T), 1012* (E), 1013 (Eton), 1014 (F), 1015 (F), 1016 (F), 1017 (F), 1018 (F), 1019 (F), 1020 (F), 1021 (F), 1021.5 (Hvd), 1022 (Hunt), 1023 (Hunt), 1024 (Bmer), 1025 (NLS), 1026 (NYPL), 1027 (NYPL), 1028 (Newb), 1029* (OSU), 1030 (O), 1031 (Pr), 1032 (TCU), 1033 (Clk), 1035 (Penn), 1036 (Penn), 1037 (V&A), 1038 (Y), 1039 (Y-E)

***1 Sir John Oldcastle* (32, 7)**: SC 1416 (BPL), 1417 (BL), 1418 (BL), 1419 (C-T), 1420* (Dar), 1421 (Eton), 1422 (F), 1423 (F), 1424 (F), 1425 (F), 1426 (F), 1427 (F), 1428 (F), 1429 (F), 1430 (Hvd), 1431 (Hunt), 1432 (NLS), 1433 (NYPL), 1434 (Newb), 1435 (Newb), 1436* (OSU), 1437 (O), 1438 (O), 1439 (PML), 1440 (Pr), 1441 (Pr), 1443 (SBT), 1444 (TCU), 1445* (Akr), 1446 (Clk), 1446.5* (Gla), 1447* (UIUC), 1448* (Leeds), 1448.5 (Penn), 1449* (HRC), 1450 (V&A), 1451 (V&A), 1452 (Y), 1453 (Y-E)

***Whole Contention* (33, 5)**: SC 1676* (BNF), 1677 (Birm), 1678 (Birm), 1679 (BPL), 1680 (BL), 1681 (BL), 1682 (C-T), 1683* (Dar), 1684 (E), 1685 (Eton), 1686 (F), 1687 (F), 1688 (F), 1689 (F), 1690 (F), 1691 (F), 1692 (F), 1693 (F), 1694 (F), 1695 (F), 1696 (F), 1697 (Hvd), 1698 (Hav), 1699 (Hunt), 1700 (Bmer), 1701 (NLS), 1702 (NYPL), 1703 (NYPL), 1704 (NYPL), 1705 (Newb), 1706* (OSU), 1707 (O), 1708 (PML), 1710 (TCU), 1711 (Clk), 1713* (HRC), 1714 (V&A), 1715* (Y-E)

***Woman Killed with Kindness* (21, 6)**: BL; BL; BPL; Cdf*; F; F; F; Gla*; Hvd; HRC*; HRC*; Hunt; LC; Newb; NLS; NLS; O; O; O; O; O; O-M; Sutro*; Swed*; V&A; Y; Y

***Yorkshire Tragedy* (25, 6)**: SC 1722 (BPL), 1723 (BPL), 1724 (BL), 1725 (BL), 1726 (BL), 1727 (C-T), 1728* (Dar), 1729 (E), 1730 (F), 1731 (F), 1732 (F), 1733 (F), 1734 (F), 1735 (F), 1736 (Hvd), 1737 (Hunt), 1737.5 (JHU), 1738 (NLS), 1739 (NYPL), 1740 (Newb), 1741 (O), 1742 (PML), 1745 (TCU), 1745.5* (Gla), 1747* (Leeds), 1748* (HRC), 1749 (V&A), 1749.5* (Will), 1750 (Y), 1751 (Y-E), 1752* (YM)

LIBRARY ABBREVIATIONS

Akr University of Akron
Auck Auckland Public Library
Birm Library of Birmingham
BL British Library
Bmer Martin Bodmer Foundation, Geneva
BNF Bibliothèque nationale de France
BPL Boston Public Library
Cdf Cardiff University
Cha Charlecote House
C-K University of Cambridge, King's College
Clk Clark Library, UCLA
C-T University of Cambridge, Trinity College
CU Columbia University
Dar Dartmouth College
E University of Edinburgh
Eton Eton College, Windsor
F Folger Shakespeare Library
Gla University of Glasgow
Hav Haverford College
HRC Harry Ransom Center, University of Texas
Hunt Huntington Library
Hvd Houghton Library, Harvard University
IU Indiana University
JCB John Carter Brown Library
JHU Johns Hopkins University
LC Library of Congress
Leeds University of Leeds
Newb Newberry Library

NLS	National Library of Scotland
NYPL	New York Public Library
O	University of Oxford, Bodleian Library
O-B	University of Oxford, Balliol College
O-M	University of Oxford, Magdalen College
OSU	Ohio State University
Penn	University of Pennsylvania
Pet	Petworth House
PML	Pierpont Morgan Library
Pr	Princeton University
Rut	Rutgers University
SBT	Shakespeare Birthplace Trust
SHL	Senate House Library, University of London
Sutro	California State Library, Sutro
Swed	Royal Library of Sweden
TCU	Texas Christian University
UIUC	University of Illinois, Urbana-Champaign
UVa	University of Virginia
V&A	Victoria and Albert National Art Library
Will	Williams College
Y	Beneicke Library, Yale University
Y-E	Elizabethan Club, Yale University
YM	York Minster Library

NOTES

INTRODUCTION

Epigraph: W. W. Greg, "On Certain False Dates in Shakespearian Quartos," *Library* n.s. 34 (1908): 113–31, 115.

1. Ibid.

2. The term "New Bibliography" seems to have been introduced only in 1945 by F. P. Wilson; see A. C. Green, "The Difference Between McKerrow and Greg," *Textual Cultures* 4 (2009): 31–53, 31. My thinking on the New Bibliography is heavily indebted to Laurie Maguire, *Shakespearean Suspect Texts: The "Bad" Quartos and Their Contexts* (Cambridge: Cambridge University Press, 1996). Maguire begins in 1909 with Pollard's announcement of the category of "bad quartos," another one of the foundational bibliographic "revolutions." Greg's discovery of what have been called the "Pavier Quartos" preceded and, I think, influenced Pollard's ideas about this other bibliographic case.

3. A. W. Pollard, "A Literary Causerie: Shakespeare in the Remainder Market," *Academy* (2 June 1906): 528–29. Pollard writes only that he saw the volume a "few years ago." But in their *Census of Shakespeare's Plays in Quarto, 1594–1709* (New Haven: Yale University Press, 1916), Pollard and Henrietta C. Bartlett record the sale to Quaritch (which occurred after Pollard saw the book) in August 1902, and the Quaritch sale to Marsden Perry in October 1902.

4. On the order of printing, see William J. Neidig, "The Shakespeare Quartos of 1619," *Modern Philology* 8 (1910): 145–63. Neidig is followed by most later scholars, for example Sonia Massai in *Shakespeare and the Rise of the Editor* (Cambridge: Cambridge University Press, 2007), 107.

5. The lack of author attribution on *Henry V* is likely due simply to the tendency in the period for reprints to repeat the information given on the previous title page; only rarely did reprinted playbooks add information to the title page. See Alan B. Farmer and Zachary Lesser, "Vile Arts: The Marketing of English Printed Drama, 1512–1660," *Research Opportunities in Renaissance Drama* 39 (2000): 77–165, 105n19.

6. The story is recounted in Stephen H. Grant, *Collecting Shakespeare: The Story of Henry and Emily Folger* (Baltimore: Johns Hopkins University Press, 2014), 85–87.

7. See "Huntington Buys Duke of Devonshire Library," *Publisher's Weekly*, 21 March 1914, 1008–10, 1009. I am grateful to Stephen Tabor for details of this purchase.

8. The Pavier volume is somewhat anomalous among surviving books once owned by Gwynn; his library does not seem to have included much English literature. For an ongoing census of his books, see https://folgerpedia.folger.edu/List_of_books_owned_by_Edward_Gwynn.

9. A. W. Pollard, *Shakespeare Folios and Quartos: A Study in the Bibliography of Shakespeare's Plays, 1594–1685* (London: Methuen, 1909), 81.

10. Seymour de Ricci is often cited as the source of the attribution to Goertz-Wrisberg; see *English Collectors of Books and Manuscripts* (Cambridge: Cambridge University Press, 1930), 28. Greg states simply that the book was "the property of Count Goertz-Wrisberg." W. W. Greg, *A Bibliography of English Printed Drama to the Restoration* (*BEPD*), 4 vols. (Oxford: Bibliographical Society, 1939–59), 3:1108. The Folger catalogue is more guarded about the attribution, flagging the bookplate's identification as questionable, although it is unclear why, since the evidence of books in other collections confirms it; see James Holly Hanford, "The Goertz Collection," *Princeton University Library Chronicle* 17, no. 1 (1955): 40–45. Greg and de Ricci may well have had private knowledge of the identity of Pollard's "German gentleman."

11. Pollard, *Shakespeare*, 81.

12. Ibid.

13. For more on Neile and his books, see Jason Scott-Warren's blog post, "In Search of 850 Lost Books," 21 October 2013, https://www.english.cam.ac.uk/cmt/?p=3716; and Tamara Atkin, *Reading Drama in Tudor England* (New York: Routledge, 2018), 175.

14. Hussey's manuscript account is at Scotney Castle, written on formerly blank pages that Hussey had bound into the binding of the volume, which he kept after the plays had been removed for auction. National Trust, NT 3112453.

15. The Hussey copy of *Whole Contention* is now at the Folger (STC 26101 copy 1), and the *Yorkshire Tragedy* is now at the Houghton Library at Harvard (STC 22341). The copies of *King Lear* and *Merchant of Venice* are at the Shakespeare Birthplace Trust [SR 35.17 (1170) and SR 35.21 (1169)], and the copy of *Henry V* may be the one at Meisei University (MR 3412). See the entries for Hussey in the index of Henrietta C. Bartlett and Alfred W. Pollard, *A Census of Shakespeare's Plays in Quarto, 1594–1709,* rev. ed. by Bartlett (New Haven: Yale University Press, 1939). In the 1916 edition of the *Census*, a copy of *Merry Wives* owned by the booksellers Dodd, Mead and Co. was also listed as Hussey's, but by 1939 Bartlett could not locate it. Several copies at the Sotheby's auction were acquired by the booksellers Pickering and Chatto; they may still be in private hands.

16. Pollard, "Literary," 528.

17. Ibid., 529.

18. On sammelbands, see Jeffrey Todd Knight, *Bound to Read: Compilations, Collections, and the Making of Renaissance Literature* (Philadelphia: University of Pennsylvania Press, 2013); and, for some qualification of Knight's thesis, Aaron T. Pratt, "The Status of Printed Playbooks in Early Modern England," Ph.D. diss., Yale University, 2016. The German capitalized terms *Sammelband* and *Sammelbände* (pl.) have traditionally

been preferred, but I follow the Rare Books and Manuscripts Section of the American Library Association and the Folger Shakespeare Library in anglicizing them; see https://rbms.info/vocabularies/provenance/tr106.htm and https://folgerpedia.folger.edu/Sammelbands.

19. Pollard, "Literary," 529.

20. Ibid.

21. Ibid. Alice Walker also argues that Capell gave the quartos "an interest and value which increased their chances of survival." Alice Walker, "Edward Capell and His Edition of *Shakespeare*," Annual Shakespeare Lecture, *Proceedings of the British Academy* 46 (1960): 131–45, 138.

22. Pollard, "Literary," 528–29.

23. Greg also showed that the woodblock printer's device used on the title page of *A Midsummer Night's Dream*, dated 1600, showed greater signs of damage than when it was used on another book printed in 1605, a logical impossibility. But he later declared this evidence "invalid" after Pollard showed him other books printed with this device even earlier than 1600 with similar apparent damage: "The astonishing fact [was] that the cracks in the blocks opened and closed and the breaks grew greater and less quite irrespective of the date of printing." W. W. Greg, "On Certain False Dates in Shakespearian Quartos, II," *Library* n.s. 34 (1908): 381–409, 384–85. These expansions and contractions derive from temperature fluctuations, the dampness of the block and the paper at the time of printing, and other accidental factors that make it hard to rely on evidence of damage to woodblocks.

24. The devices are numbers 138 and 283 in Ronald B. McKerrow, *Printers' and Publishers' Devices in England and Scotland, 1485–1640* (London: Bibliographical Society, 1913). In *BEPD* (3:1107), Greg mislabels the device on *Sir John Oldcastle* as 183 instead of 283.

25. Peter W. M. Blayney, "'Compositor B' and the Pavier Quartos: Problems of Identification and their Implications," *Library* 5th ser. 27 (1992): 179–206, 199–200n37, 181–82. Isaac took over his father's position as Printer to the City of London on 4 November 1623, at which time William was described as deceased. On the timing of William Jaggard's death, and its effects on the First Folio, see Ben Higgins, *Shakespeare's Syndicate: The First Folio, Its Publishers, and the Early Modern Book Trade*, forthcoming.

26. Greg, "Certain," 127.

27. E. K. Chambers, *William Shakespeare: A Study of Facts and Problems*, 2 vols. (Oxford: Clarendon Press, 1930), 1:136. For the entry in the Stationers' Company court records, see William A. Jackson, *Records of the Court of the Stationers' Company 1602–1640* (London: Bibliographical Society, 1957), 110.

28. W. W. Greg, *The Shakespeare First Folio: Its Bibliographical and Textual History* (Oxford: Clarendon Press, 1955), 15. In the third volume of *BEPD* (1108), published in 1951, Greg likewise continued to discuss Pavier as the main agent behind the collection, noting, for example, that it was Pavier who "took the precaution . . . of ascribing the reprints" of *Merchant of Venice* and *Dream* to the safely dead James Roberts.

29. On Bertillon's influence, see Neidig, "Shakespeare," 6. Neidig's order has been largely confirmed based on the evidence of paper stock by R. Carter Hailey, "The Shakespearian Pavier Quartos Revisited," *Studies in Bibliography* 57 (2005–6): 151–95. Hailey, however, suggests that *Merry Wives* may have preceded *Merchant of Venice*: "If the order *MV*>*MWW* is correct . . . there is a small anomaly. *MV* is the first of the Pavier quartos to bear a false date, and it seem[s] peculiar that, having decided that subterfuge was necessary, Pavier and Jaggard would have reverted to the actual date of 1619 for *MWW* before then falsely dating the four remaining titles. It it at least possible that the first gathering or two of *MWW* had been printed off before work began on *MV*, which was completed before work resumed on *MWW*" (177). I adopt Hailey's view that the printing of these two plays was at least partly concurrent, and that *Dream* was probably printed around this moment as well.

30. Greg, "Certain," 128.

31. A. S. W. Rosenbach, inscription on flyleaf of Folger STC 26101 copy 3.

32. *Mr. William Shakespeares Comedies, Histories, & Tragedies* (1623), sig. A3r. For a debate over the meaning of these phrases in relation to the 1619 quartos, see David Scott Kastan, *Shakespeare and the Book* (Cambridge: Cambridge University Press, 2001), 73–78; and Lukas Erne, *Shakespeare as Literary Dramatist*, rev. ed. (Cambridge: Cambridge University Press, 2013), 280–83. See also John Jowett, "Shakespeare Supplemented," in *The Shakespeare Apocrypha*, ed. Douglas A. Brooks (Lampeter: Edwin Mellen, 2007), 39–73, 44.

33. "False Folio," Wikipedia, en.wikipedia.org/wiki/False_Folio, edited 6 December 2018, accessed 1 March 2019.

34. Texas Christian University, PR2750.A15 1619, *Yorkshire Tragedy*, sig. D3r; *Merchant of Venice*, sig. K4v. The SC number refers to the unique identifier for each copy in the *Shakespeare Census*, ed. Adam G. Hooks and Zachary Lesser, created in 2018, www.shakespearecensus.org. I give SC numbers parenthetically in the text. The date inscription is given as "Mill[esim]o sexcentesimo septuagesimo quarto" along with the regnal year "vicesimo quinto" of Charles II. It is unclear why Walker wrote the note on *Yorkshire Tragedy* instead of Plat; given the problem he had in spelling his own first name, in which he had to go back and insert the "e" above "Jams," he may have been practicing writing. The Plat inscription appears on the first available blank page in the volume, which is probably why it was written there; it clearly refers to the entire volume, not that single play, given all the evidence (some of which I describe later) that the plays had never been sold separately.

35. I am grateful to Aaron Pratt, who examined this book with me, for this point. At several points the earlier sewing has been reinforced by the addition of a second sewing thread, without removing the older thread or creating new sewing stations. Pratt also noticed a "témoin" (or "witness"), a piece of the top edge of signature E4 in *Dream*, which must have been folded down when the rebinding was done, and which therefore escaped the binder's plow. The top edge of this témoin is dyed red, demonstrating that the earlier binding had a red edge treatment, which was removed when the book was trimmed to fit its current binding.

36. John Edmund Hodgson, *The Remarkable Story of the Shakespearian Quartos of 1619, Being a Brief Record of the Unravelling of a Puzzle in Shakespearian Bibliography and an Account of the Unlooked-for Discovery of a "Set" of the Quartos of 1619* (London: Hodgson, 1946). For information about and documentation of the sale price and provenance of the volume, I am grateful to the special collections librarian at Texas Christian University, Susan Swain.

37. *Oldcastle*: Clark, PR2867.A1 1619*.

38. *Dream*: NLS, Bute.500; *Merchant*: Bodmer, barcode 1072056516; *Merchant*: Morgan Library, 16503; *Lear*: Princeton, RHT 17th–512.

39. *Catalogue of the Famous Library . . . Collected by Henry Huth . . . which will be sold by auction by Messrs. Sotheby, Wilkinson & Hodge . . .* (London, 1911), 334–35.

40. Maguire, *Shakespearean*; Paul Werstine, *Early Modern Playhouse Manuscripts and the Editing of Shakespeare* (Cambridge: Cambridge University Press, 2013).

41. Maguire, *Shakespearean*, 66. On criticism as detection, see also Rita Felski, *The Limits of Critique* (Chicago: University of Chicago Press, 2015).

42. In this endeavor I am particularly inspired by Werstine, *Early*.

43. Pollard, *Shakespeare*, 81. Sarah Neville makes a similar point about the relationship of textual editing to air travel in "Rethinking Scholarly Commentary in the Age of Google: Some Preliminary Meditations on Digital Editions," *Textual Cultures* 12 (2019): 1–26, 1n2.

44. Pollard, "Literary," 529; Greg, "Certain, II," 390.

45. Neidig began working on the bibliographic possibilities of composite photography while in graduate school at the University of Chicago; he wrote his essay while a professor at the University of Wisconsin, Madison. He refers in his essay to photographs taken for him by others in London and at the Boston Public Library: "My distance from the quartos necessitated my entrusting the photographing of these title-pages to a photographer who could not at the best be expected to attain to the microscopial accuracy attained in the laboratory among instruments of precision" (18).

46. Pollard, *Shakespeare*, 85.

47. W. W. Greg, "What Is Bibliography?" *Transactions of the Bibliographical Society* 12 (1911–13): 39–53, 48.

48. Indeed, the collation of multiple copies is still today confined almost exclusively to the first (or otherwise "authoritative") edition—an entirely reasonable approach if one is mainly concerned with establishing the text of a work.

49. Greg, "What Is," 45.

50. Ibid., 52.

51. Ibid., 45.

52. For a discussion of microfilm, EEBO, and print copies of early English books, see Zachary Lesser, "Xeroxing the Renaissance: The Material Text of Early Modern Studies," *Shakespeare Quarterly* 70 (2019): 3–31.

53. I borrow the term "longue durée" from the Annales school of historians, and especially Fernand Braudel; see Braudel, "History and the Social Sciences: The Longue

Durée," trans. Immanuel Wallerstein, *Review (Fernand Braudel Center)* 32, no. 2 (2009): 177–203, a new translation of his classic 1958 essay. My usage does not assume some of the important context of the term in its historiographic usage, including the emphasis on long-term structural aspects of historical change. Instead I take the term in the more basic sense that Braudel sometimes intended, and in which David Armitage and Jo Guldi have recently used it, to contrast "broad historical time-scales" with "short-term horizons." Armitage and Guldi, "The Return of the *Longue Durée*: An Anglo-American Perspective," *Annales HSS* 70 (2015): 219–47, 221. Braudel similarly could use the term simply to describe one of the "two poles of time" (174) available to the historian, long-term and short-term.

54. My discussion here is influenced by Alan Galey, *The Shakespearean Archive: Experiments in New Media from the Renaissance to Postmodernity* (Cambridge: Cambridge University Press, 2014).

55. Paul Eggert, "Brought to Book: Bibliography, Book History and the Study of Literature," *Library* 13, no. 1 (2012): 3–32, 13.

56. Vivian Hunter Galbraith, *Studies in the Public Records* (London: Thomas Nelson and Sons, 1948), 3.

57. Hilary Jenkinson, *A Manual of Archive Administration Including the Problems of War Archives and Archive Making* (Oxford: Clarendon Press, 1922), 84, 93, 91. I am indebted throughout these paragraphs to Paul Saint-Amour's excellent discussion of the temporality of the archive as elaborated by Jenkinson, in *Tense Future: Modernism, Total War, Encyclopedic Form* (Oxford: Oxford University Press, 2015), 157–76. For the relationship of early bibliography to natural history, see Kathryn James and Aaron T. Pratt, *Collated and Perfect* (New Haven: Yale University Press and University of Texas at Austin Press, 2019), 12–13, 14.

58. Jenkinson, *Manual*, 11.

59. Ibid., 12–13.

60. Galbraith, *Studies*, 14.

61. Jenkinson, *Manual*, 106. See Saint-Amour, *Tense*, 159–60.

62. Jenkinson, *Manual*, 21. The only valid means of culling archives, he writes, is for the original administrator of an archive—the secretary of the war office, for instance, or the clerk of the exchequer—to destroy documents in the course of running the bureaucracy.

63. Saint-Amour writes that Jenkinson's archivist is "a member of a secular holy order who withdraws from the libidinal economy of argument in the service of the archive's intrinsic value and of all research still to come"; this is what Saint-Amour terms "historiographic celibacy" (*Tense*, 165).

64. Jacques Derrida, *Archive Fever: A Freudian Impression*, trans. Eric Prenowitz (Chicago: University of Chicago Press, 1996), 1–2.

65. Ibid., 91.

66. Henry Bradshaw, *A Classified Index of the Fifteenth Century Books in the Collection of the late M. J. De Meyer* (London: Macmillan, 1870), 15–16. On Bradshaw as a

founder of bibliographic method, see Paul Needham, *The Bradshaw Method: Henry Bradshaw's Contribution to Bibliography* (Chapel Hill: Hanes Foundation, 1988), and G. Thomas Tanselle, *Bibliographical Analysis: A Historical Introduction* (Cambridge: Cambridge University Press, 2009), 6–14.

67. Pollard, *Shakespeare*, 100–101.

68. Ibid., emphasis added.

69. Greg, *BEPD*, 3:1108.

70. W. W. Greg, "The First Folio and Its Publishers," in *Studies in the First Folio*, ed. Israel Gollancz (Oxford: Oxford University Press, 1924), 139–44, 143; Greg, *Shakespeare*, 13, 15.

71. See Maguire, *Shakespearean*, 53.

72. Stanley Wells, "Jaggard, William (c. 1568–1623), printer and bookseller," *Oxford Dictionary of National Biography*, 23 September 2004, accessed 11 February 2019.

73. See Higgins, *Shakespeare's*, chap. 2.

74. Gerald Johnson, "Thomas Pavier, Publisher, 1600–25," *Library* 6th ser. 14 (1992): 12–50, 13.

75. Johnson, "Thomas," 12; here he is quoting F. E. Halliday (1964) and David Bevington (1980).

76. Ibid., 38.

77. Ibid., 39.

78. Ibid., 21.

79. See Peter Stallybrass, "'Little Jobs': Broadsides and the Printing Revolution," in *Agents of Change: Print Culture Studies After Elizabeth Eisenstein*, ed. Sabrina Alcorn Baron, Eric N. Lindquist, and Eleanor F. Shevlin (Amherst: University of Massachusetts Press, 2007) 315–41; and Ben Higgins, "'We Have a Constant Will to Publish': The Publishers of Shakespeare's First Folio," Ph.D. thesis, University of Oxford, 2015, 148–55, and his appendix transcribing the City of London annual printing account for 1627.

80. Andrew Murphy, *Shakespeare in Print: A History and Chronology of Shakespeare Publishing* (Cambridge: Cambridge University Press, 2003), 39–40.

81. Kastan, *Shakespeare and the Book*, 57.

82. Instead, Erne argues, Pavier published the books "in contravention to the Lord Chamberlain's express order." Erne, *Literary Dramatist*, 281, 282n6, 282.

83. Massai, *Shakespeare*, 107–8.

84. See ibid., 114.

85. In this way Massai provides an explanation for the frequently repeated revisionist comment that the title pages are not sophisticated enough to have deceived stationers: "Why did Pavier make such a poor effort at covering his tracks, by issuing fraudulent title pages that did not even attempt to look like the title pages in the earlier editions he was assumedly attempting to copy?" (Massai, *Shakespeare*, 108). This frequent critique fails to account for the fact that for hundreds of years, all collectors, editors, and scholars did believe these editions were printed in the years stated in their imprints. It also misstates the New Bibliographic theory, which did not assume these title pages were designed to

fool people into believing they were copies of the same edition actually printed in that year—as Greg imagined Pavier telling a bibliographer who noted the differences between his editions and the true first editions: "have you any reason to believe that there were not two editions printed that year?" (Greg, "Certain, II," 397). And this is exactly how they were understood until the early twentieth century.

86. James J. Marino, *Owning William Shakespeare: The King's Men and Their Intellectual Property* (Philadelphia: University of Pennsylvania Press, 2011), 108. Adam G. Hooks also attributes significantly more agency to Jaggard than have most other scholars; see *Selling Shakespeare: Biography, Bibliography, and the Book Trade* (Cambridge: Cambridge University Press, 2016), 112–24.

87. Marino, *Owning*, 114.

88. Ibid., 108. See Peter W. M. Blayney, "The Publication of Playbooks," in *A New History of Early English Drama*, ed. John D. Cox and David Scott Kastan (New York: Columbia University Press, 1997), 383–422.

89. Marino, *Owning*, 128.

90. Ibid., 116.

91. Ibid., 115. Like Massai and the other revisionists, Marino draws attention to the "imperfectly" copied title pages: "Why are these quartos not facsimiles? Why, indeed, are they less perfect facsimiles than Jaggard, using less personal ornaments, might have made them? Why did Jaggard leave the clue by which his handiwork has been identified?" (113). Again, we might wonder whether the case is being viewed too much through the lens of current knowledge.

92. Cyndia Susan Clegg, "*King Lear* and Early Seventeenth-Century Print Culture," in *King Lear: New Critical Essays*, ed. Jeffrey Kahan (New York: Routledge, 2008), 156–83, 176.

93. Clegg, "*King*," 177.

94. Lukas Erne, *Shakespeare and the Book Trade* (Cambridge: Cambridge University Press, 2013), 174.

95. Tara Lyons, "Serials, Spinoffs, and Histories: Selling 'Shakespeare' in Collection Before the Folio," *Philological Quarterly* 91 (2012): 185–220, 202. See also Jeffrey Todd Knight, "Invisible Ink: A Note on Ghost Images in Early Printed Books," *Textual Cultures* 5, no. 2 (2010): 53–62.

1. GHOSTS

Epigraph: James Joyce, *Ulysses* (Paris: Shakespeare and Co., 1922), 180.

1. For detailed discussion of why these ghosts are produced, see C. H. Bloy, *A History of Printing Ink, Balls and Rollers, 1440–1850* (London: Wynkyn De Worde Society, 1967), 88–91; Vincent Daniels, "The Discolouration of Paper on Ageing," in *Papers from the 10th Anniversary Conference, 'New Directions in Paper Conservation,' Oxford, 14–18 April, 1986, Part 3*, ed. Nicholas Pickwoad, special issue of *The Paper Conservator: Journal of the Institute of Paper Conservation* 12 (1988): 93–100, 95.

2. Knight, "Invisible."

3. Cathleen Baker, *From the Hand to the Machine: Nineteenth-Century American Papers and Mediums, Technologies, Materials, and Conservation* (Ann Arbor: Legacy Press, 2010), 47–48.

4. Hailey, "Shakespearian," 177. In this section I draw from, while modifying based on later research, Zachary Lesser and Peter Stallybrass, "Shakespeare Between Pamphlet and Book," in *Shakespeare and Textual Studies*, ed. Sonia Massai and M. J. Kidnie (Cambridge: Cambridge University Press, 2015), 105–33.

5. It has done so even though Pollard himself speculated, based on his knowledge of the Gwynn, Hussey, and Capell copies, that "no order was observed when the plays were bound" and "some trouble seems to have been taken in separating *Pericles* from the *Whole Contention*" (*Shakespeare*, 103).

6. Greg, "Certain," 116.

7. A. W. Pollard and G. R. Redgrave, eds, *A Short-Title Catalogue of Books Printed in England, Scotland, & Ireland and of English Books Printed Abroad, 1475–1640*, 2nd ed., rev. W.A. Jackson, F.S. Ferguson, and Katharine F. Pantzer, 3 vols. (London: Bibliographical Society, 1976–1991). The description of the volume was revised by Erin Blake in March 2017 (after the publication of Lesser and Stallybrass, "Shakespeare"), as part of a broader revision of cataloguing of the Pavier Quartos. The current catalogue record can be found at https://hamnet.folger.edu/cgi-bin/Pwebrecon.cgi?BBID=163925; the original catalogue description can still be found (in essentially identical form) in the Holdings Details of the copy in the *English Short Title Catalogue* (ESTC), http://estc.bl.uk/S111147, accessed 31 January 2019.

8. As G. Thomas Tanselle explains, bibliographers use π to denote an unsigned *initial* gathering, and chi or χ to denote an "unsigned gathering in the body of a book for which no letter (or number) of the regular sequence is available to be inferred." Tanselle, "Title-Page Transcription and Signature Collation Reconsidered," *Studies in Bibliography* 38 (1985): 45–81, 63. The choice of chi rather than π for the title page of *Pericles* is therefore itself a bibliographical interpretation implying that *Whole Contention* and *Pericles* are a single book. I am grateful to Alan Farmer for this insight.

9. Sigmund Freud, "The Uncanny," in *The Standard Edition of the Complete Pyschological Works*, vol. 17, trans. James Strachey (London: Hogarth Press), 219–52, 245.

10. University of Pennsylvania catalogue record: https://franklin.library.upenn.edu/catalog/FRANKLIN_9915398633503681, accessed 15 December 2018.

11. Pollard, *Shakespeare*, 83.

12. Greg, "Certain," 114.

13. According to George Steevens, Garrick was "the only person who was at peace" with Capell. Quoted in George M. Kahrl, with Dorothy Anderson, *The Garrick Collection of Old English Plays: A Catalogue with an Historical Introduction* (London: British Library, 1982), 33.

14. Kahrl and Anderson, *Garrick*, 22.

15. See the bound volume of Capell's flyleaves in the British Library, which were removed from their original volumes and bound together during the nineteenth century; shelf mark 643.l.30.

16. Quoted in Kahrl and Anderson, *Garrick*, 237, emphasis altered; Garrick's copy of *Pericles* lacks the title page, and this note implies that it was already lacking in the eighteenth century, since Capell makes no mention of the unsigned title leaf that precedes the R gathering.

17. Trinity College, Cambridge, Capell Q.12. (A note on the title page of *Pericles*, which reads "Pt. 2 of what follows (no. 4)," is not in Capell's handwriting; it is likely a later librarian's note.)

18. See Kahrl and Anderson, *Garrick*, 20–21.

19. British Library, C.34.k.23.

20. On the provenance of Garrick's collection, the indispensable reference is Kahrl and Anderson, *Garrick*; see also Dorothy Anderson, "Reflections on Librarianship: Observations Arising from the Examination of the Garrick Collection of Old Plays in the British Library," *British Library Journal* 6 (1980): 1–6; and Tiffany Stern, "'I Do Wish That You Had Mentioned Garrick': The Absence of Garrick in Johnson's Shakespeare," in *Comparative Excellence: Essays on Shakespeare and Johnson*, ed. Eric Rasmussen and Aaron Santesso (New York: AMS Press, 2007), 70–96.

21. Kahrl and Anderson, *Garrick*, 16.

22. When the collection was separated into individual volumes in the 1840s, Kahrl reports, there were 1,169 books, "with 10 fragments" (Kahrl and Anderson, *Garrick*, 66).

23. British Library, C.34.k.19.

24. Capell's treatment of his own copies of these plays at Trinity College—which he did rebind in two volumes but preserved together, apparently in the original order of binding—suggests he was not responsible for disbinding the putative Garrick volume of Pavier Quartos. I have more to say later on Capell's handling of his volume.

25. In my census of bound volumes of the 1619 quartos, therefore, I include a single entry for Garrick's copy that incorporates both of these ghosts (see Appendix A). But it is impossible to be sure, based on the evidence we currently have, that these ghosts do not point toward the existence of two distinct volumes rather than one. Likewise, I have listed two distinct volumes based on ghosts on copies at the Folger, since there is nothing to suggest they traveled together, but it is impossible to rule out that they were once all found in the same volume.

26. Boston Public Library, G.126.28.

27. Elizabethan Club, Yale University, Eliz 204; Princeton University Library, RHT 17th-518; Victoria and Albert National Art Library, Dyce 26 Box 43/2; University of Texas, Harry Ransom Center, Pforz 890; Folger Shakespeare Library, STC 22293 copy 4; Folger Shakespeare Library, STC 22291 copy 1. I have not examined the Ransom Center copies personally, and I am grateful to Aaron Pratt for alerting me to this ghost.

28. Folger Shakespeare Library, STC 22300 copy 8; the Bodmer does not use shelf marks.

29. Eton College Library, Sal.4.30(2). Possibly there is a faint ghost image on this verso of a circular printer's device, and *Dream* is the only Pavier Quarto with a circular device, but if it is indeed present, it is very faint, and it is equally possible that this may simply be ordinary discoloration.

30. See the University of Virginia library catalogue (1857–1905), RG-12/12/1.119, p. 414. I say the volume "likely" burned because Sidney Lee intriguingly records the librarian at Virginia as telling him that the "books contiguous to this volume were saved, but the quarto was never seen again. It was probably stolen." See Sidney Lee, "The Shakespeare Quartos," *Athenaeum* 4238 (16 January 1909): 73. Pollard reports that the Virginia quartos "came to the library in 1853, each in a separate binding, and were bound together by a bookseller in Charlottesville in 1853 or soon afterwards" (*Shakespeare*, 84). It is possible, therefore, that the catalogue does not reproduce the original binding order; but since, as Lee reported, "in 1853 Governor Randolph made the University of Virginia a gift of quarto plays, including the nine Shakespeare quartos in question, and no other Shakespeare plays" (73), it is almost certain that the group were once bound together in a single volume. And since the order preserved in the library catalogue does not list *Pericles* immediately after *Whole Contention*, as a binder in 1853 seeing the continuous signatures would have been inclined to do barring other factors, it is quite possible that the original order was preserved. The provenance of this volume is murky, and it is not clear how much to trust the information that the plays came to Charlottesville in separate bindings. In 1853 there would have been no good reason other than a previous binding to bind these quartos together, as no one knew that they formed a set.

31. *A Catalogue of the Library of John Henderson, Esq. . . . Which will be Sold by Auction by T. and J. Egerton, Booksellers. . . . On Monday, the 20th of February, 1786, and the Five following Days* (London, 1786), 59. I am indebted to Henry Woudhuysen for suggesting that I look through early catalogues for more Pavier Quarto volumes.

32. Newberry Library, Vault Case 4A 956. The catalogue record can be found at: https://webvoyage.carli.illinois.edu/nby/cgi-bin/Pwebrecon.cgi?DB=local&v1=1&BBRecID=676078, accessed 6 December 2018.

33. I remain very grateful to both for their willingness to do this; by no means would all libraries be open to this idea, but the results bear out the scholarly rationale for doing so and confirm their professional judgment that it was worth the risk.

34. E-mail from Lesa Dowd, 12 October 2018.

35. Aaron Pratt likewise emphasizes the variable nature of the grouping, though he goes further than I do in labeling the Gwynn and Plat volumes "*sammelbände*" and in describing the 1619 quartos as simply "nine distinct editions that were available for purchase at the same time, in the same place" (Pratt, "Status," 248.) As I will demonstrate, the evidence suggests a more "tightly bound" grouping than this, but also a more "loosely bound" grouping than either the New Bibliographers or revisionists—or library catalogues—have perceived.

36. On Goodman's appointment, see Elizabeth Lane Furdell, *The Royal Doctors, 1485–1714: Medical Personnel at the Tudor and Stuart Courts* (Rochester: University of

Rochester Press, 2001), 214. Goodman's date of birth is unknown, but he is recorded in *The Political State of Great Britain, Volume LVII* (1739), page 85, as having been "aged upwards of Seventy" when he died on 25 December 1738.

37. *A Catalogue of the Entire Library of Dr. Thomas Goodman, Late Physician in Ordinary to His Majesty* (1739), 166, items 1452 and 1453. The order of plays in these two lots is identical to the Orlebar volume; given that, as I discuss, known volumes of sets of the 1619 quartos never follow the same order, it is highly likely (though not certain) that Goodman's book passed to Orlebar. If so, the division into two lots in Goodman's catalogue is probably an error, since the set was in one volume when Orlebar gave it to Percy, and since lot 1453 lacks the left brace that signals a multi-text lot elsewhere in the catalogue, indicating that the brace for 1452 was meant also to incorporate the texts that ended up listed as 1453. But it is conceivable, though I think highly improbable, that the set was in two volumes in Goodman's library and then rejoined into a single volume in Orlebar's collection. I am very grateful to Tony Russ for alerting me to Goodman's catalogue.

38. Folger Shakespeare Library, STC 26101 copy 2; transcription from Erin Blake's discussion of the volume at https://folgerpedia.folger.edu/Miss_Orlebar_copy_of_the_Pavier_quartos, supplemented by my own transcription of the struck-through passage. As Blake points out in her Folgerpedia article, since Percy refers only to "Miss Orlebars," we do not know for certain which of the three Orlebar sisters owned the volume, but it was "most likely the eldest," Mary. While Percy consistently writes the surname "Orlebars," and while Giles Dawson followed him, the more common spelling was Orlebar, which I use following Blake's Folgerpedia article.

39. Since the lists of contents in Goodman's auction catalogue and on the flyleaf now at the Folger are identical, of course, *Woman Killed* also appears as the first item in lot 1452 in the Goodman catalogue.

40. See Blake's Folgerpedia article, which also provides evidence that the original order of binding was maintained.

41. One other copy at the Folger, STC 26101 copy 1, binds *Whole Contention* (SC 1686) and *Pericles* (SC 1014) together. But this is a sophisticated volume: William Neile's signature and the added manuscript date "1622" on the title page of *Whole Contention*, both now largely erased, make clear that this was Hussey's copy, which was not followed by *Pericles* in Hussey's volume. The copy was acquired by Folger from the collector Robert Hoe (1839–1910) after it was collated by F. S. Ferguson at Quaritch on 28 May 1906 (noted at the end of *Pericles*; a similar note at the end of *Whole Contention* is dated two days earlier). Ferguson finished his collation, in other words, only a week before his friend Pollard's essay on the quartos appeared in the *Academy*. The plays were bound together in ornate style by the Club Bindery in 1907, no doubt precisely to put them in the "correct" order of signatures. Other than those discussed elsewhere in this book, I am aware of two other copies of *Whole Contention* that are bound today with *Pericles*: one at the Huntington Library (SC 1699 and 1023) and one at the New York Public Library (SC 1702 and 1027), both lacking the title page to *Pericles*. The Huntington copy was bound in the

nineteenth century by Francis Bedford, and the NYPL copy by J. Mackenzie in the early nineteenth century, so their current configurations date back at least that far, and may indeed testify to their early seventeenth-century arrangement. But the Huntington copy was once owned by Capell, who was aware of the "correct" binding of the two plays, as discussed above. And the lack of the *Pericles* title page likewise suggests that both may be later made-up copies, since the title page was far more likely to survive intact if the play was included in a bound volume from the start. Because these two are doubtful cases, I do not include them in my "Census of Known Sets of the 1619 Quartos" (Appendix A).

42. Giles Dawson, typescript note in Folger STC 26101 copy 2.

43. See Knight, "Invisible." I cite here the revised and elaborated discussion in Knight, *Bound*, 151.

44. It should also caution us against relying too heavily on digital facsimiles. While these are incredibly useful for bibliographic work, they typically do not enable the identification of ghosts—nor, for that matter, of stab-stitch holes, the key evidence discussed in the following chapter.

45. Knight, *Bound*, 154–55, 235n15; Jeffrey Todd Knight, "Making Shakespeare's Books: Assembly and Intertextuality in the Archives," *Shakespeare Quarterly* 60 (2009): 304–40, 326.

46. Erne, *Book Trade*, 223. Tara Lyons was more on track in suspecting that "this *Sammelband* may have been formed in [the Jaggards'] shop, either the product of the stationers marketing bundles of books from their press or perhaps the result of displaying or storing together similar kinds of recently printed material" ("Serials," 203). But the use of the term "sammelband" still implies that the gathering of Heywood's play with the Shakespeare plays was more or less fortuitous, the result of happenstance more than the publishers' intentions. I argue that Jaggard's intentions are an important part of the story.

47. *A Catalogue of Several Libraries and Collections of Books* . . . (London, 1774), 222.

48. Kahrl and Anderson, *Garrick*, 66–67.

49. Greg, "What Is," 45.

50. I am very grateful to Adam Hooks for alerting me to the presence of this ghost before I had a chance to visit Cambridge.

51. It is also possible that the ghost has become more visible over time, due to some ongoing reaction in the paper, even though *Woman Killed* is no longer adjacent. I am grateful to Ben Higgins for this idea.

52. See Greg, "Certain," 116.

53. I am grateful to Ivan Lupić for this point, and for photographs of some of these volumes.

54. Greg, "Certain," 116.

55. Bodleian Library, Mal. 182(2). Oddly, only the top edge of *Woman Killed* is stained, not the fore and bottom edges. But since the leaves of *Woman Killed* are significantly smaller than the others in Capell's volume, if the top edge of the play had been aligned with the rest of the book block, these other two edges may have been missed when the treatment was applied. (Capell's volumes are not uniformly stained, with some

plays receiving more or less of the green pigment.) *Woman Killed* measures 18.2 × 13.3 cm, while the plays that preceded and followed it in Capell's volume, *Henry V* and *Pericles*, are 18.9 × 13.9 cm. Once Malone acquired this copy of *Woman Killed*, he bound it along with six other playbooks in his volume bearing the shelf mark Mal. 182, but all seven plays were rebound individually in 1927. None of the other six plays has the same green edge treatment, confirming that it was done before Malone acquired *Woman Killed*. (*Technogamia*, *Witty Combat*, and *Ungrateful Favourite* do show signs of some previous edge treatment, but it is different from that on *Woman Killed*.) Furthermore, this copy of *Woman Killed* shows no evidence of stab-stitch holes, suggesting it was originally sold as part of a bound volume (see Chapter 2), while the other six plays in Mal. 182 do contain stab-stitch holes.

56. While the rival editors Malone and Capell famously detested each other, they did exchange copies at least once, perhaps explaining how Capell's copy of *Woman Killed* ended up in Malone's collection. See W. W. Greg, "Editors at Work and Play: A Glimpse of the Eighteenth Century," *Review of English Studies* 2 (1926): 173–76.

57. Capell's collection was "of Elizabethan literature generally, and there were proportionally few plays; the only dramatists well represented were Shakespeare and Beaumont and Fletcher." Since Capell seems to have viewed his own collection and Garrick's as complementary, he apparently sometimes acquired non-Shakespearean plays for Garrick rather than himself, and some plays in Garrick's collection "also bear on the title-pages his initials in red, 'E.C.'" Of these plays, no copies also "appear in Capell's collection, and it would seem that there was a decision, at least on his part, that he would not compete with Garrick in the collecting of the plays of the early dramatists, but would concentrate rather on Shakespeare and on other literary forms." Kahrl and Anderson, *Garrick*, 29–30. While Capell's *Woman Killed* did not go to Garrick, perhaps because Garrick already had a copy (BL 644.e.33), it may have ended up with Malone for similar reasons.

58. Capell's copy reminds us that more has been done to these books than appears to us at first glance. So does the Newberry copy. In that copy, even after we have peeled away the later stab-stitched blue wrapper, the evidence of previous binding shows us not only that three Pavier Quartos (*Merry Wives, Oldcastle, Whole Contention*) have traveled together for a long time but also that something peculiar has occurred with one of them. Intriguingly, *Oldcastle* has an extra sewing hole compared to the other two plays, suggesting that it may have been transferred into this grouping at some point. Since the leather thongs, glue, and remains of the leather backing persist across all three plays, such a transfer must have occurred early in the life of the volume. Perhaps this extra sewing hole testifies to a reconfiguration of the plays from an earlier, multivolume binding; perhaps the copy of *Oldcastle* that originally came with this grouping was damaged and another copy was substituted during a rebinding; perhaps the extra hole is simply a binder's error of some kind and this copy has always been present. Without further evidence, we will likely never know. The bibliographic evidence in this case answers some questions but reveals new problems.

59. It is conceivable that some of the items listed separately in my census once belonged to the same volume. For example, the BPL ghost, which gives the sequence *Pericles–Lear*, is compatible with having once formed part of the same volume as the Elizabethan Club ghost, which has the sequence *Oldcastle–Henry V*, or as the Princeton ghost that has the same sequence. Several other such combinations are possible, since ghosts provide only a sequence of two plays. The total figure should therefore be understood as an approximation.

60. Pollard, *Shakespeare*, 102. See also Greg, *Shakespeare*, 17.

61. Greg, *Shakespeare*, 9; Erne, *Book Trade*, 175; David Scott Kastan, *Shakespeare After Theory* (New York: Routledge, 1999), 106.

62. Pollard, *Shakespeare*, 102.

63. Ibid., 103. Erne writes that "several bound copies of the ten quartos survive from the seventeenth century, suggesting that the Pavier quartos were nevertheless bound and sold together" (*Literary Dramatist*, 281). It is not clear to which copies Erne is referring, since only the Gwynn and Plat copies fit this description, not "several" copies. Ten years later, in *Shakespeare and the Book Trade*, Erne describes the surviving evidence of binding more precisely—although even he underplays the extent to which the bound volume was the main object of sale when he writes: "Although only *The Whole Contention* and *Pericles* were printed with continuous signatures and the eight playbooks seem to have been issued separately, they were nonetheless part of a single commercial undertaking, and, given their generic and authorial coherence, lent themselves to joint binding" (*Book Trade*, 222).

64. Pratt, "Status," 248.

65. A ghost of the "C" in "Chronicle History" from the title page of *Henry V* can just barely be perceived on sig. 2B1v of *Pericles*; a very strong ghost of the title page of *Oldcastle* is present on sig. G4v of *Henry V*; and the ghost of "M. VV" from the first line of the title page of *Lear* can be seen on sig. D4v of *Oldcastle*.

66. I am grateful to Aaron Pratt for discussions about this ghost and its relation to the pressing process.

67. Kastan, *Shakespeare and the Book*, 57. E. K. Chambers argues similarly that Pavier and Jaggard "had already abandoned the continuous signatures and perhaps the idea of a comprehensive volume, had separately issued those dated '1619,' and had the rest ready in print. If so, rather than sacrifice their material, they took the rather hazardous course of altering the dates on these to agree with those of the last impressions, so that they might pass as not new at all. The explanation is not wholly satisfactory, since it would have been safer to substitute fresh title-pages more exactly agreeing in detail with the old ones. But it seems to be the best available." It is highly implausible that all the plays were "ready in print" by the time "the rather hazardous course of altering the dates" was made; Chambers is forced into this implausibility precisely because he cannot perceive the collection itself as the crucial goal. The high number of bound volumes we can now document helps to make that goal clear. See Chambers, *William*, 1:137.

68. Greg's account falls into the same logical error: "If the remaining six pieces were to be printed at all, it must be made to appear that they were old stock" (*Shakespeare*, 16). But why print them at all, except in order to build up a collection?

69. On *London Prodigal* and *Titus*, see Erne, *Book Trade*, 179. Pavier had acquired the rights to *Titus* by transfer from Thomas Millington in 1602, although he seemingly declined to finance an edition of the play, as the 1611 edition was published by Edward White. Pavier had apparently lent him the rights but retained control, since it was Pavier's widow who transferred the title to Edward Brewster and Robert Bird in 1626. Tara Lyons has recently argued that the principles of "seriality and historicity largely guided [Pavier's] accumulation of playbooks and thereby influenced the selection of titles in the 1619 project," at least as much as authorship per se. Many of the plays involved were "true" histories or "part-plays" or "spin-offs" ("Serials," 193–95), although *Dream* in particular is something of an outlier on this theory. And the primacy of Jaggard in the project, more than Pavier, would need to be accounted for, since the argument put forward by Lyons mainly concerns Pavier's publishing history. But her point that "the 'Shakespeare' available . . . in 1619 was still a serial, historical 'Shakespeare'" (200) is an important one.

70. See Massai, *Shakespeare*, 108; Lyons, "Serials," 193–203.

71. John Jowett, *Shakespeare and Text* (Oxford: Oxford University Press, 2007), 70.

72. Marino, *Owning*, 107.

73. Ibid., 120. Marino also claims that Shakespeare's name appears on the title page of *Henry V*, but it does not, which complicates his argument that "the assignment of the three *Henry* plays and of *Oldcastle* to Shakespeare, the 'correct' and 'incorrect' attribution, must be considered part of one process," one assertion that a penumbra of literary property covered all of them (121).

74. Massai, *Shakespeare*, 119.

75. Of course, that risk could be offset to some extent, as Massai notes, by selling the plays individually as well, but the stunt itself, on this theory, focused on the bound set. The median length of quartos listed in the *STC* and published between 1558 and 1640 is thirty-eight leaves, and the average is about eighty-two leaves, demonstrating just how lengthy a bound set of Pavier Quartos was. I am grateful to Alan Farmer for these figures (which exclude nonspeculative editions such as royal proclamations, blank forms, and so on).

76. Massai, *Shakespeare*, 107–8.

2. HOLES

Epigraph: Stationers' Company, Liber A, f. 50r, 25 March 1586, digital facsimile, *Literary Print Culture: The Stationers' Company Archive, 1554–2007*, Adam Matthew Digital, http://www.literaryprintculture.amdigital.co.uk/, accessed 4 February 2019. The order seems to have been imposed on the Stationers' Company through outside pressure to the Court of Alderman of London.

1. In the most extensive study of stab-stitching undertaken to date, Aaron Pratt shows that "in terms of content, stab-stitched books range widely, from what we would expect to what we perhaps would not." Aaron T. Pratt, "Stab-Stitching and the Status of Early English Playbooks as Literature," *Library* 7th ser. 16 (2015): 304–28, 314. For recent studies on stab-stitching and its ramifications, see also Roger Chartier and Peter Stallybrass, "What Is a Book?" in *The Cambridge Companion to Textual Scholarship*, ed. Neil Freistat and Julia Flanders (Cambridge: Cambridge University Press, 2013), 188–204; and Alan B. Farmer, "Playbooks and the Question of Ephemerality," in *The Book in History, The Book as History: New Intersections of the Material Text*, ed. Heidi Brayman, Jesse M. Lander, and Zachary Lesser (New Haven: Beinecke Rare Book Library and Yale University Press, 2016), 82–125. I draw on Lesser and Stallybrass, "Shakespeare," for its discussion of stab-stitching as well.

2. Pratt, "Stab-Stitching," 304. Pratt is specifically describing a copy of *The London Prodigal* at the Folger (STC 22333 copy 2); pamphlets might be stab-stitched through two or four holes as well, although three seems to have been the norm.

3. Pratt, "Stab-Stitching," 322. Still, some collectors, including Frances Wolfreston and Henry Oxinden, simply kept their books stab-stitched, never combining them into bound sammelbands (326).

4. Ibid., 315, 318.

5. Pratt also provides evidence that "booksellers were responsible for a significant proportion of binding transactions in London—that they were commissioning bindings on behalf of their customers and selling ready-bound copies of some titles" (ibid., 321n29). On this question, see also Stuart Bennett, *Trade Bookbinding in the British Isles 1660–1800* (New Castle, Del.: Oak Knoll Press, 2004). Ben Higgins alerts me to Edward Blount's preface to *Horae subsecivae* (1620), where the publisher tells the reader: "If the Booke please you, come home to my Shop, you shall haue it bound ready to your hand" (sigs. A3r–v).

6. Pratt, "Stab-Stitching," 312.

7. University of Pennsylvania, PA6666.A1 1581 (Seneca) and PR2659.L9 A6 1632 (Lyly).

8. Pratt, "Stab-Stitching," 305–6.

9. As Pratt notes, it is "relatively easy to conclude with confidence *that* a book was certainly stitched." But it is "much harder to determine that it definitely *was not*, that it was traditionally sewn from the beginning," not only because of the logical impossibility of proving a negative but also because the holes are sometimes hidden in a tightly rebound book, or have been expertly repaired, or cropped entirely (ibid., 312).

10. Ibid., 314; on median length, see Alan B. Farmer and Zachary Lesser, "The Popularity of Playbooks Revisited," *Shakespeare Quarterly* 56 (2005): 1–32, 24.

11. Pratt, "Stab-Stitching," 313.

12. On these regulations, which are complicated by the fact that they (apparently accidentally) omit the quarto format, see the discussion in Farmer, "Ephemerality," 110–11. Pratt notes, importantly, that "there is no evidence in the form of fines or penalties that

this order was ever implemented or enforced—for any format" (Pratt, "Stab-Stitching," 314n22). Farmer and Pratt revise earlier discussions by David Foxon, "Stitched Books," *Book Collector* 24 (1975): 111–24; and Joad Raymond, *Pamphlets and Pamphleteering in Early Modern Britain* (Cambridge: Cambridge University Press, 2003), 81–83.

13. This figure includes fourteen copies that I have not been able to see personally. Six copies at Ohio State University (*Whole Contention, Pericles, Merry Wives, Henry V, Oldcastle, Dream*) formed part of Pratt's study; five copies at the Bibliothèque nationale de France were examined for me by Liza Blake; two copies at Glasgow University were examined for me by Robert MacLean; and one copy at York Minster Library was examined for me by Sophie Coulombeau.

14. While the sample sizes for individual plays are too small to enable fine-grained comparisons, the highest rate of stab-stitching is only 50 percent (*Lear*), and it falls to as low as 21 percent (*Dream*).

15. It is true, as Pratt notes, that the lack of stab-stitch holes does not necessarily mean "that the sets were prepackaged by Jaggard or any other stationer. Because many bindings were evidently commissioned through retail booksellers and not standalone bookbinding shops, a reader could order a fully custom sammelband of quarto publications that had never been stab-stitched" (Pratt, "Status," 245). The consistency with which these very same plays (with or without *Woman Killed*) were bound together, however, strongly suggests that they were in fact prepackaged.

16. Folger *Whole Contention*, STC 26101 copy 1; Shakespeare Birthplace Trust *Merchant of Venice*, SR 35.21, and *King Lear*, SR 35.17; Harvard University, Houghton Library *Yorkshire Tragedy*, STC 22341. The whereabouts of the other plays in the Hussey volume are now unknown, with the probable exception of a copy of *Henry V* at Meisei University in Japan, which I have not been able to examine for stab-stitching. The Folger copy of *Pericles* now bound with the Hussey *Whole Contention* may also be Hussey's, and it too does not have stab-stitch holes. Unfortunately the later stab-stitching that attached the blue wrapper to the book block of the Newberry copy has made it impossible to look for earlier holes.

17. It is also possible, given the example of the Newberry volume, that copies could be stab-stitched *after* they had been taken out of a bound volume, but this was surely very rare.

18. Pratt notes numerous sammelbands with some items stabbed and others not: since books were often warehoused in sheets, customers could commission some new works to be bound up with others purchased previously and stab-stitched, resulting in a bound volume that includes some texts with and some without stab-stitch holes ("Status," 245–46). This is unlikely to have been what happened in the case of the ghosted Pavier Quartos copies with stab-stitch holes, since all the plays were printed in the same year (except for *Woman Killed*), but other narratives are imaginable. The absence of stab-stitch holes in a particular copy might, in an exceptional case, be explained by other factors, such as its having been warehoused in sheets until much later; or its having been purchased in sheets and only later incorporated into a reader's sammelband. But these cases are not the norm.

19. Pollard, *Shakespeare*, 85; see also T. A. Birrell, "The Influence of Seventeenth-Century Publishers on the Presentation of English Literature," in *Historical and Editorial Studies in Medieval and Early Modern English*, ed. Mary-Jo Arn and Hanneke Wirtjes (Groningen: Wolters-Noordhoff, 1985), 163–73, 166: "The highest survival rates for Shakespeare quartos are among the famous group published in 1619. . . . Now this is because they were issued *en bloc* and then bound up."

20. These figures are rounded to the nearest whole number and are derived from the *Shakespeare Census*, www.shakespearecensus.org, ed. Adam G. Hooks and Zachary Lesser, created 2018, accessed 14 May 2020. I include all plays listed in the *Shakespeare Census*, even those now generally considered apocryphal. The 1617 edition of *Woman Killed* survives in twenty-eight copies, but without a better basis of comparison, it is hard to know how typical that figure is. *Woman Killed*, it seems clear, was sold as part of a bound volume of Pavier Quartos less frequently than were the other plays in the group.

21. Farmer ("Ephemerality," 111) finds that books of a length just under the limits for stab-stitching established in the 1586 regulations do not survive in numbers significantly different from those of a length just over the limits, suggesting that, contrary to what many scholars have argued, stab-stitching *in itself* may not have increased the ephemerality of books compared to binding. But at 326 leaves, the Pavier Quartos as a set (even without *Woman Killed*) would have been among the longest 4 percent of all quartos published for retail sale from 1558 to 1640. The length of the bound volume may have been as important as its binding. Farmer also concurs with Oliver Willard that "when a text has been reprinted in multiple editions . . . there are usually fewer copies of the early editions and more of the later ones" (ibid., 91). See Oliver M. Willard, "The Survival of English Books Printed Before 1640: A Theory and Some Illustrations," *Library* 4th ser. 23 (1942): 171–90. Five of the Pavier Quartos (*Whole Contention*, *Yorkshire*, *Henry V*, *Dream*, *Oldcastle*), plus *Woman Killed*, were the final early edition of the play. Still, other Shakespeare plays that were last editions survive in an average of 24.4 copies, far fewer than the Pavier Quartos that were last editions (39.6 copies, not including *Woman Killed*).

22. Indeed, Farmer explains the similar survival rates of books just above and just below the threshold established for stab-stitching in precisely this way: "This similarity in loss rates may have resulted from owners routinely binding short publications into *Sammelbände*, thereby transforming what had been stab-stitched books into ones with sewn bindings" ("Ephemerality," 111).

23. My work on stab-stitching in *Woman Killed* derives from my collaboration with Peter Stallybrass in "Shakespeare." The copies without stab-stitch holes include one at the Bodleian (Mal. 182[2]); one at the BPL (G.3972.33); two at the Folger (STC 13372 copy 1 and copy 2); one at Glasgow (Sp Coll BD1-c.87); one at Magdalen College, Oxford; one at the Ransom Center at the University of Texas (Pforz 488 PFZ); one at the Victoria and Albert (Dyce 26 Box 20/1); and one at Yale (Ih H519 607wc). Of these twenty-six copies, I have seen twenty in person. Another copy that I have examined, at the Newberry Library, is excluded from these figures because it is inlaid and hence any stab-stitching evidence has been destroyed. Aaron Pratt examined the two copies of *Woman Killed* at the

Ransom Center for me, and Robert MacLean the copy at Glasgow. Joshua McEvilla provided photographs of the copy in the Royal Library of Sweden, Jose Guerrero did the same for the copy in the Sutro Library, and the Special Collections and Archives department at the University of Cardiff did so for their copy: while these are often not sufficient to identify stab-stitch holes, in these cases they were clearly visible even in photographs. McEvilla has also compiled a census of extant copies of the edition, which independently confirmed my own; see the "Editions and Textual Matters" section of "VIII: Renaissance Drama, Excluding Shakespeare," *Year's Work in English Studies* 98, no. 1 (2019): 445–94.

24. A copy of *Woman Killed* at the Harry Ransom Center, University of Texas (Wh H519 607wb), shows a spattering of red at the top of the last page, resulting from a previous edge treatment, a good indication that it once was part of a bound volume. But this may have been a later sammelband, especially since this copy does have stab-stitch holes. E-mail from Aaron Pratt, 18 December 2018.

25. Pollard, *Shakespeare*, 100–101; Greg, *BEPD*, 3:1108; see also Chambers, *William*, 1:135; Johnson, "Thomas," 37.

26. See Massai, *Shakespeare*, 112; Jowett, "Shakespeare Supplemented," 46. Massai herself notes that Pavier "probably collaborated with the stationers who held the rights," but the acceptance of Pavier as originator of the collection leads to the uncharacteristic lapse of simultaneously claiming that the imprints on *Merry Wives* and *Lear* are "misleading" because they make the books "appear to have been printed for Arthur Johnson and Nathaniel Butter" (*Shakespeare*, 114, 112).

27. *STC* 2.326, 325.

28. In the following paragraphs I draw on Lesser and Stallybrass, "Shakespeare."

29. *A Catalogue of Several Libraries and Collections of Books . . .* (London, 1774), 222.

30. Jaggard copublished the 1607 edition with the bookseller John Hodgets. The play was never entered in the Stationers' Register, but the imprint is typical for this kind of arrangement—"Printed by William Iaggard dwelling in Barbican, and are to be sold in Paule's Church-yard. by Iohn Hodgets. 1607"—and Jaggard seems to have retained the right to copy. He also printed most of the 1607 *Westward Ho*, and perhaps helped to finance the edition, but that imprint does not include his name: "Printed at London, and to be sold by Iohn Hodgets dwelling in Paules Churchyard." Since the play was entered in 1605 by Henry Rocket, the publishing arrangements behind this edition remain murky. (One and a half sheets of this play were printed by George Eld, according to Adrian Weiss, "Bibliographical Methods for Identifying Unknown Printers in Elizabethan/Jacobean Books," *Studies in Bibliography* 44 [1991]: 183–228, 211.)

31. The numbers for "sold by" imprints are small (four of ten) but nonetheless suggestive, I think. I exclude five items where Pavier's involvement is merely a conjecture because only his shop address is listed (two cases) or the book survives only in an imperfect copy (three cases).

32. Both Marino (*Owning*, 114) and Hooks (*Selling*, 120) likewise refer to the group as the "Jaggard Quartos," though for somewhat different reasons. So too do Kahrl and Anderson in their catalogue of the Garrick collection, where the quartos are called "W.

Jaggard's Collection of 1619" (*Garrick*, 237). See also Clegg, "*King*," 177. Higgins notes that both F. E. Halliday and Edwin Willoughby suggested that Jaggard had been responsible for publishing at least *Merchant* and *Dream*, the plays with the "James Roberts" imprint ("We Have," 124).

33. It is true that Bishop Percy removed *Woman Killed* and the pseudo-Shakespearean *Yorkshire Tragedy* from the volume at some point, but then he also took out *Lear*, while leaving in the pseudo-Shakespearean *Oldcastle*.

34. See Jeffrey Knapp, "What Is a Co-Author?" *Representations* 89 (2005): 1–29.

35. Aston Cokain, "To my Cousin Mr. Charles Cotton," in *A Chain of Golden Poems* (London, 1658), sigs. G6r–G7r. Knapp notes that "the Beaumont and Fletcher folio was the very first collection of explicitly co-authored plays to be published in England," but that even here most of the collaboration it included went unacknowledged ("What," 8).

36. It is therefore an overstatement, I think, although a usefully provocative one, to call the Shakespeare First Folio "an unstable entity (or, rather, a collection of variant copies) made up of removable parts that must be bound together" (Hooks, *Selling*, 117). Occasionally some of the preliminaries in the 1623 Shakespeare folio are found in a different order, but not the plays. Compared to the Shakespeare First Folio, the 1616 Jonson folio has a fairly clear register and pagination, but voluminous variant states; on its printing, see David Gants, "The 1616 Folio (F1): Textual Essay," *The Cambridge Edition of the Works of Ben Jonson Online*; James A. Riddell, "The Printing of the Plays in the Jonson Folio of 1616," *Studies in Bibliography* 49 (1996): 149–68; and Mark Bland, "William Stansby and the Production of *The Workes of Beniamin Jonson*, 1615–16," *Library* 6th ser. 20 (1998): 1–33. Bland writes that the ordering of texts in the volume "is part of its meaning as a book" (30). The second and third volumes of the Jonson folio (1631, 1640), however, involved a more complex register, and in extant copies sections "were combined in different orders"; see Peter Happé, "The 1640–1 Folio (F2(3)): Textual Essay," *The Cambridge Edition of the Works of Ben Jonson Online*. On the printing of the Beaumont and Fletcher folio in multiple shops, see Johann Gerritsen, "The Printing of the Beaumont and Fletcher Folio of 1647," *Library* 5th ser. 3 (1949): 233–64; while the catchwords in this folio are often wrong, the plays are nonetheless bound in the order listed in the table of contents; see Gerritsen, "Printing," 252; and W. W. Greg, "The Printing of the Beaumont and Fletcher Folio of 1647," *Library* 4th ser. 2 (1922): 109–15. See also Greg's entries for these collections in volume 3 of *BEPD*.

37. The page is unsigned and unpaginated, appearing on the verso of the last leaf of the index of scriptural references and an advertisement for other books sold by the publisher, John Saywell. I am grateful to Aaron Pratt for alerting me to this example.

38. On collections before the Shakespeare and Jonson folios, see Tara Lyons, *Assembled Plays: Reading Drama in Collection in Early Modern England* (forthcoming). In this discussion, I exclude very short "collections" of two-part plays such as *1 & 2 Edward IV* and *The Conspiracy and Tragedy of Charles Duke of Byron*. For her own reasons, Lyons does include them, with important consequences.

39. In both Lyly's *Six Court Comedies* (1633) and Brome's *Five New Playes* (1653), however, the initial play (*Endymion* and *A Mad Couple Well Matched*, respectively) lacks a separate title page; perhaps these title pages were accidentally omitted or perhaps they were considered unnecessary for the play leading off the volume, which had a general title page.

40. In the case of nonce collections, noncontinuous signatures were inevitable, and I therefore exclude these volumes from my comparison here, which in any case is not meant to be exhaustive.

41. During the printing of Lyly's collection, several stop-press corrections were made to the title page, and the *STC* lists two variant issues for the volume (STC 17088, 17089; see *DEEP: Database of Early English Playbooks,* ed. Alan B. Farmer and Zachary Lesser, created in 2007, deep.sas.upenn.edu, 5098, 5099). Since these variants do not affect my study of binding order, I have surveyed copies of both issues. In my survey of all of these small-format drama collections, I have ignored copies that are wanting the majority of the plays.

42. The disparity in the register is likely due to the fact that one printing house produced the first three plays and another the last two (Greg, *BEPD*, 3:1021). Brome's collection was issued with two variant title pages, one dated 1653 and the other 1654, and with different information in the imprint; see *DEEP* 5153 and 5154. I include copies of both issues in my survey. A copy of the 1654 issue at the Folger (B4871) erroneously includes the 1653 title page and preliminaries bound at the end and conjugate with G1–G3 of *Damoiselle*, showing that these preliminaries were printed last, along with the final forme of the intended order of plays. See the Folger catalogue record for this copy: http://hamnet.folger.edu/cgi-bin/Pwebrecon.cgi?BBID=145581.

43. Duke, PR3142 1653 copy 1; Haverford, Phillips 103; University of Pennsylvania, EC Sh665 B653a; Morgan Library, 18715. The copy at Haverford includes a blank leaf between *Court Secret* and *Cardinal* that reveals the order of plays was manipulated at some point. The verso of this blank leaf includes a ghost image of the title page of *Court Secret*, while the recto includes a ghost of the text on the last verso of *Court Secret*. In other words, this blank leaf appears now to exist impossibly in two different positions, bound both immediately after *Court Secret* and immediately before it. The paradox suggests that at one point either the plays appeared in title-page order (hence binding *Court Secret* after this blank leaf) or the blank leaf once appeared between *Imposture* and *Court Secret*. I suspect the latter option is more likely, since the former requires us to believe that the plays once appeared in title-page order but were later rebound "incorrectly."

44. John Creaser, "The 1631 Folio (F2(2)): Textual Essay," *The Cambridge Edition of the Works of Ben Jonson Online*. I have substituted "bind" where Creaser writes "print," since he is actually describing how the texts were bound, not the order in which they were printed.

45. University of Illinois, Urbana-Champaign, IUA11409. This copy includes *The Gentlemen of Venice* and *The Politician*, printed together in 1655 as a supplement to the *Six*

New Playes; the last gathering of *Brothers* is swapped with the last half sheet of *Gentlemen*.

46. National Library of Scotland, H.3.d.5.

47. Hailey, "Shakespearian," 176.

48. Greg speculated similarly: "The original intention may have been to produce a collection with signatures continuous throughout and a general title dated 1619. But no rigid plan was followed. The first title was left undated and the next two items were begun without providing for separate titles" (*BEPD*, 3:1107). Nearly all of the plays in the Jaggard Quartos include head titles that would seem perfectly ordinary for a collection of plays preceded by a general title page. The exception is *Oldcastle*, in which the Prologue intervenes between the title page and the head title, but that play may well have been the last printed, long after the idea of a general title page had been scrapped.

49. There is another possibility that could explain the absence of any evidence of *Whole Contention* and *Pericles* being bound consecutively. Maybe some volumes bound with the two plays consecutive were in fact sold in 1619 or shortly after, but our surviving archive is preselected against them, perhaps because they were destroyed?

50. As discussed above, Pratt notes several sammelbands in which some items have and some lack stab-stitch holes. In these cases readers probably bound up some of their already purchased plays at the moment they bought some new ones, which therefore lacked stab-stitch holes ("Status," 245–6). While some of the Jaggard Quarto copies without stab-stitch holes could conceivably have been bound in this way by readers, all the other evidence suggests this is not the best explanation.

51. On the Boys volume, I am indebted to the forthcoming monograph by Aaron Pratt. I am very grateful to him for sharing his ongoing research in this area.

52. Greg, "What Is," 45.

3. RIPS AND SCRAPES

Epigraph: Max Schweidler, *The Restoration of Engravings, Drawings, Books, and Other Works on Paper*, trans. Roy Perkinson (Los Angeles: Getty Conservation Institute, 2006), 118–19.

1. I say "true enough" because the location of *Merry Wives* in the sequence remains problematic. If it was truly printed after the falsely dated imprints began with *Merchant*, as Neidig argues, then the fact that *Merry Wives* is dated 1619 is hard to explain. Hailey tentatively suggests based on watermark evidence that "at least the first gathering of two of *MWW* had been printed off before work began on *MV*, which was completed before work resumed on *MWW*" ("Shakespearian," 177).

2. Boston Public Library, *Pericles* G.176.28; *Yorkshire* G.176.57; *Merry Wives* G.176.20. I am very grateful to Jay Moschella for everything to do with the BPL copies, especially for alerting me to the pen facsimiles and for locating the relevant passages in the Barton correspondence quoted later in the chapter.

3. See David McKitterick, *Old Books, New Technologies: The Representation, Conservation and Transformation of Books Since 1700* (Cambridge: Cambridge University Press, 2013), 37–56. For a similar argument about the need to contextualize historically the "sophisticated" books that Thomas Wise created, see Pratt, "Perfect," in James and Pratt, *Collated*, 38–39.

4. Thomas Rodd, *Elegant Literature: Part IV. of a Catalogue of an Extensive Collection of Books* (London: Compton and Ritchie, 1845), 357–64. Rodd lists two copies of *Henry V* and *Pericles*, and one each of *Whole Contention, Yorkshire, Merry Wives, Merchant, Dream,* and *Oldcastle*. Barton had already purchased from Rodd his copies of *Henry V* (in 1842) and *Merchant* (in 1843); the provenance of his other Jaggard Quartos is as yet unknown. Clearly many copies of Jaggard Quartos were readily available in the mid-nineteenth century.

5. Letter, Thomas Rodd to Thomas Pennant Barton, 30 December 1846, Boston Public Library MS f G.52.8.

6. "Books obtained since I last wrote to Mr. Rodd," Boston Public Library MS f G.52.8; the item is undated but is bound between letters dated November 1848 and January 1849. While the reference to Rodd here is oblique, the note probably represents Barton's accounting of books that had arrived (late) from Rodd since he last wrote to the bookseller asking when this shipment would be coming. Thanks again to Jay Moschella for finding this document and helping to date it.

7. As Pratt points out, this explains why some eighteenth-century collectors trimmed and inlaid all the leaves of their prized books into new volumes: "The techniques available for closing tears and filling losses paled in comparison to those possible a century later: completely removing margins, as Kemble did, obviated most of the need for awkward repairs." Pratt, "Perfect," 26–27.

8. Janet Ing Freeman, "John Harris," *Oxford Dictionary of National Biography*, https://doi.org/10.1093/ref:odnb/37514, accessed 18 January 2019; see also McKitterick, *Old Books*, 39, 105–8; and Emma Smith, *Shakespeare's First Folio: Four Centuries of an Iconic Book* (Oxford: Oxford University Press), 323–26. I am grateful to Henry Woudhuysen for first suggesting that Harris may have been responsible for the pen facsimiles. For an earlier facsimilist, and the development of a modern understanding of historical preservation, see Sonja Drimmer's account of Eliza Dennis Denyer (1765?–1824) in "A Medieval Psalter 'Perfected': Eighteenth-Century Conservationism and an Early (Female) Restorer of Rare Books and Manuscripts," *Electronic British Library Journal* 2013, article 3, http://www.bl.uk/eblj/2013articles/article3.html.

9. [William Roberts], "John Harris, Facsimilist," *Times Literary Supplement* 888 (23 January 1919): 48. *The Times Literary Supplement Historical Archive*, http://tinyurl.galegroup.com/tinyurl/8qrmZ4, accessed 22 January 2019.

10. *Reports by the Juries on the Subjects in the Thirty Classes into which the Exhibition Was Divided* (London, 1852), 3:892.

11. Robert Cowtan, *Memories of the British Museum* (London: Richard Bentley and Son, 1872), 335.

12. See Roy Perkinson, introduction to Schweidler, *Restoration*, 10.

13. Alfred Bonnardot, *Essai sur la restauration des anciennes estampes et des livres rares* (Paris, 1846), 51: "Provision d'anciens papiers de toute époque et de toute nature, provenant de vieux livres ou des marges de mauvaises estampes sacrifiées." My translations.

14. "J'ai vu chez un peintre en miniature, habile en ces sortes de réparations, des lacunes si adroitement comblées, qu'à peine distinguait-on en transparent l'endroit précis de l'application de la pièce. Les bords du trou, ainsi que ceux du morceau de rapport, étaient amincis au grattoir et ajustés avec tant de précision, que toutes les dentelures s'enchevêtraient les unes dans les autres sans laisser aucune trace de jonction. . . . Quelques artistes comblent les lacunes par un procédé plus expéditif, mais aussi moins parfait: ils posent, avant le mouillage, la gravure, à l'endroit troué, sur un papier identique pour la teinte, le degré d'encollage et les vergeures; puis il rasent net toutes les bavures du trou, au moyen d'un canif bien tranchant. On conçoit que du même coup ils découpent la pièce avec une grande précision. . . . Dans ce système, les lignes de raccord sont un peu crues; le morceau ajouté ne peut guère se dissimuler" (ibid., 51–52). The preferred method described here is essentially the same as the modern "chamfered" repair; see Perkinson, introduction to Schweidler, *Restoration*, 9.

15. By the twentieth century, Schweidler could "implant" wire lines in paper by carving them with a knife, but it is unclear whether this technique was available in the early 1800s; Bonnardot stresses the selection of suitable paper rather than the faking of the lines. Schweidler, *Restoration*, 118–19.

16. Letter, Thomas Pennant Barton to John Russell Smith, undated, Boston Public Library, Thomas Pennant Barton Papers. The New York collector James Lenox likewise wrote to his bookseller in 1855 that any missing title pages should be done by Harris (McKitterick, *Old Books*, 106).

17. Boston Public Library, G.176.41 and G.176.2.

18. James Mascarene Hubbard, *Catalogue of the Works of William Shakespeare Original and Translated Together with the Shakespeariana Embraced in the Barton Collection of the Boston Public Library* (Boston: Boston Public Library, 1880), 71, 185.

19. Library of Birmingham, S336.16; University of Akron, Rare Vault PR2812.A1 1619.

20. *Catalogue of the Valuable Library of the Late William Holgate, Esq . . . sold by auction, by Messrs. S. Leigh Sotheby & Co.* (London, 1846), 45.

21. At one point the librarian of the Sterling Library (books donated by Louis Sterling, now part of the Senate House collection, University of London) wrote to the booksellers Lionel and Philip Robinson, who sold the copy to Sterling, asking them to reinspect the copy because "I could detect no facsimile anywhere on the title page, either of a word of the imprint or of the date." The Robinsons "examined the King Lear quarto" and "agreed that the word 'Printed' and the date were probably in facsimile. New paper with matched chainlines had been taken right across the bottom of the leaf" (letter, J. H. P. Pafford to Lionel Robinson, 30 July 1958; MS annotation by "C.D." on letter, D. T. Richnell to Philip Robinson, 6 August 1958; correspondence in the Senate House Library

files). This description matches with my own sense. Since the new paper includes the rest of the imprint, however, possibly the entire imprint is in pen facsimile, or possibly the bottom portion of the title page of another copy was used to repair this one. Such cannibalizing of incomplete or otherwise undesirable copies was not uncommon in the nineteenth and early twentieth centuries.

22. Quaritch's "Rough List" #143 (London, 1894), item #491, with the Senate House *Lear* also listed at #488; Henkels's catalogue #1238 (Philadelphia, 1919), lot #129. In Quaritch's catalogue 267 (July 1908), there is a listing for a *Merry Wives*, item #424, with "the outer corners of the title, which is backed and has tears mended, defective, the figure 9 in the imprint being missing" (p. 35); as described, however, this seems more like accidental damage than deliberate alteration.

23. *Catalogue of . . . William Holgate,* 45. The *Merchant* description of "some leaves mended" would not alone suffice to identify it with the Birmingham copy (and Bartlett does not so identify it), but combined with the binding description it makes the identification highly likely, since it is listed in a Sotheby's catalogue (22 July 1910, lot 296) as "blue morocco extra, g.e. by C. Lewis." Bartlett describes the Birmingham copy as "Bound in black morocco, by Lewis," but this is the same copy, with each person perceiving the color differently. (In fact, the binding appears to be very dark green; where some has worn away, a brighter green shows through.) Both Sotheby's and Bartlett's descriptions include the detail of a small hole on B1 as well as the facsimile repair to the corner of the title page. Bartlett also lists "Lauder" as the purchaser (with no first name), and "Lauder" was noted in *Book-Auction Records* for 1910 (7:540) as having bought the copy for £155, indicating that Bartlett believed it was the same copy but decided to change the color description (see Bartlett, *Census,* 1939 ed., 59).

24. The *Henry V* cannot be the Akron copy, and the *Dream* cannot be the one described in the Quaritch "rough guide," because the binding details do not match. The *Yorkshire* is bound in red morocco like the BPL copy, while the *Merry Wives* lists no binding details. Conceivably these two could be the repaired copies, but presumably those repairs would have been listed, since the others were.

25. *Catalogue of . . . William Holgate,* 23.

26. At the Holgate sale, the repaired *Pericles* was purchased by the bookseller Joseph Lilly, according to the annotated catalogue. Rodd must have acquired it in the following two years before selling it to Barton around the end of 1848.

27. *Rare First Editions of Famous Writers to be sold on the afternoon of Thursday, January 14, and the afternoon and evening of Friday, January 15, 1926 . . .* (New York: American Art Association, 1926), lot 657. The copy was also described as having Holgate's bookplate, confirming it was the copy listed in that sale.

28. McKitterick, *Old Books,* 45. I am grateful to Jay Moschella for suggesting that Lewis may have been responsible and likely had such a "hospital" in his bindery.

29. *Catalogue of the extensive and very valuable library of . . . George Smith, Esq. . . . which will be sold by auction, by Messrs. Sotheby, Wilkinson, & Hodge. . . . On Wednesday,*

10th of July, 1867 (London, 1867), 150. Bartlett reports that this copy was purchased by Halliwell-Phillipps (Bartlett, *Census*, 1939 ed., 134).

30. Bartlett, *Census*, 1939 ed., 153.

31. *Catalogue of a small but highly interesting collection of the rarest old plays in the English drama . . . which will be sold by auction, by Mr. Sotheby, on Wednesday, April 12, 1826 . . .* (London, 1826), 10–11.

32. The Inglis *Yorkshire Tragedy* (SC 1751), however, is now at the Elizabethan Club, still in its signature binding, and so it cannot be the tear-and-repair copy.

33. I am grateful to University of Pennsylvania conservator Sarah Reidell for suggesting this comparison of the gilt edges. The Akron *Henry V* does not have gilt edges, suggesting it was bound at a different time (probably earlier) and perhaps by someone else.

34. The BPL *Merry Wives* and the Senate House *Lear* show no sign of stab-stitching, while the BPL *Pericles* and *Yorkshire Tragedy* and the Birmingham *Merchant* have stab-stitch holes. (I have not been able to examine the Akron *Henry V* personally.) As discussed above, however, the presence of stab-stitch holes does not preclude that copy from having been sold as part of a bound volume.

35. Bartlett measures *Merry Wives* at 7 1/16 × 5¼ inches, and *Henry V* at 7 1/16 × 5 3/8 inches. I have been unable to get precise measurements of the BPL *Yorkshire Tragedy*, since it was unavailable while the library was undergoing renovation, but secondhand measurements via a digitized copy (with digitized ruler) yield an identical binding size. Thanks to Jay Moschella for measuring the BPL copies for me. In his catalogue of the Clawson collection, Seymour de Ricci measures the Akron *Henry V* at 18.1 × 13.6 cm. Seymour de Ricci, *A Catalogue of Early English Books in the Library of John L. Clawson, Buffalo* (Philadelphia: Rosenbach, 1924), 267.

36. Pratt makes a similar point in "Perfect," 44.

37. Folger, STC 22230 copy 6.

38. Folger, STC 22287 copy 5. A note on the flyleaf dating from 1841 indicates that the repair had not yet been made: "The date (cut off) of this Edn. is 1622." An auction record from 1852 records, again, "*last line of imprint cut away*," but by 1874 it had had its "*title mended and date restored*." I am grateful to Abbie Weinberg for alerting me to this fascinating copy. Both the Folger catalogue and Bartlett (*Census*, 1939 ed., 24) claim that only the date is in pen facsimile, but the paper repair line shows that the entire last line of the imprint has been added later. Furthermore, while the original printed line has a comma between "gate" and "1622," the Folger copy has a period, a mistake by the facsimilist, who may have been working from a copy that was closely trimmed, as in the George III copy at the BL (C.12.g.21), in which the loss of the tail on the comma has made it appear as a period. Auction records from the Utterson sale (1852) and Tite sale (1874): *Catalogue of the Principal Portion of the Valuable Library of Edward V. Utterson . . . which will be sold by auction, by Messrs. S. Leigh Sotheby & John Wilkinson . . . on Monday, April 19th, 1852, and seven following days* (London, 1852), 124; *Catalogue of the Extensive, Important and Valuable Collection . . . of the late Sir William Tite . . . which will be sold by*

auction, by Messrs. Sotheby, Wilkinson & Hodge . . . on Monday, the 18th of May, 1874, and five following days, and on Wednesday, the 27th of May, and nine following days (London, 1874), 198. Bartlett is incorrect that this copy was sold as part of the Halliwell sale at Sotheby's in 1857; that genuine copy of the 1622 edition is at the BPL.

39. Yale, Eliz 96. This copy was acquired from the auction of the Robert Hoe collection in 1911, where it is described as having the "lower portion of title cut, 10 letters and date supplied in facsimile, and several corners also supplied." *Catalogue of the Library of Robert Hoe of New York . . . to be sold by auction beginning on Monday, April 24, by the Anderson Auction Company* (New York, 1911), 227. I have been unable to trace its previous provenance. The copy of the 1594 *Coblers Prophesie* at the Harry Ransom Center (Pforz 1073) is similar: the paper has been repaired around the imprint (probably by the binders Rivière and Son around 1920), with pen facsimile supplying the missing text. The repair seems not to have touched the date but rather cuts a somewhat meandering line across the right-hand side of the three lines of the imprint above the date, as well as portions of the printer's ornament. (Thanks to Aaron Pratt for alerting me to this repair.)

40. The copy of *1 Henry IV* (1639) now at the Martin Bodmer Foundation (SC 270) has the entire lower portion of the imprint in facsimile, and again the paper is ragged and decayed; a copy of *Merchant* (1637) now at the Folger (SC 681) has the entire imprint, everything below the printer's device, in facsimile; a 1630 *Othello* at the Beinecke (SC 871) has almost all of the title-page text and the printer's device in facsimile; the title page of the copy of *Richard II* (1634) at the BPL (SC 1256) is heavily damaged, and various letters are supplied in facsimile throughout the text, in addition to the imprint date; the title page on another copy of *Richard II* (1634) at the Beinecke (SC 1255) is frayed, and the bottom of not only the title page but also other interior leaves has been lost straight across the page; the title page of yet another copy of the same play at the Bodmer (SC 1245) is damaged throughout, and not only the date but the entire bottom portion of the page has been restored, including the entire second line of the imprint. (Bartlett claims this last repair affects only the "lower corner," but the new paper clearly runs across the entire page; see Bartlett, *Census*, 1939 ed., 96).

41. De Ricci, *Catalogue*, 266.

42. Letter, E. H. Dring to A. W. Pollard, National Library of Scotland, MS 14307, 82r–v, 84r. Dring thought the pen facsimiles were done "in the [eighteen] fifties and early sixties," but, as discussed above, they must have been done earlier, given the evidence of the bindings and the Holgate auction catalogue. Kerney speculated that "most of them were mended & the dates filled in by Harris." I am grateful to Henry Woudhuysen for alerting me to these letters, and to Aaron Pratt for photographs of them.

43. Dring to Pollard, 82v.

44. *Henry V* would have appeared like a third edition, or perhaps like a second edition if the owner had never seen a copy of the rare 1602 quarto.

45. British Library, C.12.g.26.

46. Greg, *BEPD*, 2:406, 3:1108. Peter Blayney writes similarly that the copy "has the last two figures of the date '1619' erased, and '08' stamped in their place—presumably by

the printer, Jaggard." But as this is a brief reference in a footnote, it may simply be based on Greg, not on Blayney's own bibliographic analysis. Peter W. M. Blayney, *The Texts of King Lear and Their Origins: Volume 1, Nicholas Okes and the First Quarto* (Cambridge: Cambridge University Press, 1982), 253.

47. I have been informed here by discussions with Elisabeth Berry Drago, Christina Duffy, Steven van Impe, and Sarah Reidell; I am very grateful to Duffy for her willingness to photograph the imprint with a microscope and a multispectral imaging setup.

48. https://discover.elgar.govt.nz/iii/encore/record/C__Rb1968894, accessed 24 January 2019.

49. If the altered dates were in fact hand-stamped, of course, it is possible that Jaggard used a different font of numerals for the job. But the zeros do not match between the two copies, so they were not hand-stamped at the same time with the same type.

50. See BL 102.gg and 103.gg, "MS Classed Catalogue of the Library of George III., acquired by the British Museum in 1823. Compiled by Sir F. A. Barnard," vol. 10, fol. 34e. The catalogue lists two copies of *Yorkshire Tragedy*, both "for T.P.," which distinguishes them as the 1619 quarto, since the imprint on the genuine 1608 quarto gives Pavier's name in full. One is listed as 1608 and one as 1619. These clearly refer to the two George III copies of the 1619 quarto at the British Library, one with the date alteration (C.12.g.26) and one without (C.12.g.17). The genuine copy of the 1608 *Yorkshire Tragedy* currently in the British Library was acquired later and so cannot be the copy listed in the Barnard catalogue.

51. Grey knew the date was false when he bought the book, as he indicated in a note on the flyleaf: "This is the edition of 1619 altered by some former possessor." According to Donald Jackson Kerr, Grey bought it from the 1862 catalogue of the booksellers Thomas and William Boone, and the Auckland Libraries have Grey's purchase record indicating he bought it from the Boones. See Donald Jackson Kerr, *Amassing Treasures for All Times: Sir George Grey, Colonial Bookman and Collector* (New Castle, Del.: Oak Knoll, 2006), 177. But the catalogue listing itself does not quite match this copy: not only does it make no mention of the altered date, which might be explained by the Boones' lack of interest in condition, but it also indicates that "the headlines are, in a few instances, cut off," and yet Auckland librarians report that no headlines are damaged in their copy. *Catalogue of a Very Choice Selection of Rare and Valuable Books* (London: T. and W. Boone, 1862), 124. The listing also describes the binding as by Rivière, but the Auckland binding is unsigned, and George Bayntun booksellers, the inheritors of the Rivière shop, report that the "Greek key" design on the turn-ins of the binding was not made by one of Rivière's binding tools, which they still have. Edward Bayntun-Coward proposes the date of circa 1820 for the binding. George Bayntun (@GeorgeBayntun), "So it seems it's not one of our rolls—Edward Bayntun-Coward thinks that it looks earlier—circa 1820ish," 31 January 2019, 12:06 P.M., Tweet, https://twitter.com/GeorgeBayntun/status/1091004865093009409.

52. National Library of Scotland, Bute.485. I am grateful to Aaron Pratt for alerting me to this copy.

53. Whoever corrected the date by adding the awkward handwritten top loop of the 8 was probably not the same person who wrote "Second Edition Perfect" on the title page, since this note seems to have been written by someone who thought it was a copy of a second edition printed in 1600, much like other plays in the Jaggard Quartos. (It is possible, however, that the two marginalia were in fact written by the same person and work together to "correctly" identify the edition as the "second" edition of 1608, because this person was unaware of the rare, actual second edition of 1602.) Bartlett thinks this owner was the collector Richard Forster, who is recorded as purchasing George Steevens's copy of the play at the auction of his books in 1800, and whose own books passed into the collection of the Marquis Bute, ultimately ending up at the National Library of Scotland (Bartlett, *Census*, 1939 ed., 35). (Bartlett does not, however, note the manipulation of the date in the imprint.) But the auction catalogue for the Steevens sale gives the correct date of 1608 (*Bibliotheca Steevensiana: A Catalogue of the Curious and Valuable Library of George Steevens, Esq . . .* [London, 1800], 81). Perhaps the correction had already been made, therefore, by the beginning of the nineteenth century. Or perhaps the Steevens catalogue simply lists the correct date without noting the specific condition of the imprint on this copy, not an uncommon practice in catalogues in the period. Or perhaps this is not, in fact, the same copy.

54. The *Yorkshire Tragedy* numbering is from the 1791 catalogue; the *Henry V* from the 1792.

55. *Catalogue of . . . Edward V. Utterson*, 123, emphasis mine; NYPL, *KC 1619 (Shakespeare, W. Whole Contention betweene the two Famous Houses, Lancaster and Yorke) copy 1, MS note on flyleaf, emphasis altered; Tite *Catalogue*, 196.

56. This appears to be the same copy as the one described by Sidney Lee in his 1905 census of *Pericles* editions: "An unbound detached copy, sold at a miscellaneous sale Sotheby's, on February 25, 1901, with minute fragments of the date rubbed off, but otherwise perfect, ending Bb1, was purchased by B. F. Stevens, the American agent, for £100." Sidney Lee, *Shakespeares Pericles* (Oxford: Clarendon, 1905), 44. The Huntington copy was bound by the Club Bindery in 1901, presumably after it was purchased unbound by Stevens.

57. A fascinating pair of copies of *Taming of the Shrew* (1631) offers a suggestive comparison. Both the copy currently at University of Pennsylvania (SC 1497) and the one at the University of Edinburgh (SC 1482) were once owned by Halliwell-Phillipps. The date on the Edinburgh copy has been neatly inserted onto the title page, and the date on the Penn copy has been neatly excised and replaced by a blank patch of paper. A note by Halliwell-Phillipps on the flyleaf of the Edinburgh copy explains: "The date is genuine, absolutely so, being taken by F. Bedford from my other copy of the same edition. The copy has not been made up in any other respect" (University of Edinburgh, JA 3706). Bedford worked under Charles Lewis before taking over his shop, and the insertion of the date on this copy is quite similar to the patch on the BPL *Yorkshire Tragedy*, except for being printed rather than pen facsimile. If the BPL *Yorkshire Tragedy* was damaged through scraping, the date may have been excised and replaced in a manner much like the treatment of these two copies of *Shrew*.

58. Greg, "Certain, II," 397.

59. Arthur Conan Doyle, *The Sign of Four* (London: Spencer Blackett, 1890), 93.

60. On "possible," "probable," and "demonstrable" claims in bibliography, see Fredson Bowers, *Bibliography and Textual Criticism* (Oxford: Clarendon Press, 1964), 77–79.

61. Greg, "Certain," 115.

62. The missing copies are *Henry V* (Bartlett, *Census*, 1916 ed., #245), *Lear* (Bartlett, *Census*, 1916 ed., #352), *Merchant* (Bartlett, *Census*, 1916 ed., #441), and *Merry Wives* (Bartlett, *Census*, 1939 ed., #717; Bartlett, *Census*, 1916 ed., #494).

CONCLUSION

Epigraph: Agatha Christie, *Thirteen at Dinner* (New York: Dodd, Mead, 1933), 152.

1. For the argument that the lost edition was printed between 1607 and 1617, and is therefore Q2, see K. M. Sturgess, "The Early Quartos of Heywood's *A Woman Killed with Kindness*," *Library* 5th ser. 25 (1970): 93–104. More recently, M. J. Kidnie argues that the lost edition was actually Q1, printed before 1607; see Thomas Heywood, *A Woman Killed with Kindness*, ed. Kidnie, Arden Early Modern Drama (London: Bloomsbury, 2017), 111–12, 118–19.

2. I am grateful to Stephen Tabor at the Huntington for measuring the ghost image for me, and to Erin McCarthy for measuring the copy of the 1607 quarto at the British Library.

3. See, for example, the 1610 Geneva Bible (STC 2212), which misprinted "Iudas" for "Iesus" in John 6:67. Several extant copies have a printed slip with "Iesus" pasted in. For more on this example, see Sarah Werner and Mitch Fraas, "Keeping Your Jesus and Judas Straight," https://collation.folger.edu/2015/04/keeping-your-jesus-and-judas-straight/; and more generally, Sarah Werner, "Correcting with Cancel Slips," https://collation.folger.edu/2015/04/correcting-with-cancel-slips/, both accessed 4 February 2019.

4. E. R. Wood, "Cancels and Corrections in *A Discovery of Errors*, 1622," *Library* 5th ser. 13 (1958): 124–27, 126; for Brooke, see the entry for STC 3832 (*STC* 1:169–70).

5. I am grateful to Aaron Pratt for this point (personal communication, 7 May 2019). Further examination of Jaggard's entire printed output might shed light on his choice of these numerals for the quartos.

6. I am very grateful to Sarah Wheale for sending me her spreadsheet of Bodleian items arranged by Malone's original volumes, which are otherwise difficult to reconstruct. For Garrick's collection, see Capell's flyleaves now found at BL 643.l.30; for Capell's, see W. W. Greg, *Catalogue of the Books Presented by Edward Capell to the Library of Trinity College in Cambridge* (Cambridge: Cambridge University Press, 1903). The only duplicates I find in Capell's collection are: two copies of *The Two Noble Kinsmen* (1634), bound at S.4.6 and S.27.1; three copies of John Davies's 1599 *Nosce Teipsum*, two bound in the same volume but not consecutively (Q.9.1, Q.9.3, S.36.4); and two copies of *The Second Part of the Faerie Queene* (1596), bound at R.7 and S.18.1. Capell

also owned two copies of the first edition of *Paradise Lost*, bound consecutively as S.10 and S.11 (not in the same volume), but these are two different issues with different imprints, which he likely would not have thought of as duplicates. On his collecting and its relation to his editorial practice, see Claire M. L. Bourne, "Bibliography, Book Design, and Edward Capell's 'Shakespeariana' Collection," paper presented to the annual meeting of the Shakespeare Association of America, 2019; and her forthcoming work on the subject.

7. A copy of *Pericles* at the Huntington (SC 1022) seems to display ghosting from warehousing; see Pratt's forthcoming essay on this copy. Joseph Moxon describes the system of warehousing sheets in *Mechanick Exercises; or, The Doctrine of Handy-Works. Applied to the Art of Printing* (London: Joseph Moxon, 1683–84), 349–50. See also Philip Gaskell, *A New Introduction to Bibliography* (New Castle, Del.: Oak Knoll Press, 1972), 142–45. For a counterargument, see Philip Tromans, "The Collation of John Hawkins's *Troublesome Voyage* (1569), and Its Wraparound Blank," *Library* 18 (2017): 325–29; but also Pratt's rebuttal, forthcoming.

8. See Tromans, "Collation." As Tromans notes, Greg had earlier inferred this practice from the evidence of variable soiling of title pages and final blanks.

9. At some point the Huntington *Henry V* seems to have lost its original title page, since the one currently bound with the volume appears to be a sophistication from another copy. We do not know when this occurred, however. But if the copy lacked a title page for some part of its history, obviously the ghost could not have been made from this same copy during that time.

10. One other possibility seems less likely to me. Jeffrey Peachey has discussed eighteenth-century printing manuals that describe the process of "beating" sheets so as to compress them before sewing them into a binding. Some of these texts mention that the gatherings are shuffled in the process of beating, the better to create a uniformly crisp appearance to the text block. Peachey writes: "Most late eighteenth- and nineteenth-century manuals caution to be alert for set-off, although examples of it, in my experience, are unusual." Theoretically, this practice could account for some offset of the title page of a book onto its final blank. But the texts that Peachey discusses describe the beating of about six signatures at a time, with their order being shuffled, not the shuffling of all the gatherings in a book. It is not clear that the first and final gatherings of longer books like the Jaggard Quartos would ever come into contact in this way. And importantly, the transfer that Peachey describes is true printer's "set-off," in which the still-wet ink from one page touches another, not the kind of ghost image I have been discussing throughout this book. The ghostly "1608" on the Huntington *Henry V* looks just like these ghosts, not like printer's set-off. Jeffrey S. Peachey, "Beating, Rolling, and Pressing: The Compression of Signatures in Bookbinding Prior to Sewing," in *Suave Mechanicals: Essays on the History of Bookbinding, Volume 1*, ed. Julia Miller (Ann Arbor: Legacy Press, 2013), 317–82, 335–36. I am grateful to Aaron Pratt for alerting me to this article.

11. Harry Ransom Center, Ag Sh15 623jb.

12. If Jaggard indeed used a cancel slip for *Woman Killed* with the date 1608, that choice might tell us something about the lost edition of Heywood's play, even though the ghost does not derive from a copy of that edition. Since the false dates on the Jaggard Quartos usually correspond to the date of an actual early edition of the play, perhaps this choice suggests that the lost edition of *Woman Killed* in fact dates from 1608. But the appearance of 1608 on *Henry V* (the date of no known edition of that play), and the fact that the dates chosen for the other Jaggard Quartos are all those of the first editions, should caution us against inferring too much from this evidence.

13. Chartier and Stallybrass, "What Is," 195.

14. The device was cut for Richard Jones, and bears his initials; he used it in the 1590s. It was later used by John Windet in 1606 on STC 7019, before Jaggard took it over. Since Windet was Printer to the City of London before Jaggard gained the position, it seems likely that the device was transferred along with the title. The device with the arms of the city of Geneva, used only on *Dream*, had been cut for Rowland Hall, who had worked in Geneva in 1559–60; it passed to Richard Serle in the 1560s, to John Charlewood by the 1580s, to Richard Jones by the 1590s, to James Roberts by 1599, before ending up in Jaggard's hands. The common strand in the provenance of both devices—Richard Jones to William Jaggard—suggests that Roberts too may have possessed the "HEB DDIEV" device at some time before Windet and Jaggard came to own it, although the device does not appear on any extant copies of Roberts's work. See R. B. McKerrow, *Printer's and Publishers Devices in England and Scotland, 1485–1640* (London: Bibliographical Society, 1913), devices #283 and #136.

15. Marino, *Owning*, 111; Hooks, *Selling*, 114. This trend is continued in Erne, *Book Trade*, 179: "The collection as a whole is now rightly considered Pavier's."

16. By contrast, as Hooks notes (*Selling*, 118), in Pavier and Jaggard's earlier collaborations it was Pavier's device that had appeared on the title page. Higgins notes that Jaggard's own publications "usually featured his full name and his publisher's device" ("We Have," 136).

17. See Higgins, *Shakespeare's*, chap. 2.

18. Thomas Heywood, *An Apology for Actors* (London, 1612), sigs. G4r–v. As Hooks notes, however, the order in which the two title pages were printed is not certain (*Selling*, 111–12). Basing this part of his argument on Lesser and Stallybrass, "Shakespeare," Hooks explicitly links the episode to the 1619 quartos: "Once again in 1619, Jaggard adds something written by Heywood to which he held the rights, to a collection that is marketed as (mostly) Shakespearean" (123). On the history of scholarly interpretation of these title pages, and the Heywood epistle, see Higgins, "We Have," 112–23.

19. About the fraudulent imprints, Gerald Johnson argues similarly that "it must be assumed that the ruse succeeded, or that, as is more likely, the officers of the Company simply winked at the affair. Perhaps the acting company considered that the faked dates sufficed to indicate to potential customers that they were being offered old goods" ("Thomas," 40). As I discuss later in this Conclusion, however, the new evidence of

post-printing manipulation of the imprints suggests strongly that the false printed dates alone did not suffice. James Marino considers the undated quartos of *Romeo and Juliet* (c. 1623) and *Hamlet* (c. 1625) published by John Smethwick to be analogous to the 1619 quartos. Smethwick "takes an approach less spectacular than Jaggard's, withholding dates rather than forging them, but his apparent goals are the same: to continue asserting his right to publish King's Men's plays, including in individual editions, without the King's Men's leave or perhaps without that of Smethwick's partners in the Folio" (Marino, *Owning*, 126). Perhaps these quartos are like the Jaggard Quartos in another way: another partner in the Folio project (Smethwick) works out an arrangement with the King's Men that allows publication so long as there is enough of a facade that the publications are not so closely contemporary with the Folio.

20. Greg, "Certain, II," 397.

21. Johnson, "Thomas," 39.

22. Greg sometimes expressed a similar view: "In view of the uncertain nature of the enterprise and the obvious risks involved, the players . . . may have had some difficulty in finding a stationer prepared to venture upon it. They may have met with rebuffs, and Jaggard may not have been their first choice" (*Shakespeare*, 10). But he also wanted to shift the agency to Pavier, exporting that desire back to the King's Men: "For the sake of their own collection they could afford to overlook [Jaggard's] part in what they no doubt regarded as Pavier's piratical attempt" (*Shakespeare*, 10–11). Blayney points out that "Jaggard was, moreover, the best possible person to negotiate acceptable terms with Pavier (who owned four of the plays to be included in the Folio) and with two other publishers (each owning one play) who had probably also been involved in the illicit activities of 1619." Peter W. M. Blayney, *The First Folio of Shakespeare* (Washington: Folger Shakespeare Library, 1991), 4.

23. Giles Dawson, typescript note in Folger STC 26101 copy 2.

24. On some copies, for instance, I thought I could see some ghosting but could not be certain. The copies with possible ghosting, which should certainly be investigated further, are: SC 660 (Morgan Library, *Merchant*, on blank last verso); SC 728 (Folger, *Merry Wives* copy 8, on the title page around the "A" of the title); SC 731 (Bodmer Foundation, *Merry Wives*, on the title page around the "A" of the title and just below); SC 1033 (UCLA, Clark Library, *Pericles*, on the blank last verso); SC 1039 (Yale, Elizabethan Club, *Pericles*, on the blank last verso); SC 1427 (Folger, *Oldcastle* copy 5, on the blank last verso); SC 1751 (Yale, Elizabethan Club, *Yorkshire Tragedy*, on the blank last verso). On SC 341 (Bodleian, *Henry V*), some paper has transferred onto the title page (likely due to glue) from the last verso of a text that used to be bound immediately before it: "full au . . . / Roman . . . E . . . / . . . ni 17."; I have not been able to locate this text, but it does not appear to be a Jaggard Quarto.

25. Thanks to Ben Higgins for pointing me to the possible parallel with *The Malcontent*. Copies with this type of excision include those at the Bodleian (Mal. 252[4] and Mal. 195[5]), BPL (G.3977.50), Folger (STC 17481 copy 2), and Victoria and Albert (Dyce 26 Box 28/2, crudely repaired by a later reader). See John Marston, *The Malcon-*

tent, ed. G. K. Hunter, The Revels Plays (Manchester: Manchester University Press, 1975), xxix.

26. On domestic tragedy, see the survey of critical opinion in Sean Benson, *Shakespeare, "Othello" and Domestic Tragedy* (London: Bloomsbury, 2012), 81–82, quoting the introduction by M. R. Ridley to his Arden edition of *Othello*; on how readers may have understood texts encountered in sammelbands, see Knight, *Bound*.

INDEX

In references to individual copies, library abbreviations follow the list given in Appendix C.